HEALING HOME

Health and Homelessness in the Life Stories of Young Women

Based on research that was awarded the Governor General's Academic Gold Medal, *Healing Home* is an exploration of the lives and health of young women experiencing homelessness. Vanessa Oliver employs an innovative methodology that blends sociology and storytelling practices to investigate these women's access to health services, their understandings of health and health care delivery, and their health-seeking behaviours. Through their life stories, Oliver demonstrates how personal and social experiences shape health outcomes.

In contrast to many previous studies that have focused on the deficits of these young people, *Healing Home* is both youth-centric and youth-positive in its approach: by foregrounding the narratives of the women themselves, Oliver empowers a sub-section of the population that traditionally has not had a voice in determining policies that shape their realities. Applying a strong, articulate, and systemic analysis to on-the-ground narratives, Oliver is able to offer fresh, incisive recommendations for health and social service providers with the potential to effect real-world change for this marginalized population.

VANESSA OLIVER is an assistant professor in the Department of Sociology at Mount Allison University.

Healing Home

Health and Homelessness in
the Life Stories of Young Women

VANESSA OLIVER

UNIVERSITY OF TORONTO PRESS
Toronto Buffalo London

ISBN 978-1-4426-4531-8 (cloth)
ISBN 978-1-4426-1344-7 (paper)

Printed on acid-free, 100% post-consumer recycled paper with vegetable-based inks.

Library and Archives Canada Cataloguing in Publication

Oliver, Vanessa, 1980–
Healing home : health and homelessness in the life stories of young women / Vanessa Oliver

Includes bibliographical references and index.
ISBN 978-1-4426-4531-8 (bound) – ISBN 978-1-4426-1344-7 (pbk.)

1. Homelessness – Health aspects – Ontario – Toronto – Case studies.
2. Homeless women – Ontario – Toronto – Case studies.   3. Homeless
women – Ontario – Toronto – Biography.   4. Women – Health and hygiene
– Ontario – Toronto – Case studies.   5. Health services accessibility – Ontario – Toronto – Case studies.   6. Toronto (Ont.) – Social conditions – 21st
century – Case studies.   I. Title.

RA564.9.H63O45 2013   362.1′0425   C2012-906819-5

University of Toronto Press acknowledges the financial assistance to its
publishing program of the Canada Council for the Arts and the Ontario
Arts Council.

Canada Council   Conseil des Arts
for the Arts   du Canada

ONTARIO ARTS COUNCIL
CONSEIL DES ARTS DE L'ONTARIO
50 YEARS OF ONTARIO GOVERNMENT SUPPORT OF THE ARTS
50 ANS DE SOUTIEN DU GOUVERNEMENT DE L'ONTARIO AUX ARTS

University of Toronto Press acknowledges the financial support of the
Government of Canada through the Canada Book Fund for its publishing
activities.

To my mothers
Susan Phillips Oliver
&
Nellie Green Oliver
Who taught me the most valuable things I know:
Love
Compassion
Determination

Contents

Preface: A Room of One's Own

Virginia Woolf (1948) once said, "If you do not tell the truth about your-self you cannot tell it about other people." This is a complicated quotation with which to start, but I have chosen it intentionally. Although to cite Virginia Woolf is to engage with early and influential feminist thought, it is also to privilege a voice of privilege – the voice of a woman who could write because she was part of the elite, and who at times spoke from an elitist, classist, and racist perspective. In many ways, Woolf is an example of the sort of feminism that postcolonial feminists seek to problematize. For this she is not to be excused. But Woolf was more complex, as we all are, than these descriptions allow. She was also a survivor of childhood sexual abuse, a brilliant storyteller, a woman who sometimes sought the sexual companionship of women, and a sufferer of depression, to which she would eventually succumb, drowning herself in 1941 (DeSalvo, 1990; Sproles, 2006). Virginia Woolf and her words speak to the power of stories: what they tell and what they obscure, what they say about particular times and places, and how they, like the people who tell them, are never simply one thing but always complexly becoming.

Most feminist thought believes that there is not a singular truth to be discovered, but rather multiple truths that depend on how one sees the world (Ramazanoğlu & Holland, 2002). To tell the truth, then, is to say what one believes to be true at the particular moment and place when one is asked. To say the truth about others is even more complex. This book relies on the voices of eight young women living in extraordinary circumstances who tell their truths through their own stories – stories that have not often been heard before. Through my research I aim to tell their stories while remaining true to the way that they told them to me, and, in so doing, to communicate their experiences through the 300-page story that is this book.

This research would not have existed or been nearly as powerful without the help of the First Stop Woodlawn women's shelter and its staff, who believed in my story and my work enough to tell me to stop being a one-track academic and write some interview questions that mattered. This story cannot be told without the eight young women who told me that their stories needed to be heard. Through the course of this research, I hope that you will, as I have, come to hear them and to better understand their truths, their fictions, and their lives.

Throughout this work I will argue that, due to multiple marginalizations ranging from their age to the social stigmatization of homelessness to inequitable policies, homeless young women face unique barriers to accessing health and social services and also, therefore, to achieving their full human potential. The subsequent chapters and discussion explore the ways in which the women's narratives contribute a personal face and an authoritative voice to the most pressing issues facing young people living in exceptional circumstances. Their thoughts, feelings, and suggestions for change reflect the need for renewed focus on social safety nets and inclusive citizenship for all.

Acknowledgments

To my father, Norman Oliver, who has always been, above all things, my Dad. And who, with strength and love enough for two, raised a little girl who wanted to make the world a better place.

To my sister, Melissa Oliver Doucette, who gave the world the three most perfect people I know: Brandon, Caleb, and Camryn Doucette.

To my Uncle Clayton Oliver for teaching me humility.

To my Uncle Ross Magill for teaching me vulnerability.

To Isobel Richmond Oliver for doing the caring work that allowed me to do this.

To my family of friends, for love, life, and laughter: Kelly Burrows, Laura Carr, Matthew Coppins, Jennifer Esmail, Francesco Fiore, Christopher Grouios, Christopher Huey, Kathryn Hum, Caroline Hume, Jane Hutton, Clare Frejd, Adrienne Palmer, Daniel Reid, Michael Sung.

To an amazing group of women, academic colleagues and friends, with the utmost gratitude for support, enthusiasm, and motivation: Pat Armstrong, Susan Braedley, Diana Majury, Nancy Mandell, Sarah Flicker, Tamara Daly, Nora Jacobson, Morgan Seeley, Wendy Winters, Melba Cuddy-Keane, Sylvia Soderlind, Asha Varadharajan.

To the eight young women who trusted me enough to tell their stories. You are the heart of this story.

HEALING HOME

Health and Homelessness in the Life Stories of Young Women

1 The Story behind the Story: An Introduction

More than 300,000 Canadians experience homelessness annually – the number of shelter beds in Canada jumped by 22 per cent in one year to 26,872 in 2007, and by 2011 this number had increased to 28,495 (Shapcott, 2008; Homelessness Partnership Secretariat, 2012). Providers of social services in Toronto have estimated that there are between 1,700 and 2,000 homeless or under-housed youth living in the city on any given night (Gaetz & O'Grady, 2002). In 1999, 6,310 youth between the ages of 15 and 24 used Toronto's shelter services, equalling 21 per cent of the total number of people who used these services. This number is especially startling in light of the fact that youth comprise only 12 per cent of the general population of the city (Novac et al., 2002). Researchers believe that females represent anywhere from one-third to one-half of the urban street youth population in Canada (ibid.). In all likelihood these statistics are conservative given that Canada lacks national data on homelessness and that homeless youth comprise a hidden population of people with no fixed addresses and loose or no ties to social services. A study published in 1999 demonstrated that in the past 25 years there has been a 450 per cent increase in the number of youth shelter beds in Toronto alone (Toronto Community Foundation, 2009). Clearly, these large and escalating numbers of homeless youth warrant the serious and sustained attention of researchers and policy-makers.

To date, Canadian research on the health of homeless youth has been scant. Much of the extant literature takes a biomedical approach to young people's clinical issues, focusing on quantitative measures and epidemiological outcomes. While this research generates important knowledge, biomedical approaches sometimes obscure the role of social, political, and economic forces in creating the conditions that lead to homelessness, ill health, and poverty. Moreover, considerations of gender, race, and social location have been conspicuously absent from the bulk of research on youth, which homogenizes this population under the category of "homeless youth." Lack of social analysis has contributed to a view of youth homelessness that tends to advocate "solutions" that fit too neatly into a neoliberal discourse of individual responsibility and curative, single-solution responses. We know that youth often end up on the street and that they are vulnerable to a wide range of illnesses, but we know very little about the ways in which they make sense of their situations or what factors precipitate their decisions to engage, or disengage, with particular kinds of services (Finkelstein, 2005). Recently, there has been growing awareness of the import of taking social locations into account, and more researchers are beginning to grapple with issues of gender, race, sexuality, and age (Benoit et al., 2007; Gaetz, 2004; Ensign, 2001; Kidd, 2007). My research is situated within the context of this emerging corpus of work that is concerned with the social and political implications of homelessness.

As Ensign and Panke (2002) note, there is a scarcity of research on self-perceived health-seeking behaviours, as homeless youth are not usually invited to share their perspectives on their own lives. Gaetz (2004) agrees that we need a better understanding of service usage, especially in gaining insight into those environments that are viewed as positive spaces for homeless youth. He calls for research that seeks to uncover the barriers that "prevent or discourage members of specific sub-populations of the homeless from accessing services" (p. 58). In response to these calls, my research utilizes a qualitative, narratological approach to analyse the life histories of eight young homeless women; I investigate the factors they perceive to have impeded or facilitated their ability to access health services and how these factors have influenced their overall health and well-being. This research was conducted in downtown Toronto, recognizing that barriers, such as availability of services, differ in different social and geographic locations. The intent of this study is to interrogate the ways in which relations of gender and power are fundamental to the understandings and practices of health access, health delivery, and health-seeking behaviours of homeless youth.

This book explores the lived health experiences of homeless youth, the meanings they attach to their health and health experiences, and the factors they describe as barriers and facilitators to their access to health services. Employing feminist methodologies, I have sought to privilege the narratives of young women in order to empower a subsection of the population that traditionally has not had a voice in determining the research and policy that shape their realities.

Exceptional Circumstances

But the real problem in pursuing questions of definition and identity is not one of reducing ambiguity or refining terms. Nor is it a question of the way definition betrays the irreducible complexity of lived experience. The problem lies in the homelessness of our times.

(Jackson, 2002, p. 81)

This project is based on qualitative, participatory interview research with eight young women who live in exceptional circumstances. Wolcott (1995) reminds us that "what we don't label others will, leaving us at their mercy. We are better to supply labels of our own and be upfront about the identifications we seek" (p. 81). I try to use the term "exceptional circumstances," as employed at the shelter, as much as possible in deference to the women's preference to not be labelled as "homeless" or "street involved." These women are constantly in transition – between group homes and shelters, between streets and parents' homes, between friends' couches and their own apartments; their circumstances are not those of typical housed women of their age, but they are also not immutable, abnormal, or deserving of stigma. I will rely on the terms "homeless" or "street involved" despite their inadequacies, however, given that they are the terms most commonly used in the research literature.

For the purposes of this research, health-seeking behaviour is the search for, and access to, health services and healthy situations that enable young women to treat illness and preserve wellness. The life narratives of young women explain how they define their own health, what health issues they are experiencing, which services they use in seeking to care for themselves and what factors they perceive as having influenced their access to health services.

The questions guiding this analysis explore the connections between young women's understandings of health and the ways in which their social and physical locations impact both their definitions and their experiences of health and health services. How young women define and experience health over time and across space is also impacted by gender, culture, and power in health and social services experiences. This research focuses on the ways in which young women themselves see these factors impacting, or not impacting, on their lives and health-seeking behaviours. In other words, what factors do homeless young women identify as facilitators and barriers in their health services experiences? How do they experience and define health? What roles do space and place play in those experiences?

The Health of Women and Girls

Renewed interest in the field of women's health in the past decade has produced a number of understandings of what "women's health" actually entails. Although it varies from discipline to discipline and from individual to individual, women's health still tends to be narrowly and traditionally defined under the medical model as reproductive health. This understanding of women's health reflects an important biomedical and physiological conception of the differences in the health of women and men, but excludes a large piece of the puzzle. While physiology certainly accounts for many of the health differences manifest between men, women, and intersex people, the context afforded by a gender lens offers a more nuanced analysis of the complex web of biology and interrelationships that constitute a broader definition of women's health. A serious and sustained gender focus assumes that socio-political factors influence women's health owing to women's unequal power and control over material resources, their greater exposure to domestic violence, and their differing social roles.

Sherwin (1998) draws attention to the fact that health care interactions are, by their very nature, political. By overlooking the political dimensions of women's health, one also overlooks the power imbalances that create inequitable conditions in health care. These inequalities are pervasive at all levels of health care. As a result, when women are given a set of medical instructions as opposed to a number of options, they are not always provided with the medical advice that best suits the context of their lives. So, while they may be receiving medical care, women's own personal responsibilities or employment obligations may prevent them from following medical advice, and may also result in a non-compliance notation in their medical files. Recognizing the constraints of social conditions is especially crucial in cases where non-compliance is seen as a reason to withdraw or discontinue treatment. Farmer (2003) underscores that those least likely to comply are those least able to comply.

In a study such as this – which attempts to understand the ways in which politics, in their many forms, shape the health and morbidity of women patients and providers in the urban setting – women's health encompasses health services delivery, health care decision-making, political negotiation, providers, patients, caregivers, and communities. When health is defined broadly, the services that contribute to the good health of young women also include appropriate social services. Women's health involves ensuring that all women have access to high-quality, equitable care that recognizes the complexities of women's lives and allows them to make decisions, remaining mindful of their obligations to partners, friends, family, and work.

In order to better understand the complex relationships that frame women's health, we must begin with the understanding that all health services are women's health services. A commitment to women's health means ensuring that the delivery of care is equitable and inclusive – services must be delivered in ways that are particularly sensitive to the needs of underserved communities. Health for women means providing options that are responsive to their everyday lives.

Youth and Adolescence

Youth, as a life course stage, has been seen by some to be expanding at both ends. Children are being exposed to what is typically considered youth culture at earlier ages as a result of pervasive marketing and music video culture, while changing labour and housing markets as well as shifting views on marriage and childbearing are delaying transitions to adulthood (Hollands, 2001). New global economies and technologies are catalysing shifts in youth culture around the world, prompting youth studies researchers to pay attention to the new realities of youth in this particular historical moment. Importantly, these shifts are sending confusing signals to youth who are immersed in a culture that worships at the fountain of youth, marketing it as seductive and highly coveted, while at the same time denying young people access to power in terms of citizenship and economic gains. These effects are magnified for homeless youth who lack economic power, and whose life experiences are far removed from those of Paris Hilton or Hannah Montana.

Problematizing the terms "adolescence" and "youth" represents one of the challenges of engaging in research with this population. Adolescence is, for the most part, a twentieth-century Western construction that signals a departure from childhood, but also a distancing from adulthood. The differing age ranges that serve to quantify youth, anywhere from 12 to 30 years of age, are proof that youth is a social construct rather than a biological given. Typically, adolescence is a time when young people begin to accept more responsibility for their own decision-making and learn the skills necessary for independent living; however, many adults characterize youth as awkward and immature, thus thwarting their agency. As Kelly and Caputo (2001) signal, these stereotypes serve adult interests in retaining control of and cordoning off adult spaces. These instruments of control intensify in periods of rapid social change. The appearance of homeless youth in spaces defined as adult spaces or, at best, homeless adult spaces, disrupts these carefully constructed boundaries between adults and children. These images are troubling because homeless youth appear to be outside the control of adults. Critical youth researchers call for youth-centred studies in which young people represent their own interests and are "actively involved in the production and reproduction of themselves, their cultures, and their social realities" (ibid., p. 47)

Homeless Youth

Gaetz (2009) defines homeless youth as "young people up to the age of 24 who are no longer living with parents or guardians, and who lack stable housing, employment and educational opportunities." Homeless young people are a heterogeneous group who struggle to live independently and "whose lives are characterized by the inadequacy of income, health care supports and importantly, the kinds of social supports that we typically deem necessary for the transition from childhood to adulthood" (ibid.).

The tangle of terminology used in research with "youth" and "homeless" populations is often contradictory and divergent. As discussed above, which age range constitutes youth varies from source to source; similarly, definitions of homelessness change depending on the context. Agencies that assist homeless youth usually specify the age range of their clientele as between 15 and 24 years old. The United Nations specifies the same age range in its definition of youth. Young, low-income women with dependent children blur the lines of child, youth, and adult – and are much less likely to seek health care options than are low-income men or higher-income people of either gender (Acosta & Toro, 2000).

For the sake of this project, youth is defined as a socially constructed life stage that occurs in the life course of an individual in between childhood and adulthood. I would also add that age is a social determinant of health – where this determinant is recognized, the emphasis tends to be on older adults rather than on youth. According to Callaghan and colleagues (2002), individuals who are homeless are those who have no home and who live either outdoors or in emergency shelters or hostels, and people whose homes do not meet the United Nations' basic standards of adequate protection from the elements, access to safe water and sanitation, secure tenure and personal safety, and accessibility to employment, education, and health care (p. 8). Again, my aim is to define these young women by who they are, not what they lack. In accordance with Jackson (2002), I attempt to make the term "homeless" "a site of intersubjectivity rather than biography" (p. 81). The women's biographies are the stories told herein. Homelessness is but one aspect of the telling.

One of the several negative repercussions of labelling groups "homeless" is that the label misrepresents the heterogeneity of the population and often leads to one-size-fits-all decision-making. This holds true within the group labelled "homeless female youth." There are many refugee and immigrant youth living in shelters. Lesbian, bisexual, and transgender girls navigate the fraught territory of homophobia and transphobia in addition to poverty. Aboriginal girls are the most over-represented group within the shelter system. Relational elements of gender, race, class, ethnicity, ability, sexual orientation, health status, and age intersect with one another to create what Young (2002) has called "structures of constraint," restricting the choices and access of young homeless women and girls. These individuals are highly mobile, diverse, and resistant to fixed categories that fail to represent their unique situations. Homelessness can be all-encompassing at some points in an individual's life course and non-existent at others; either way, homelessness is just one piece of a complex person's life.

Further, gendered complexities exist within definitions of homelessness. Popular public perceptions of homelessness tend to fall back on images of visible homelessness: the types of homelessness that exist when people sleep rough in public spaces unintended for human habitation, such as alleyways, ravines, and park benches. While there are many women whose living situations constitute visible homelessness, the gendered nature of their experiences tends to create a more invisible form of homelessness for women and girls. Invisible homelessness includes those situations in which an individual or family is staying on friends' sofas, in overcrowded or unsafe dwellings, or with a violent or abusive intimate partner or relative. Urban geographers have focused on the ways in which streets and public areas become masculinized spaces, and how this construction has rendered homeless women particularly invisible as they either seek male protection or seek shelter in one of the aforementioned locations (Williams, 2002). Independence, caring relationships, and economic options are often very different for girls and women than they are for men and boys (O'Grady & Gaetz, 2004). Fear of sexual and physical assault and gender discrimination creates added risks for females. Young women, especially those engaged in substance use, often become dependent on older men for shelter, for which they exchange sex, domestic service, and other forms of labour. These men often have considerable control over the actions and options available to those who are under their protection (ibid.).

The "othering" of homeless women and girls also contributes to public misconceptions about homelessness. Unable to deal with the contradictions between the reality of women and youth on the streets and middle-class ideals, people view homeless women and youth as deviant, victimized, or crazy, further alienating those who find themselves without homes. The homeless label also speaks to one of the longest-standing feminist debates: politicizing the personal. The artificial boundary between home – constructed as an off-limits, personal space – and homeless needs to be redefined and opened up. Houses are not always homes and women's dependency on men often makes what should be their "home" a place of violence and insecurity. Masculinist and neoconservative discourses have created an artificial naturalness around the association of women, home, and private spaces, reinforcing nuclear families and the economic dependency of women on men. When a young woman becomes homeless, she is an outcast on male-dominated streets, socially alienated, and divorced from the home environment that she has been socialized to see as feminine space (O'Grady & Gaetz, 2004). This research proposes to complicate and expand the narrow definitions and perceptions of the "homeless" label. Homeless young women require the same access and supports as other homeless people, but they also require policies that demonstrate an awareness of their differing access to power, their heterogeneity, and their in-between child and adult social status.

The Role of the State

Neoliberal governments and policies have played a significant role in undermining public support for those living in poverty. With their focus on free markets, individual responsibility, and economic competitiveness, neoliberal agendas eschew collective responsibility and social transfers in favour of so-called employment initiatives. These same agendas have also been particularly effective in impeding political opposition from activists and advocates, especially given the constant devolution of responsibility from one level of government to the next, as has been the case with social services transfers from the provincial to the municipal level (Poland et al., 2000). As Peck (2001) argues, labour market deregulation not only allows for income inequality, it actually promotes it in order to ensure a willing and inexpensive (read: "competitive") labour force. These changes have had the most devastating impact on those who are most vulnerable (Klodawsky, 2006). Accompanied by punitive social programs such as workfare, neoliberal policies discipline and punish rather than assist and support. With the aim of downloading social responsibility onto family and community, these same policies have forced women into caring work, often on top of their paid employment responsibilities. This return to "family values" has had the worst effect on single mothers, children, and youth.

As my research was conducted in Toronto, I focus on the Ontario context in explaining the punitive measures that neoliberal and neoconservative policies have instated. In 1995, Ontarians elected a Conservative government that almost immediately enacted a 20 per cent reduction in the welfare rate and ceased to fund social housing. Unsurprisingly, homelessness grew at an amazing rate throughout the 1990s. By 2001, Ontario had 6,100 people living in assistance shelters, while Quebec had 3,365 and British Columbia had 1,085 (Klodawsky, 2006). Simultaneously both federal and provincial governments clawed back core funding for community agencies, forcing agencies to rely on limited-term project and services funding that was constantly being redefined and thus not guaranteed from one project to the next. A 1996 survey of youth agencies demonstrated that 40 per cent of the available youth programs lost paid staff as a result of government cuts (Novac et al., 2002). While agencies including the Children's Aid Society and mental health facilities were gutted, retributive powers of the police and courts were enhanced; today, criminalizing social problems remains the most popular method of obscuring them. As the condition of social housing stock declines, markets continue to inflate housing costs, leaving youth with fewer housing options.

Government emphasis on employment through such initiatives as the Youth Employment Strategy, which ties social assistance to labour market participation, has functioned in complex ways for youth and has in fact made them more, rather than less, vulnerable. There is a popular perception that homeless youth are unemployed because they are lazy and unmotivated. In reality, homeless youth who have dropped out of school usually end up working in casual, unskilled, often unsafe jobs that barely provide enough to get by. These young people form a reserve army of labourers who have little choice but to work "flexible" hours for very little pay (Hollands, 2001). In the mid-1990s, this sort of insecure employment was combined with punitive social assistance rules, which deemed that 16- and 17-year-olds – including single mothers – are unable to receive social assistance in their own names. Still today, such assistance is only available through reliance on a trustee or guardian and youth are entirely ineligible for assistance unless they can prove they attend school (Novac et al., 2002).

Too often youth fall into the liminal space between child and adult benefits, especially as many youth leave state care at the age of 16. If 16- to 18-year-olds are out of wardship and not in school, they are expected to find jobs; given that these youth often do not have money for first and last months' rent, and therefore have nowhere to shower, dress, and eat, finding a job can be difficult. Health access is also compromised for homeless youth because of the requirement that one must have an Ontario Health Insurance Plan (OHIP) card to see most physicians – a card which is easily lost or stolen, or which parents refuse to turn over to their children (ibid.). Uninsured health services, dental care, and prescription drugs are virtual impossibilities for homeless people. These realities are especially troubling in light of the *Canada Health Act* (1984), which promises public administration, comprehensiveness, universality, portability, and accessibility of services.

Risk

Homeless individuals contend with the same illnesses as the rest of the population; however, homelessness itself exacerbates a range of health problems: foot problems, respiratory illnesses, nutritional deficiencies, tooth decay, and skin infections (Public Health Agency of Canada, 2006). Quantitative and biomedical studies have shown that homeless youth are 10 to 12 times more likely than other youth to contract blood-borne infections and sexually transmitted infections (STIs) (ibid.). Cuts, burns, and bites are easily infected when exposed to unsanitary conditions, and youth often suffer from "street sickness," a condition of constant malaise caused by exposure, sleep deprivation, and poor hygiene (Wingert et al., 2005). Mental health issues and substance misuse are also of particular concern with homeless populations (ibid.). Women and girls often engage in survival sex practices that make them more susceptible to STIs, abuse, and pregnancy (Ensign & Panke, 2002). Lack of access to money to buy menstrual supplies combined with lack of privacy also places women in an especially precarious situation (Whitzman, 2006). Qualitative researchers must be aware of these epidemiological factors so that attempts can be made at addressing the ways in which homeless individuals go about coping with, and understanding the implications of, these health services issues. At the same time, we must remain cognizant of Foucault's (1973) critique of medicalization as a form of social control, that is, to recognize the social and political hierarchies that structure biomedical discourses and the tendency to medicalize women's bodies. Similarly, discourses of risk also tend to undermine the examination of the structural factors that contribute to homelessness and ill health in the first place. Researchers must ask the questions: Who benefits from, and who loses out as a result of, this label? How does the label "at risk" contribute to vilifying homeless youth, while simultaneously letting decision-makers and the public at large off the hook for providing them with adequate social support? If "at risk" signals victimization, what agency do homeless youth have to self-represent?

Citizenship

As a result of dominant neoliberal ideology, citizenship, too, has come to be constructed around market exchange and consumer power: those who are employed in the paid labour market and funnel money into the economy are those who are considered full members of society and entitled to all the privileges of citizenship. Homelessness, then, removes people from these normative ideals and casts them as deviant and unproductive (Chouinard, 2006). Bylaws and legislation, like the

Safe Streets Act (1999), are passed in order to prevent homeless people from carrying out monetary exchanges in the informal economy, such as squeegeeing car windshields. These laws construct homelessness as disorderly, while privileging "safety," "citizenship" and "civility" as protecting "the public" by ensuring that the streets are safe (Hermer & Mosher, 2002). Claims such as these beg the question: safe for whom? Criminalizing facets of homelessness obscures the structural causes of homelessness and forces youth into invisible forms of exchange, most notably sex work and drug dealing. These exclusionary ideals of citizenship are further complicated in the case of homeless youth who can work, consent to sex, seek and consent to health care, and drive a car, but cannot vote if they are not 18 or do not have a fixed address. Although the state controls and regulates their actions, homeless youth under the age of 18 are unable to voice dissent or support for those who create policies that often affect their ability to live healthy and secure lives.

Chapter Structure

Chapter 2 – Once upon a Time: "Storying" Feminist Theory in Neoliberal Times

This chapter presents the theoretical approaches and key concepts with which the book engages. Drawing on critical insights from feminist theory, the second chapter highlights the need for intersectional approaches to the study of social phenomena by recognizing the import of social locations, such as gender, age, race, and socio-economic status, in speaking to broader systemic issues such as homelessness. Feminist political economy provides a guiding light throughout the following chapters in its concern with understanding the ways in which inequalities and health disparities are produced and perpetuated by socially and politically determined structures, and by the historical and material circumstances that give them form. For these reasons, the roles of the state and social policy are discussed in order to situate homelessness in the broader political context. The second chapter also explores the role of subjectivity in the lives of homeless young people, concluding that although young women are often subject to the edicts of public policy and social norms, they are also agents involved in the process of co-determining the outcomes of their lives. While their choices may be constrained, they are nevertheless making decisions and creating spaces for themselves on a daily basis.

The chapter concludes with the discussion of the related concepts of social inclusion and resiliency. Social inclusion theory, it is argued, provides evidence that social attachments and social capital (such as networks, education, and income) make for healthier individuals. The health of homeless young people is crucially attached to this notion of belonging and forming attachments and trust with care providers. Likewise, resiliency theory, as it has been adapted by social science, demonstrates that resilience in the face of trauma is strongly correlated to a young person's level of social inclusion within communities, families, and peer groups.

Chapter 3 – Girl, You'll Be a Woman … Soon: A Narrative Project

This chapter outlines the methodology for the study, including life-history interviewing, feminist methodologies, narrative theory, and qualitative research. Expanding upon the concepts of narrative theory and methods, such as life-history interviewing, I operationalize the ways in which narrative data are obtained, scrutinized, and analysed. Ethical issues, particularly around consent and vulnerable populations, are elaborated upon. New views on ethical obligations to homeless research participants are outlined and presented as crucial to improving research processes to protect more vulnerable populations. Speaking to intersecting subject positions and conceptions of youth, I outline some of the challenges of working with youth in exceptional circumstances. This chapter covers the conceptualization of the project and speaks broadly to the critical concepts that are foundational to the book as a whole.

Chapter 4 – Girls Aloud: Narratives and Self-Stories

Here, the stories of eight unique young women struggling to gain ground against backgrounds of abuse, to build successes against histories of poverty, and to find a sense of belonging against landscapes of invisibility, are presented in their verbatim form. Their voices and language have not been changed, although their accounts have been condensed. In this regard, I state my editorial position and justify my selection of the particular stories. Although the young women discussed their health narratives at length, they also returned to their social positions and locations to contextualize the barriers and challenges they face in health services encounters. These social, material, and historical circumstances are presented in this chapter to create a broader picture of the terrains these young women have travelled and continue to navigate. The stories told here are meant to provide a point of focus for the remainder of the analysis. It is my hope that readers will come back to these larger stories as they are reintroduced to the young women through smaller segments of their accounts in the chapters that follow.

Chapter 5 – Sugar and Spice and Everything Nice: Age, Space, Place, Gender, and Health

This chapter describes the political economy of youth homelessness, engaging with the literatures on health and place in terms of their gendered implications for youth. I discuss the role that traditional discourses around childhood have played in limiting the options of young people in exceptional circumstances, both in terms of access to public and private spaces, and to the social assistance they require. Drawing on the narratives of the young women, I show how factors such as age, gender, and immigration status support, challenge, and complicate current theoretical work in health, social geography, and childhood studies. I also employ empirical evidence to highlight the ways in which young women create spaces for themselves despite the many constraints and systemic barriers they face – often by relying on creative innovation and the manipulation of the very discourses of childhood and femininity that limit them in other areas of their lives. In these ways, individuals become relationally connected to multiple health-promoting and health-damaging spaces across their life course. This chapter examines the ways in which those who inhabit them in both visible and invisible ways negotiate spaces such as shelters, group homes, and streets. Analysing the multiple and interconnecting relationships between the state, its institutions, law enforcement, social services, and the various actors that people them, this chapter seeks to interrogate assumptions about youth, gender, and homelessness. Ultimately, the chapter turns to the crucial role of belonging in places over time to underscore the role that people, and through them, spaces, play in expanding opportunities for young women.

Chapter 6 – Seen and Not Heard: Negotiating Health and Wellness

From theorizing the spatial and relational contexts of young homeless women's lives, this chapter explores participants' specific health concerns. Although the analysis to this point has looked at health more broadly, I here concentrate on the two areas of health most commonly discussed by the participants: mental health and sexual and reproductive health. In so doing this chapter not only details the health concerns most relevant to these young women, but also examines the ways in which young women understand their health and the way that those understandings are impacted by visits to clinics, experiences of stigmatization, and troubled relationships. Youth in exceptional circumstances experience health conditions that are both similar to and different from those of their housed peers; they access services differently and for different reasons, based on a range of health concerns – some of which are directly related to their homelessness status and others which are not. For instance, most youth are exploring issues of sexuality at this stage of their life course, but not all youth are trading sex to survive. This analysis extends to show that young homeless women are not well-served by models of care that treat symptoms as individual or solely biomedical, and that they do not have the same supports that are available to most young people. These two factors are key in exploring innovative models of caring for youth who do not have the guidance of a trusted adult or who are facing a number of health concerns concurrently. Importantly, these health concerns are not solely the result of homelessness, and often, especially in the case of mental health, extend from neglect, abuse, or poverty in their early childhood development.

Much quantitative research has been undertaken to determine which conditions homeless youth are likely to suffer from, but very little research has sought to explore the ways in which young people themselves view the health and social services landscape. This chapter reveals the ways in which the narratives of the young women are sometimes internally inconsistent, let alone inconsistent with the stories of the other women. Keeping an eye on points of similarity and divergence, this chapter theorizes the ways in which gender, power, and social position interact to create complicated health maps that are, for a number of reasons, often difficult to navigate.

Chapter 7 – Begging for Change: Barriers, Facilitators, and Implications for Policy and Practice

Following from the analysis of the health issues that most concern young women in exceptional circumstances, this chapter analyses care access by examining the barriers and facilitators that young people confront when, and if, seeking services to manage their health concerns.

I divide the health services barriers that young people face into three categories that assist in delimiting the characteristics that impede access: structural characteristics, clinical characteristics, and characteristics of space and place. Health services barriers are understood as the constraints produced by the ways in which health care is financed, delivered, and organized. Barriers discussed include fee-for-service remuneration for physicians, institutionalized health care environments such as hospitals and clinics, and a perceived lack of privacy and confidentiality. Notably, the barriers faced by street youth are at once similar and different from those faced by shelter youth as issues of safety, criminalization, and theft create another layer of barriers for those living on the streets. Social locations such as race, ethnicity, sexuality, and citizenship status are also significant contributors to young women's inability or reluctance to access services. The failure of decision-makers to account for these inequalities has often made for ineffective policy and programming. Cuts in funding, the fragmentation and downloading of services, and even constraints faced by physicians seeking to care for vulnerable populations combine to build fences rather than bridges for homeless young people

Despite these many barriers, however, there are significant actions and supports that help homeless young women get on the path to achieving better health outcomes and seeing overall improvements in their daily lives. In the clinical setting these facilitators include developing relationships with providers, continuity of care, integrated service delivery, and guarantees of confidentiality. When young homeless people do exhibit personal strength and create their own opportunities, they are often labelled "resilient youth." The last section of this chapter theorizes that resiliency is not so much an inherent personal characteristic, but a result of a supportive community. In examining the relationships that homeless young women value, create, and nurture it becomes apparent that healthy relationships with providers, peers, and family are key to sustaining and supporting youth through difficult times.

Chapter 8 – Living in a Material World: Challenges and Change

The final chapter addresses questions of gender relations and power structures in the broader context of neoliberal policies and social relations, commenting on the implications for equity, policy, health services delivery, and population health. Discourses of risk and criminalization are tied to the destructive emphasis on citizenship through market mechanisms, demonstrating the ways in which the hollowing out of social services has been justified by an ideology of individuality that fails to recognize our shared vulnerability. The attribution of personal responsibility to social problems that are deeply rooted in systemic inequalities effectively privatizes the experiences of those young women who struggle with housing insecurity and homelessness. Policies that allow youth one chance to get independent living right fail to understand the very nature of a life course stage that is characterized by trial and error. For example, for many young women direct entry into the workforce is a flawed solution when maintaining employment depends so heavily on being healthy, housed, stable, and supported. From this understanding of the role of policy, the focus of the chapter turns to broader notions of citizenship and the creation of socially inclusive communities. In so doing, issues of what constitutes political engagement and meaningful participation are discussed to highlight spaces and places of inclusion that warrant more sustained attention: the Internet and public forums for consultation. Finally, I conclude the book by discussing the overall analysis and significant findings of the research, focusing on developing the solution space that will assist young women in achieving their ambitions by knocking down barriers and replacing them with bridges.

2 Once upon a Time: "Storying" Feminist Theory in Neoliberal Times

Introduction

This book seeks to blend art and science to tell a story about young women living in a particular time and space. Feminist theory informs the questions I pose and underlies my understanding of the role of power, place, and intersubjectivity in the lives and well-being of homeless young women. I begin with Foucauldian conceptions of power, while remaining cognizant of the gender-blindness suffered by Foucault, and by many health care workers and administrators, social policy-makers, and health and youth scholars. The critical intersections of race, class, gender, sexuality, age, and ability are foregrounded throughout these chapters. This chapter in particular engages with feminist theories and epistemologies, drawing especially on feminist political economy in the understanding of neoliberalism and government policy and their relationship to women's health and illnesses. While ill health is quite visible in a young woman's life, the social determinants of health status are less apparent. As Dorothy Smith (1999) notes, social relations are organized from "elsewhere," but a strong social analysis can provide people with a thorough understanding of social organization and social relationships. Furthermore, social analysis can help explicate "the social relations and organization pervading her world but invisible in it" (Adams & Sydie 2001, p. 215). Smith believes that such analysis can have emancipatory potential in that it brings seemingly divergent issues together to highlight the complex web of relations omnipresent in people's everyday lives. This chapter attempts to shine a light on those various relationships that intersect to create and maintain homelessness.

Power, Resistance, and Narrative

Foucault (1978, 1980) famously asserts that power is pervasive and that discourse sets limits and imposes restrictions on who and what has power in society. The social, cultural, and political worlds of homeless youth are closely monitored and vigilantly policed, and the decision-making that shapes those worlds is often obscured from the view of the young people who move within them. This type of governance often leads to young people feeling helpless or insignificant (Goodley et al., 2004). Indeed, the young women involved in this project reported feeling powerless in shaping their daily lives. However, while existing power and knowledge relations undoubtedly contribute to the inequalities experienced between and among citizens, power is not static or impermeable to change from below. The local, the transgressive, and the marginal, without which the mighty and the mainstream could not exist, construct difference and form opposition. For this reason it is helpful to understand power as being socially constructed and never entirely the property of one actor or another, creating space for negotiation and change (Petchesky-Pollack, 2003; Plummer, 1995). Narratives too can be understood through these lenses of discourse, power, and historical conditions.

Tamboukou (2008) sees narratives as the effect of power/knowledge relations whereby power produces truth, knowledge, and subjectivity. She calls for attention to be paid to both dominant and marginalized narratives, noting that power shapes the conditions that allow some stories to be told while others are silenced. My goal in this work is to examine those silencing conditions while creating conditions in which the stories of marginalized individuals can be told and heard. "Storying" is a phenomenon that occurs universally – if one has language, whether verbal or visual, one has a story to tell. Plummer (1995) refers to humankind as *homo narrans* – the born storytellers – to underscore the human need for stories and to signal the ways in which communities are built and strengthened by the stories they tell (p. 5). However, it often seems that the need for stories becomes most acute when one feels isolated or ostracized from one's community (Jackson, 2002). For many participants in my study, telling their story seemed strange at first: previously, no one had asked, no one had cared, no one had been non-judgmental. The stories they eventually told were of experience, family, hurt, loss, and resilience. Their stories described a human experience that many people judge, but very few know. Herein lies the value of life-history interviewing that studies the "storied nature of lives, [...] honouring the individuality and complexity of individuals' experiences. It goes beyond the individual or the personal and places narrative accounts and interpretations within a broader social context" (Cole & Knowles, 2001, p. 20). In this way the researcher is allowed to view subjectivity as an amalgamation of the individual and her interaction with social structures, history, culture, and power. Through this lens each participant is not a "homeless youth," but a daughter, mother, friend, worker, student, lover, and struggling citizen. This recognition is central to the tenets of feminist theory.

Feminist Theory and Feminist Political Economy

Feminism has never just been feminism, insofar as it has almost always been characterized by multiple or coalitional feminisms. That said, most feminist scholars would not object to bell hooks' (2000) definition of feminism as "a movement to end sexism, exploitation and oppression," (p. 1). Feminist theorizing, then, necessitates discussing the marriage of privilege and oppression and interrogating the complicated dynamics of privilege/oppression, academy/community, and global/local, while retaining an awareness that these apparent binaries are more effectively conceptualized as spectrums along which women's multiple identities are constituted. As Mohanty (2003) asserts, feminist scholarship must take place on multiple levels: on the level of everyday life, on the level of collective action, and in the form of emancipatory education. In other words, feminist scholarship aims first to understand the world, and then goes beyond understanding to change it. In emphasizing thinking from contradictory positions that value difference and equity over control and privilege, Harding's (1991) conception of standpoint epistemology continues to provide a unique point of entry to the study of women's issues and women's lives. Feminist epistemologies recognize relations of ruling, and draw attention to standpoints, reflexivity, and history (Fonow & Cook, 1991; Maynard & Purvis, 1994; Smith, 1999). Feminist theorizing takes into account the multiple subject positions from which a woman views the world, recognizing especially that factors such as race, class, gender, sexuality, and ability are critical to the ways in which women experience the world. In response to some postmodern critiques of woman-as-subject, Modleski (1991) suggests that retaining the category "woman," while recognizing that each individual is in the process of redefining and constructing that category, remains the most important point of feminist theorizing.

The past, present, and future of anti-racist feminist thought are also fundamental to my conception of feminist theory. Scepticism around the notion of a "universal sisterhood" of feminists became markedly clear in the early writing of Black feminists who sought to expose the racist and classist nature of much White, middle-class feminism in the 1980s (Davis, 1981; hooks, 1984; Lorde, 1984). Many feminists argue that even White middle-class feminism had its internal schisms, which prevented the unification of women solely on the grounds of womanhood. Many women of colour wrote about White women's inability to appreciate the privileges that their whiteness entailed and women of colour and working-class women found it difficult to relate to, let alone subscribe to, a movement that made gains at their expense and that did not speak to their experiences. Thus, rather than identifying as a feminist, hooks (1984) suggests that a person (whether female or male) should employ the language of "advocating feminism," demonstrating that being feminist does not preclude organizing around other identities simultaneously. At the same time that these discussions took place, the epistemologies of academic feminism were also problematized – as they continue to be today – for many of the same reasons (Yee, 2011). For example, theorists such as Trinh (1989) articulated the power imbalances inherent in academic writing and in written language itself, while writers such as Maracle (1996), Morrison (1992), and Mohanty (2003) detailed the subversive and empowering potential of women's oral narratives.

These ideas became central to feminist thought as theorists began to explore the complex intersections and contradictions that were key to constructing identities as unstable and in constant transition. The lived experiences of those both on the periphery and in the mainstream are constructed by location, socio-economic status, race, history, and sexuality – categories that must be taken seriously in order to understand the political realities of difference. These realities were made that much more apparent, and explicit, with the advent of anti-globalization, anti-colonial, and anti-racist feminist studies (Dua & Robertson, 1999; Yee, 2011). At the same time, the field of postcolonial studies has been critiqued for prematurely declaring an end to colonialism, especially as globalization theorists reveal the ways in which First-World identities cannot be separated from Third-World identities (McClintock, 1995; Mohanty et al., 1991; Smith, 1999). This critique is particularly relevant to discussions of homeless young women who have refugee or immigrant status here in Canada.

Stanley (1992) argues that narrative autobiographical accounts are very similar to theoretical accounts, suggesting that creating a binary between theory and experience creates a hierarchy between those who analyse experience and those who experience. In this view epistemology and ontology are not separate but symbiotic. In most feminist research, the relationship between the researcher and her participants has liberating or empowering intentions. The researcher/participant dynamic assumes that the participant is the expert on his or her own life and, as much as possible, attempts to keep the relationship equal. At the same time, however, the researcher must remain aware of her position, her own assumptions, and her relative power vis-à-vis the participant.

Inextricably linked to feminist thought, of course, is the concept of gender. I take Connell's (2002) view of gender as the "structure of social relations that centers on the reproductive arena, and the set of practices (governed by this structure) that brings reproductive distinctions between bodies into social processes" (p. 10). The use of the term "gender" signals the socially constructed nature of masculinity and femininity. Society, with its complexity of socially and culturally determined structural and institutional conditions, determines what are most often unequal relations between men, women, and transgender people. Women are among the most impoverished groups around the globe largely because of their unequal access to power and resources (Doyal, 2000). While biology, or sex, certainly has a crucial role to play in the differing health status and health conditions of men, women, and trans people, gender is a health determinant that can be made health-promoting through more equitable social and systemic change. Moreover, recent criticism refutes the dichotomy between sex and gender, indicating that the categories are mutually constitutive (Hughes & Dvorsky, 2008).

The feminist political economy approach that I adopt in this research recognizes the intersections of institutions and relations that maintain social hierarchies, as well as the social, cultural, and household systems involved in their production and reproduction. Political economy is concerned with how and why inequalities are produced and understands that the choices people make are socially and politically determined by the structures and contexts in which they live (Armstrong et al., 2001; Coburn, 2001). Accepting that human subjects and social structures are mutually constitutive also lets the researcher see the individual as a fit subject for social research, allowing that interviewing a small number of participants, although not representative of the entire population, can yield rich scientific data. In this case, individual lives cannot be spoken about without reference to the historical, material, and social conditions that shape them. A feminist political economy approach to narrative theory, then, highlights women's individual responses, which yield particular life stories, and simultaneously analyses the social constraints that have informed, or even imposed, those responses. As the Personal Narratives Group (1989), an early collective of feminist narrative theorists, contends: "Only by attending to the conditions which create these narratives, the forms that guide them, and the relationships that produce them are we able to understand what is communicated in a personal narrative" (p. 12).

Subjectivity

Feminists have long been working on understandings of subjectivity that allow theorists to re-conceptualize the mutually constitutive relationship between self and society (de Lauretis, 1984; Smith, 1993b). Mama (1995) claims that postmodern theorization of subjectivity provides an apparatus for combining the social and the individual, which allows for the interplay between self and society to flow bidirectionally: the individual is a product of social interaction, while society is the product of the individuals within it. In this line of thinking, then, the self is not unitary or unchanging, but rather is fluid and evolving over time and from interaction to interaction. As Scheman (1997) argues, claims of a unified self require that one projects onto others "the parts of [oneself] deemed too messy or too embarrassing to acknowledge" (p. 126). Allowing for the fragmentation of subjectivity opens up several possibilities. First, that individuals change based on their situation, privileging certain pieces of their identity at certain times and demonstrating the hybridity of identities available to any one person. In this analysis, for example, homelessness is but one aspect of a young woman's identity; youth and gender are others. Second, projecting one's "less desirable" characteristics onto others creates divides between people instead of bringing them together in shared experience, recognizing our common vulnerabilities. Perhaps most important for this project, however, this characterization allows young women to work through multiple identities over their life course and from day to day. In their ability to recreate identity, homeless young women and trans people can be empowered by not having to adhere to a single identity, label, or diagnosis in their struggles to rise above their current situation. Conceptualizing subjectivity in this way also demonstrates how, although their decisions are constrained by societal norms and regulations, young people are active in resisting those constraints.

The concept of multiplicity allows that a person may experience two seemingly contradictory identities simultaneously depending on a given social interaction and that she may be struggling to create a sense of self among competing perceptions of who and what she is (Mama, 1995; Weedon, 1987). This understanding of subjectivity is particularly relevant when storytellers struggle with competing conceptions of who they are depending on their proximity to power in relation to the other actors or structures in the story. Using this lens of subjectivity is crucial to understanding behaviours that are sometimes seen as pathological, but may, in fact, be resourceful negotiations of instances in which a young woman may face varying degrees of "coercion and choice, otherness and affinity, and alienation and belonging" due to multiple subject positions (Rice, 2003, p. 36). Within these spectrums lie opportunities for resistance, co-option and, ultimately, decision-making. Moreover, these understandings of subjectivities break down binaries between mainstream and margin, self and other, judger and judged. In this relational conception of subjectivity we see that privilege and marginality are two sides of the same coin and yet, as a general rule, only one side of the coin draws attention for being "other." For this reason it becomes imperative to understand subjectivity as the product of interaction within and between people and groups, observing that each person possesses attributes that are both privileged and marginalized. A young woman living in a shelter, for example, may be a university student by day, and a patient at a clinic for homeless youth in the evening. These two dimensions of her identity alone create different perceptions of the same young person. As a student she has access to the instruments of the educated, while at the clinic she is stigmatized by her lack of housing.

Subjectivity, then, is created in the here and now, as well as in the past. It both constrains and creates choices; it is social and personal. The social locations of gender, race, culture, age, ability, sexuality, and citizenship status combine to create unique points of entry to young women's narratives and lives. Each characteristic confers a set of social roles and rules, power, and privilege, which influence the ways in which one is able to access resources, how one is treated by others, and where one is situated relative to the hegemonic power structures of a given society. Intersectionality means that selves are fluid and adaptable and that space is created for complexity in negotiating between the role of social structures and the role of individual agency. For the purposes of this research I take Rice's (2003) definition of subjectivity to reflect my thinking on this set of relationships: "An inner landscape formed through the interplay of participants' experiences and cultural meanings available for interpretation; a multiple and contradictory site comprised of their many identities and multi-faceted selves; a site split between subjected and agentic parts that are outcomes of 'othering' and affirming experiences; and a dynamic and creative process of becoming" (p. 31). The participants in my research are never only one thing or another but, like all of us, a product of relations between the social, political, economic, and historical. The more one engages with these structures, the more one comes to understand one's relationship – both in constituting and being constituted – to them. The tensions that exist within the discourses to which young women are exposed are used as signposts in the development of their adult subjectivities. Within dominant discourses that frame young homeless people in certain ways, the youth that inform this research negotiate who and what they are told they are by the media, policy-makers, service providers, peers, and any number of other actors and institutions they engage with daily. Their narratives are evidence of the ways in which they seek out and create counter-narratives and more empowering discourses in developing their subjectivities, while simultaneously internalizing discourses that limit and devalue them. In navigating this landscape of contradiction youth cannot be seen as either bad or good, powerless or powerful. Subjectivity as conceived in the way I have described it here creates space for any range of combinations and possibilities – space for abjection and agency, proscription and possibility.

Neoliberalism and Social Policy

Following Smith's (1990) feminist direction to make visible the often invisible structures of social power and organization, discussing neoliberal discourses and their effects on social policy and, therefore, on the social determinants of health, is critical to paint this theoretical landscape. According to Farmer (2003), neoliberalism advocates "the dominance of a competition-driven market model. Individuals in society, if viewed at all, are viewed as autonomous, rational producers and consumers whose decisions are motivated primarily by economic or material concerns" (p. 5). Langille (2004) characterizes neoliberal governments as those that are fiscally conservative and interested in keeping spending and taxation low. As a result, neoliberalism is related to higher degrees of impoverishment and income inequality and poorer health status within and among nations (Coburn, 2004).

For example, in 2007, the Canadian Centre for Policy Alternatives (Yalnizyan, 2007) released a study that found that the richest 10 per cent of families earns more than 82 times the income of the poorest families in Canada. The researchers conclude that despite the economic boom in the 1990s, a factor that has traditionally been thought to have helped close the income gap, inequality has continued to increase. As income inequality balloons, people are unable to find stable employment and precarious employment is on the rise (ibid.). Furthermore, income inequality, arguably *the* primary determinant of health, is aggravated by the neoliberal agenda that controls public policy here in Canada and globally – an agenda that has seen social programs cut while corporate and personal taxes are lowered (Coburn, 2004). For decades, research into the social determinants of health and political economy has refuted claims that the privatization of health care systems and trickle-down economics help ensure the health of populations; research has shown that, on the contrary, these conditions are aggravating morbidity and mortality (Raphael, 2004b). Politics, health, and economic agendas are obviously interconnected.

Feminist research has demonstrated, however, that the ramifications of these processes of restructuring and capital accumulation cannot be fully understood without an analysis of social reproduction (Bezanson & Luxton, 2006). The unpaid labour of women, while invisible in these processes, is severely impacted by the neoliberal agenda, which intensifies women's subordination and diminishes their health as they continue to be overworked and unrecognized for their double contribution in the paid workforce and at home. This impact was made manifest throughout my interviews with young women who spoke of their mothers' and grandmothers' hardships in the labour market, working several low-paying jobs or experiencing frequent layoffs as they struggled to provide food and secure housing for their families.

The state has a role to play in ensuring the health and income status of women; however, in recent years under neoliberal agendas, many welfare reform measures have continued to cut all but the "most deserving" from the eligibility list (Gilmour & Martin, 2003). Redistributive factors are meant to have an equalizing effect in raising the incomes of those on the bottom through transfers, and lowering the incomes of those at the top through taxation. But as a study from the Canadian Centre for Policy Alternatives (Yalnizyan, 2007) shows, these measures are not being liberally applied. Furthermore, neoliberalism's largest impact in Canada has been on the erosion of the welfare state that has traditionally decommodified citizens' relations with the market (Coburn, 2004). Citizens are now expected to purchase services that were once provided by the state. Homeless youth are especially vulnerable as they do not have the means of purchasing the goods and services they need to survive. They often end up on streets and in shelters when the state is unable or unwilling to provide adequate income or housing support. Despite political assertions that governments need to exercise fiscal restraint, Raphael and Curry-Stevens (2004) note that federal spending as a percentage of GDP in 2004 was at 1950s levels. Resources are less limited now than they have ever been. If indeed the federal government has more resources than ever before, there is a disconnect between the types and levels of support being offered to young people and those they actually need and that could be made available.

Galabuzi (2004) notes that poverty is a key cause of social exclusion and emphasizes that the racialization and feminization of poverty generate multiple marginalities, creating an even greater net impact on the health status of these individuals. Given the clawbacks in welfare policies, many women are forced to live with the threat of violence from partners on whom they are dependent for housing, forced to sacrifice other necessities to pay rent, or forced to move into overcrowded or insecure accommodations (Bryant, 2004). As my interview data demonstrates these clawbacks have very real consequences for children who must also live under insecure conditions.

Facing an economic crisis, Stephen Harper's Conservatives tabled their 2009 federal budget promising job creation, tax cuts, and extended Employment Insurance (EI) (Department of Finance Canada, 2009). Their job creation program, however, focused on "shovel-ready" projects, signalling investment in physical infrastructure in industries that are traditionally male-dominated, such as construction and engineering. Tax cuts came at a time when public money could have been used to bolster the already underfunded social programs that faced escalating numbers of clients in the wake of the economic downturn. Moreover, these tax cuts primarily benefit Canadian middle- and upper-income earners, while taxpayers on the lower end of the spectrum see very few savings, to say nothing of the most vulnerable members of society who are unemployed or who make so little that they do not pay into the taxation system (Canadian Centre for Policy Alternatives, 2009). The 2009 budget extended EI benefits by five weeks, but only to those who meet rigid requirements. Those who fail to qualify – many of whom are women – are still without assistance (ibid.). New requirements included working between 420 and 700 insurable hours in the past 52 weeks, depending on the unemployment rate in the region at the time of filing the claim for benefits, and working a minimum of 910 hours in the qualifying period if one has entered the work force for the first time, thus creating even more rigid requirements for the young (Service Canada, 2009a). The 2009 budget did little to nothing to support social infrastructure – not least to mention failing to provide funding for daycare spaces, which many women rely on as they try to find and pursue paid employment (ibid.).

Lack of government social support is not a new problem in Canada, however. Even the *Canadian Charter of Rights and Freedoms* (1982) fails to give positive rights to society's most vulnerable. The right to adequate housing is not explicitly referenced at any level of government, nor does the *Charter* include clear provisions to positively guarantee social and economic rights (Porter, 2001). The crucial struggle, then, is to have these rights recognized as inherent in section 15, which addresses the protection of equality rights, and in section 7, which declares the right to "life, liberty and security of the person." Owing to the lack of expressed guarantees in the area of social rights, Canada's Supreme Court justices are required to interpret the *Charter* in order to resolve which rights are protected, and to what extent, under the umbrella of sections 7 and 15. In periodic reviews in 1993 and 1998, the Canadian government assured the UN Committee on Economic, Social and Cultural Rights that section 7 of the *Charter* promises, at least, that people are not *deprived of* basic necessities such as food, clothing, and housing (ibid.). This interpretation of the law ensures that laws and policies do not infringe on the right to life, liberty, and security of the person, but it does not guarantee a positive right to those basics (ibid.).

Still other federal legislation enacted to protect the vulnerable has been ignored or eroded by conditions such as "user fees" or "extra billing." The *Canada Health Act* (1984), which guarantees that all Canadians have universal access to comprehensive, publicly administered health care, has been weakened by the advances of private interests. Several of the young women who lend their voices to this study testify that the care they receive is not on the same level as the care received by the gainfully employed; independent young people living below the poverty line do not have access to universal health care. While they can receive care in clinics and emergency rooms, where such facilities exist, young homeless women do not have access to many of the supports accessible to those in the general population, such as drug benefits. This research is an attempt to demonstrate how those who are living under the label of homelessness experience these policies and their associated discourses.

Conclusion

Each of these theoretical approaches is an integral part of the overall analysis presented here. Feminist theory and feminist political economy provide the overarching framework for the following chapters, especially in their emphasis on heterogeneity, intersectionality, and social structures. Broader issues of subjectivity and power across time and space have serious repercussions in the lives and, therefore, the health of homeless young women. Subjectivity occurs in the clash between the individual and her encounters with social structures, history, and politics. For this reason, then, although many of the challenges faced by young women are due to systemic barriers, women themselves are not entirely without agency; they are active participants in their own lives and environments. In fact, it is for this reason that I emphasize the utility of narrative theory in allowing the voices of young women to resonate against, alongside, and in-between simultaneously occurring discussions around the role of policy, neoliberalism, and political processes. Each of these points of discussion is intimately related to the social determinants of health. As neoliberal policies result in the clawing back of services, dilapidated social housing stock, and vulnerable members of society sleeping on sofas and street corners, in cars and alleyways, those same people are getting sicker and less able to access the basic necessities of life. Privileging the accounts of young women demonstrates the heterogeneity of the population, exposes the multitude of pathways into homelessness, and blends life and theory without pointing to singular causal factors. Through the health narratives of the young people involved in the research, we hear that social inclusion, although called by many different names, is a determinant of health. Creating spaces in which young homeless people feel included and at home can make a significant impact on their future success.

3 Girl, You'll Be a Woman ... Soon: A Narrative Project

Introduction

This chapter provides an overview of the methodological underpinnings of this work. I start with a discussion of the recruitment of participants and the ethical implications of working with homeless young women so as to emphasize the importance of protecting those who are often unprotected while also valuing their critical contributions to improving the services which assist them in their quest to live fulfilling, independent lives. The narrative theory and methodology that drive the content of this book are rooted in these same goals. The narrative project undertaken in this research aims to highlight the insights of the young people whose lived experiences provide a wealth of advice and information that can be used to improve health and social services in their communities. More than this, however, the narrative approach also strives to partner with young people to empower them through the knowledge that their stories matter and that their voices are being heard.

Locating Participants

In recruiting for this study, my goal was to attract participants who shared social locations in terms of age range, gender, and housing status. The eight young women who participated are reflective of the diversity and the racial and cultural makeup of Toronto's shelter system. Although I want to avoid making generalizations in this study, I have seen, and social and mental health workers have verified, that their cases are not atypical. The sample was selected mainly with a view to reflect the diversity of the youth homeless population and to provide a relevant range of examples. Theoretical sampling techniques were employed to ensure that this was the case, allowing me to form comparisons between participants and to develop theoretical discussion (Patton, 2002). The process of finding participants began with a cursory search of Toronto's shelter system. I soon learned that there is only one shelter in all of Toronto that caters specifically to female and trans youth – the YWCA's First Stop Woodlawn shelter. I approached its director and asked if she might meet with me to discuss my proposed research.

Once I was granted access to the facility I attended two meetings at the shelter, one with staff and one with residents of the house. The meeting with the residents was crucial to the recruitment process as it gave the young women a chance to see me and ask questions about my intentions and motivations. After this meeting I posted flyers and sign-up sheets in the communal areas of the shelter and in the hallways outside the young women's rooms. Interested individuals were invited to contact me or to sign up directly. After interviewing five participants, I realized that I was missing the perspectives of youth who were not attached, or only loosely attached, to the shelter system. With the help of a street outreach worker, I began to recruit participants directly from the streets. At the end of the final interview, I asked each participant to complete a demographics form; their responses are noted in Table 1.

Ethics

The ethical considerations involved in this project were manifold. Working with "vulnerable" populations, such as those that experience homelessness, is a consideration in and of itself, and working with "vulnerable" minors considerably complicates the researcher's ethical obligations. The *United Nations General Assembly Convention on the Rights of the Child* (1989) requires signatory states to "assure to the child who is capable of forming his or her own views the right to express those views freely in all matters affecting the child" and affirms children's rights to freedom of expression, including the "freedom to seek, receive and impart information and ideas of all kinds, regardless of frontiers" (Article 12(1) and 13(1)). To this end it benefits children, and the societies in which they live, to have their voices heard and counted in public discourses such as academic research. The challenge, then, is to design research that is youth-centred and sensitive to the particularized needs

Table 1. Background of Participants in Study

Participant	Age	Ethnicity	Sexuality	Education	Most Worrisome Health Condition	How Do You Rate Your Health Care?*
Danika**	21	West Indian	Hetero	Some university	Stress	6
Radha	19	South Asian	Mostly hetero	Grade 12	Depression	5
Jean	20	Ojibwe	Lesbian	Grade 12	Mental health	8
Savannah	20	Native Canadian	Hetero	Grade 12	Alcoholism	9
Arielle	20	Congolese	Hetero	Some high school	Stress	10
Faith	17	Métis	Mostly lesbian	Grade 10	Kidneys	9
Raven	16	Caucasian	Mostly lesbian	Grade 9	Trans issues	4
Erin	15	Caucasian	Hetero	Grade 8	Homelessness	5

* Rating based on a scale from 1 to 10, with 10 indicating total satisfaction
** All participants' names have been anonymized for their protection. Participants chose their own aliases.

of young people. Mayall (1996) suggests that these goals are best ac-
complished by ensuring that the research regards young participants
as competent and reflexive, gives young people a voice by taking their
contributions seriously, and aims to work for the benefit of young people. Working with homeless young women requires particular care not
only in research design, but also in recognizing the ways in which youth
policy often renders them even more vulnerable to exploitation. In the
absence of adult legal rights and social benefits, young people often feel
unable to speak out against treatment they regard as questionable or
discriminatory (Bessant, 2005). These factors have often meant that research is *on* youth rather than *with* youth, suppressing young voices in
favour of the more paternalistic, "authoritative" voice of the researcher.
For me, working with youth does not mean ignoring the unequal relations of power between researcher and participant, but rather acknowl-
edging that those power relations are the exact reason that the opinions
of young women need to be heard.

In our discipline we rely on our own moral and ethical leanings, and
on guidelines from ethics committees, to protect the vulnerable. Article
5.2 of the Tri-Council Policy Statement on Ethical Conduct for Research
Involving Humans (Canadian Institutes of Health Research, Natural
Sciences, and Engineering Research Council of Canada, and Social Sciences and Humanities Research Council of Canada, 1998) affirms that:
"although ethical duties to vulnerable populations preclude the exploitation of those who are incompetent to consent for themselves for research purposes, there is nonetheless an obligation to conduct research
involving such people because it is unjust to exclude them from the
benefits that can be expected from research." The policy statement's
current guidelines state that in minimal risk research involving participants 16 years of age and older, parental consent is not required; for
more than minimal risk research involving participants 16 to 17 years of
age, parental consent may be required; and for participants under the
age of 16, parental consent is required.

The ethical guidance provided by this statement, however, seems
only to apply to "typical" young people; it relies on parents to make
decisions on behalf of their children, while recognizing that "in some
situations adolescents can be regarded as competent and provide their
own consent." Beyond this, the policy statement does not specify particular guidelines in the case of adolescents who have not reached the
age of majority, but who are without legal guardianship or who are living independently. Conducting research with homeless youth under

the age of 18, then, presents a number of issues in obtaining informed consent, especially given many have no ties to their birth families, and weak or no ties to extended family or caregivers.

To that end, the York University Human Participants Review Committee (HPRC) recently requested that researchers working in the area of homelessness draft a set of guidelines that could be employed to ensure that this type of research is conducted in such a way that the dignity of participants is promoted and the safety of homeless minors is given considerable weight (Office of Research Ethics, 2010). The resulting guideline document recommends the following requirements be met when working with young people in these circumstances:

- The young person who is homeless has given his/her consent.
- For young people under the age of 16, research must be deemed minimal risk by HPRC.
- Counselling services and supports for youth participants are arranged beforehand and are accessible following the research encounter. Ideally such supports should be provided by homeless community service providers with expertise working with this population.
- Research participants must be informed of the availability of such supports and provided with information about how to access such supports, prior to the interview.
- If interviews and research are conducted in settings where such supports are not provided "on site," the researcher must make an attempt to provide the young person with access to such service, including arranging transportation where necessary, for example, in the form of public transit or cab fare.
- In obtaining HPRC ethics approval, the researcher must clearly demonstrate the procedures put in place to offer protection to research participants under the age of 18.

Each of these recommendations was taken into account and met by this research.

Feminist Narrative Research

The function of the researcher is [...] to give voice and the printed page to those who require mediation to get their voices into the public arena.

(Wengraf, 2000, p. 140)

The goals of the feminist researcher are decidedly different from one working from a positivist perspective – feminist research claims to be neither value-free nor impartial. As a result, the voice of the researcher and her chosen methodology will necessarily shape the production of knowledge (Harding, 1991). The approach to interviewing used here, for example, is viewed as a collaborative effort between researcher and participant; however, the researcher remains cognizant of power differentials and the implications and limitations of aspiring to a shared voice. The fact that I take a feminist perspective, especially when the majority of my participants do not, certainly plays a role in shaping the final product of my study, although not in the telling of the stories themselves (Goodley et al., 2004). While my research is explicitly grounded in the feminist tradition that values women's experiences, it is not based solely on the stories of the eight participants. Individuals are not able to explain everything about their lives and the social forces that impact upon them, just as researchers cannot patronizingly assume to know everything about their participants' lives. Employing a feminist methodology demands both experiential knowledge and critical reflection thereon (Harding, 1991). Storytelling does not aspire to an objective truth, but rather to the truths as the storyteller sees them. As the Personal Narratives Group (1989) posits in their reflection on women's life stories,

> unlike the Truth of the scientific ideal, the truths of personal narratives are neither open to proof nor self-evident. We come to understand them only through interpretation, paying careful attention to the contexts that shape their creation and to the world views that inform them. (p. 261)

Hill-Collins (1991, 2000) also reminds researchers that participants at the intersection of positions, like race and class, in the development of any particular point of view are more likely to experience multiple forms of oppression. Theirs are the stories that need to be heard and understood as complex creations generated by structures and relations of power.

Narrative Theory

Narrative becomes the vehicle through which lives, social relations, and structures of power come to be perceived. Through narrative each of the aforementioned theoretical perspectives intersects. As Jackson

(2002) suggests, "rather than perpetuate [the] unhappy antinomy between science and art, fact and fiction, I think we should try to see that each is necessary to the other" (p. 102). Jackson's sentiment entirely echoes my own view that the merging of art and science has the potential to create a different type of social science research – the type of research that in its transdisciplinarity appeals to the many rather than to the few. Having come to social science from an arts background, I wanted to try to harness the universality of stories to the specificity of individual marginalized voices. Drawing on the narrative work of Arendt (1958), and its extension by Jackson (2002), and on the "sociology of stories" proposed by Plummer (1995), I see this project as socially intertextual: it is a story (a book written by a social actor inside a social institution) about the stories (of systemic barriers, political failings, and social opportunities) inside of stories (told by young social actors) (p. 17). The sociology of stories seeks to move beyond the more literary theory–influenced reading of narratives as texts, towards a vision of stories as social actions performed by social actors in social worlds (ibid.). This blending of the subjective with the broader social order creates one way to construct reality and validate multiple ways of knowing and to see truth not as static or singular, but multiple and context specific. As Ifekwunigwe (1999) states: "Stories meld the macrostructural of history and politics with the microstructural concerns of identity politics as they are manifest, negotiated and reinvented through the simultaneous prisms of gender, generation, race, class and ethnicity" (p. 47). Seen from this perspective, once-unobtrusive texts take on political significance in their ability to illustrate the complex web of relationships between individuals and the structural, institutional, and normative conditions of their societies. Narrative theory, then, allows investigation to occur on the ground at the individual level, but recognizes that neither the individual nor the wider social order can be analysed without the other. Seen as a political process and as a tool that is almost universally accessible, the sociology of stories is indeed powerful.

Today, Western society is witnessing the fetishization of autobiography, with the popularization of confessional talk shows such as Oprah, parasocial obsessions with the lives of celebrities, social media such as Facebook, and reality TV. Much of this phenomenon is related to the cult of individualization being advanced by neoliberal ideologies; however, self-storying also has a more noble and potentially subversive place in our lives. As Arendt (1958) makes clear, storytelling is a social act in which stories are created and recreated, where meanings are transitory and changeable. I share her view that storytelling is not simply personal or simply social, but rather a "subjective in-between" that recognizes a dialogue between the two, recognizing that they are mutually constitutive (p. 182). Following Arendt's work, Jackson (2002) theorizes that stories have at least two strategic functions: to transform private meanings into public meanings, and to help individuals maintain agency in times of hardship or oppression. But telling and hearing stories can also result in two different outcomes. Hearing the stories of others can allow listeners to feel justified in their preconceived notions, to "other" the marginal voice of the storyteller and, in so doing, validate prejudices that allow one to maintain one's hold on "the Truth." On the other hand, hearing another's story can cause one to question what one knows, to eschew stereotypes, to embrace rather than to fear difference so as to "push back and pluralize our horizons of knowledge" (ibid., p. 25). It is this latter outcome that I hope to invoke through this project and encourage readers to meditate upon.

Like narrative-based theory, identity-based feminist theory has sometimes been criticized as anachronistic in postmodern, poststructuralist conceptions of subjectivity and identity. But narrative feminist approaches are postmodern in their rejection of "grand narratives," and go beyond simple rejection to demystify the often manipulative power of discourse by reflecting on the nature of knowing, and the institutional and political functions served by labels such as "homeless" and "youth," and by remaining attentive to fragmented subjectivities (Goodley et al., 2004). The narrative and feminist theory that guide this work are informed by poststructuralist thought in its attention to the nature of power, the plausibility of truth claims, and the status of the subject (Weedon, 1999). Certainly these influences have altered the way feminist theorists think about their research; however, many feminist scholars have critiqued postmodernism's over-privileging of language, which makes its ideas virtually inaccessible to a larger non-academic audience, a phenomenon that is referred to as the "linguistic turn" in postmodern feminist research (hooks, 1984; Weedon, 1999). Likewise, and for similar reasons, Smith (1999) claims that feminist postmodernism eliminates the link between social science and political activism in failing to examine the structural relations of inequality and in divorcing discourse from the local realities of everyday lives. Instead of entirely dismissing these developments, feminist scholars have demonstrated the productive ways in which postmodern and poststructural ideas can be incorporated into a materially grounded approach to feminist studies. Brooks' (1997) helpful division of postmodernism into "strong" and "weak" allows that strong postmodernism is characterized by a lack of political strength, while advocating weak postmodernism that does not erase the subject, but rather questions the process of its construction. In so doing one is able to highlight difference, while avoiding the relativism for which postmodernism is often criticized. Identity, then, can be grounded in social fact as an active process of self-definition that can become a part of a larger collective, diversified movement (Bannerji, 2000).

Narrative theorists too have given careful consideration to the strengths and pitfalls of postmodern and poststructural thought, and while there remains some conflict between humanist and poststructuralist narrative traditions, the two are united by their shared view of narratives as modes of resistance to dominant forms of power (Andrews et al., 2008). In short, the two are brought together by the politicizing role of narrative. Andrews and colleagues agree that the ideal approach to narrative theorizing synthesizes the two by borrowing the singular, unified subject from humanism and combining it with the poststructural assertion that narrative is negotiable and negotiated, socially constituted and socially constituting. Likewise, in line with the postmodern and poststructural theories, narrative researchers counter the positivist contention that this type of research cannot yield credible empirical evidence as autobiographies are neither "accurate" nor "inaccurate" accounts of some quantifiable "real" experience, but are instrumental in giving form to experience and day-to-day lives (Stivers, 1993).

Feminist and narrative theorists contest the postmodern claim of the impossibility of the subject on the grounds that, although we are inundated with competing stories from various media, people continue to interpret their daily experiences. The vehicles people use to formulate identity have changed greatly as a result of new technologies and global media, yet Crawley and Broad (2004) maintain, "it is the times that are most postmodern, but the process of making sense of them for the everyday actor remains" (p. 66). Creating a sense of self is, for the most part, a narrative process. People understand themselves and others through stories of contact with the world and with one another; they use stories to order and make sense of their lives. Therefore, narrative approaches to subjectivity are not a distortion of reality, but rather a confirmation of life's proceedings (Stivers, 1993). The stories we tell allow us to explain ourselves to others, and help us explain ourselves to ourselves. In short, as *homo narrans*, our stories create our worlds.

In his Massey Lectures entitled *The Truth about Stories,* writer Thomas King (2003) discusses the ways in which the telling and retelling of *particular* stories come to shape our understandings of ourselves. He tells his audience the story of his own youth, his absent father, and the ways in which that story has come to define him: "I tell the stories not to play on your sympathies but to suggest how stories can control our lives, for there is a part of me that has never been able to move past these stories, a part of me that will be chained to these stories as long as I live" (p. 9).

In telling our stories we share our lived realities – our pasts, presents, and futures – with others who may or may not relate to, understand, or learn from them; regardless of what others take away from our stories, they come to see us as human like they are. In this way storytelling is a way of repossessing one's humanity and identity, of "turning object into subject, givenness into choice, what into who" (Jackson, 2002, p. 105). This reclamation of the self is especially important to the young women I have worked with. Accustomed to being seen as objects ("street kids"), in telling their stories they become subjects with names and faces and voices. In response to postmodernism, then, we must not advocate the erasure of a subject who is actively in the process of self-definition, but rather question the process of her stories and the construction of her identities.

From this point it is critical to explain narrative theory's perspective on "truth" and "lies" in storytelling. From the positivist perspective it would seem that stories are an unreliable, unscientific form of research because one never knows what is truth and what is fiction in autobiography: people lie, stories change, two people will tell the same story in opposite ways. However, storytelling does not claim to unveil an "ultimate truth" because, as I have outlined above, truth is relative to where one is positioned, to whom one is speaking, and any other number of variables. Arendt's (1965) understanding of this contention was that narrative does not seek to uncover some essential element buried just beneath the surface, but rather seeks to foreground new or different understandings through social interactions. Jackson (2002) also reminds us that human life does not run like the plot of a story, moving linearly from beginning to middle to end, resulting in a neat ending with all the strings neatly tucked away. I find it helpful to envision the storyteller as the author of the story, rather than as the story itself, which is garnered from viewing the narrative as a social construction, shaped by interactions between the teller and social structures. In narrative research, a researcher who has heard someone tell their life history does not assume that she has been given "the whole story"; she recognizes that she hears a truth, but not *the* truth. The goal is to hear a story, take it at face value, and understand that it was told to you on that specific day, in that place at that time. The narrative identity garnered from autobiography is simultaneously fictitious and real, revisable and ongoing, creating the possibility for future change (Martin, 1995).

In the case of this particular research I realized that there are innumerable reasons that dictate one's ability or desire to tell a story: language, safety, fear, mistrust, socio-economic status, and so on. In accordance with Plummer (1995), narrative researchers quickly learn that "the power to tell a story, or indeed not to tell a story, under the conditions of one's own choosing, is part of the political process" (p. 26). Inundated by stories as we are, through film, literature, and day-to-day interactions, we are able to easily recognize "good stories" – those that are clear, well-developed, and logical. In narrative research with vulnerable populations "good stories" are not always possible or desirable. For example, when listening to a participant with mental illness, one cannot disregard or dismiss a story that seemingly has no direction, meaning, or logical order, because to do so is to invalidate a particularized and unrepresented voice (Barham & Hayward, 1991).

Secrets, too, have a fundamental place in the social significance of storytelling. They are used when truth becomes too overwhelming, or for self-protection, and can be critical to one's sense of power, especially when telling too much creates vulnerability (Plummer, 1995). Jackson (2002) makes the important distinction between "truth effects" that preserve and bolster social order, and those that are related to personal existential struggles. Many fiction writers have contended that their genre often allows them to tell the truth about injustice and corruption in a way that would be impossible in a non-fictional medium. Camus reminds us that to write fiction is "to say more than is true, and, as far as the human heart is concerned, to express more than one feels" (cited in ibid., p. 28). As the women's stories and my analytical chapters will show, fiction plays an enormously important role in coping with difficult daily realities.

The most powerful effect of narrative research is to bring lived realities to bear on psychosocial tensions between subjectivity and alterity, and although the narratives of these young women are often inconsistent, they challenge political discourse as much as political discourse challenges them (Ifekwunigwe, 1999). In narrative research there is the potential to shift the balances of power discussed above. Stories are told within what Plummer (1995) calls "interpretative communities" of tellers and listeners that are political, cultural, and social actors. For this reason, he attests, personal narratives may function as calls for representation from the disenfranchised. Because this research represents differing accounts of youth homelessness it destabilizes common perceptions of what it is to be "homeless," thus demonstrating the multiple identities and faces of the label (Goodley et al., 2004). The voices of young people reveal complex subjects rather than objects of scorn or pity. This line of argumentation, Stivers (1993) maintains,

> makes room in critical social science for personal narrative, since it melds life and theory without insisting on there being only one story, and thus provides the grounding for an impulse toward social change that still acknowledges the fundamental (though not absolute) authenticity of an interpretation based on direct experience. (p. 423)

Narrative research does not position experience against knowledge but, like feminist research, understands experience as a valuable form of knowledge in conversation with theory and analysis. Arendt's (1994) work is especially valuable here in reminding us that the power of narrative is not simply knowing something about the other, but rather communicating with the other through interpersonal exchange. In these narratives the listener is invited to discover the personal side of a phenomenon she may assume she already knows, in hope that she might find that she did not really know it at all.

Life History

> It is to the artistic to which we must turn, not as a rejection of the scientific, but because with both we can achieve binocular vision. Looking through one eye never did provide much depth of vision.
>
> (Eisner, 1981, p. 74)

Studies like Connell's (2005) *Masculinities* and Ifekwunigwe's (1999) *Scattered Belongings* have aptly demonstrated the efficacy of life history studies in the fields of sociology and gender studies. Drawing on Sartre, Connell (1991) chooses life history methods because of their ability to "document social structure, collectivities, and institutional change at the same time as personal life" (p. 143). Life history is not simply unstructured narrative analysed as an end in and of itself. Instead it requires an understanding of the social structures that surround and assist in creating the narrative and the individual. Second-wave life history analyses adopt a "small story" approach, which focuses on the contexts surrounding narrative rather than on the pattern or preferences of language as is often done in traditional literary analysis (Phoenix, 2008). In so doing, the life history methodology can be used to study identities through local places, spaces, and behaviours, while remaining effective in the face of non-linear or incoherent narratives, like those often told by people living with mental illnesses (ibid.). The epistemology of this social strain of life story research is therefore hermeneutic, qualitative, specific, and constructive, and seeks authenticity over validity, valuing content over form (Goodley et al., 2004).

This type of storying, in comparison to that of literary analysis, conceptualizes participants and their stories as being produced by the dynamic tensions between circumstance and resources, or a lack thereof, and by the resulting social actions that they produce (Crawley & Broad, 2004). Life history methodologists believe that gaining insight into the lives of particular individuals allows for the understanding of broader communities and, by extension, for the partial explanation of broader social conditions (Cole & Knowles, 2001). In so doing, relations of power and dominant discourses that may have been otherwise obscured become clearer. In his book *Telling Sexual Stories*, Plummer (1995) looks at the Kraft-Ebbing studies of sexuality that infamously pathologized homosexual behaviour. Whereas Kraft-Ebbing looked at sexual stories to find deviance, Plummer looks to find normalcy, recognizing that shifting the stories that are told, and how we tell them, can change the relations of power. I position my own work in this school of life storying, not as an attempt to normalize teenage homelessness, but rather to demonstrate that each young woman presented here lives the life of a teenager. While many people view homelessness as a form of social deviance, I seek to convey the message that many of the young women sought to convey to me: homeless young women are ordinary young women living under extraordinary circumstances. Under neoliberalism especially, young people are challenged with the task of creating meaningful adult identities that conform to accepted social norms while also navigating the cult of individuality, mostly defined by their consumer choices. Many theorists have argued that constructing a coherent life story is a critical part of this challenge (Giddens, 1991; McAdams et al., 2006; Singer, 2004). The inability or reluctance to create a well-articulated self-defining adult narrative may therefore signal a sort of perpetual childhood. As demonstrated in the interview data, a lack of narrative coherence often inspires paternalistic and judgmental behaviours from others, which obstruct a young person's ability to access the resources required to live independently. Life history methodology asserts that although a storyteller's narrative may at times become tangential or confused there is still great value in listening to, and truly hearing, a story for the first time.

One of my primary motivations for using a life history approach was the particular age of the participants I sought to work with. Life history is often conceived of as an end-of-life, or at least middle-age, phenomenon. Boenisch-Brednich (2002) argues that adults tend to form essential narratives of their lives as a result of key events in their past. Over time, she says, repeated tellings of a story lead to the creation of a well-polished presentation that one can recite almost without thinking about it. Therefore, this particular sort of interviewing with young people avoids the rehashing of tried and true adult narratives and opens up the field of life history to fresh voices. At their particular life stage, the life history narratives of the participants in my research are either newly minted or in the process of becoming. Like adults, however, youth – and independently housed youth in particular – already occupy a number of subject positions. They are daughters, friends, partners, workers, students, lovers, and mothers who have created deep and complex life histories – even in the course of only 14, 17, or 20 years.

Life history employs particular methods to achieve its ends, the most important of which are in-depth semi-structured interviews, followed by thematic interpretation, analysis, and theorization (Cole & Knowles, 2001). This methodology involves the close inspection of stories and those things that comprise them: actors, actions, institutions, and the communications between and within them. Asking questions about who produces particular stories, as well as why, under what circumstances, for what purposes, and in which places they do so, is essential to the projects of feminism and life history (Gubrium & Holstein, 2009). Using this methodology also requires the researcher to question his or her own preconceived notions and categorizations, allowing the participants' voices to guide the analysis. Keeping with the goals of feminist research, this methodology allows for the politicizing of the personal, exploring the relationships and symbiosis between two sides of a dichotomy: personal and private, self and other, actor and institution (Leavy, 2007). In this way the storyteller remains at the centre of her story while the researcher studies particular concepts as a means of understanding the contexts within which the narrator lives (ibid.). Creating linkages between biographies and social structures provides the researcher with a more complete picture of the ways in which individuals and their environments become mutually constitutive. In the case of research with marginalized populations, life history brings to light alternative ways of knowing, taking what might typically be seen as the stories of "problem kids" and emphasizing the multiple subjectivities at play when young people are confronting an often harsh set of circumstances (Rice, 2003). In-depth interviews, then, last significantly longer than typical research interviews as they mine for greater detail and broader understandings of given situations. For this reason, the researcher usually spends several sessions with the storyteller over the course of weeks or even months (Leavy, 2007).

Life history methodology requires that the researcher view herself as an active listener, paying close attention to the subtleties and silences within the narrator's story and resisting urges to control the conversation. As Leavy (2007) notes, individuals vary greatly in their ability to completely and freely express how they feel about a given issue or set of circumstances. For this reason, deep listening to voices that have traditionally been barred from dominant discourse is key to creating a broader and more inclusive understanding of the human experience (ibid.). When listening to an in-depth interview, the life history researcher must also consider what the storyteller might think is the desired answer to a particular question, and take into account the ways in which the storyteller might feel pressure to conform to, or to resist, particular narratives (Gubrium & Holstein, 2009). Many speakers as well as listeners internalize a set of guidelines against which they judge what is and is not a good story, including linearity, plot, and forward momentum. In the case of marginalized individuals, especially those with mental health conditions, applying such criteria would mean excluding these crucial, seldom heard narratives. Once again, social structures and expectations can have a profound influence on who gets heard and why. In working with individuals who may not have all the tools to tell a well-constructed story, or who may not wish to adhere to traditional chronological forms of narrative, researchers must anticipate brief descriptions, seemingly tangential storylines, repetition, and contradiction, all of which are telling in and of themselves to those who are engaged in deep listening (ibid.). In conducting interviews in this style, the researcher must think about silences, moral judgments (both her own and the storyteller's), how social expectations and structures are shaping the story being told, and the ways in which the narrator's speech style (slang, nervousness, repetitions) influences the story that is told (Leavy, 2007). Life historians must also be mindful of the ways in which different styles of communication can be central to the story. One's positioning within a particular culture or country can influence not only what is said, but also how it is said and how these factors reflect a particular method of storytelling (ibid.). For instance, one participant in my research, Arielle, is Congolese and often spoke in parables, becoming frustrated if I was unable to see the significance in a given story or metaphor, or if I required clarification: "Listen, it means that in my country we speak in parables and if you don't understand that is too bad. The rice and bread represent people, women who have men." Life history research is not just simple information transfer, but rather narrative work that requires attention to detail, context, and collaborative constitution between storyteller and listener (Gubrium & Holstein, 2009).

Narrative Construction

Presenting the data in this type of study is difficult: abbreviation is necessary, but the goal of life history research is to present just that: a life history. I decided to work in this capacity and draw on this methodology with the explicit goal of allowing those who are rarely heard to tell their stories in their own voices. Ultimately, however, the telling of these stories is mediated by my interests as a researcher, my particular lens, and my understanding of the essence of these stories (Chamberlayne et al., 2000). Where it was possible, each of the young women read and approved the version of her story that appears in the next chapter. In three instances the participants were untraceable and therefore unable to validate the final version of their story. I have been as faithful as possible to their accounts, use of language, and idiosyncrasies. The degree to which the young women are able to articulate themselves varies greatly from participant to participant depending on a number of factors, particularly mental health status.

In the young women's stories, I have also consciously left in words and phrases that may be considered offensive to some, including homophobic and racist remarks. These examples are revealing in that they demonstrate how particular individuals feel about sensitive issues but, more importantly, they illustrate how personal opinions are shaped by social worlds thereby creating further complexity in an already complex landscape (Leavy, 2007). While one participant indicates that she struggles with homophobic attitudes from other shelter residents, another participant uses the word 'gay' to signify something she thinks is inferior, demonstrating ways in which homophobia, whether subtle or overt, acts as a barrier for LGBT2Q-identified youth. Through these inter-narrative comparisons, the reader is exposed to the conflicts that happen between homeless young people. I have tried to capture the unique personalities of each of the young women in the condensed and chronological version of their stories. In the data chapters, I select smaller segments of their stories to document the processes I attempt to explain and problematize therein. The following chapter introduces each young woman as a real person who, like all of us, struggles with and celebrates moving forward through her life. I make no claims that these stories speak for all young women who live in exceptional circumstances, even those who share similar social identities. But they do in some ways resonate with, and shed light on, the lives of other women – homeless and housed, rich and poor, old and young. I hope each of us sees a piece of our adult or teenage self reflected back in these pages, for it is in identification that we find compassion.

4 Girls Aloud: Narratives and Self-Stories

Each of us has that right, that possibility, to invent ourselves daily. If a person does not invent herself, she will be invented. So, to be bodacious enough to invent ourselves is wise.

Maya Angelou

Introduction

This chapter reflects the voices of the eight young women I spoke to over the course of four months. Although the transcript of each individual's interviews was over one hundred pages long, here I have condensed each into four to seven pages. Choosing which of the many stories to tell was by far one of the most difficult tasks of this project. In each case I decided to convey the significant or formational life events and life stories that brought these young women to where they were at the point of interview. Each interview began with the probe: Tell me about yourself. The first line of each story begins there.

These stories introduce the young people whose voices inform the subsequent chapters, giving readers a more holistic picture of who these women are and the formative events of their lives. The young women's stories demonstrate that their lives and health statuses are not the result of poor choices or personal failures, but rather the result of any number of structural inequalities that are engineered into the fabric of social and legal systems. Real people create and enforce policy and real people suffer the consequences or share in the benefits. Despite a multitude of constraints, however, these young women are making decisions daily and carving out spaces for themselves. They are advocating for themselves and others on a regular basis. They are engaged in resistance.

The stories allow the reader to understand that homelessness is not only a matter of material circumstance but also, and perhaps more importantly, a matter of the meaning that young women ascribe to their experiences, a demonstration of the ways that interactions with others have both helped and hindered their personal progress, and a testament to how the confluence of social and political factors influences the ways in which they understand themselves. Each of these factors ultimately influences the health and well-being of young people in exceptional circumstances: mapping the routes between social and health inequality requires consideration of the material, emotional, and intellectual scope of everyday people's everyday lives (Neal, 2004). In a sense, then, the stories are cartographic projects – "life maps" that allow the reader to travel alongside the young women as they trace their paths to their present circumstances (CRISIS UK, 2007, p. 11). In many cases their journeys began even before these young women were born: in residential schools, colonized countries, or broken homes. Homelessness is a process, and for these young people it is but one part of their becoming – creating pieces of who they were, who they are, and who they want to be.

Rather than passively seeing snapshots frozen in time, the reader is instead provided the opportunity to understand homelessness journeys as spatial and temporal, occurring every day from an early age and continuing beyond the scope of the passages provided here. The starting points of each map are different, as are the stops along the way and the ultimate destinations; however, through these stories one can see some well-worn pathways connecting the eight women to similar housing situations, patterns of service usage, and health concerns. Although this chapter does not explicitly discuss the young women's health concerns or their health histories, the stories told here provide the critical context for understanding their health narratives. In introducing the young women, this chapter also introduces the social determinants of health, such as poverty, gender, and social and physical environment. What is said here cannot be separated from, and is in all cases a correlational factor in, their health status.

To protect the identities of the tellers all names have been fictionalized. I have intentionally resisted editorializing and did not write a conclusion to this chapter because I want the voices of the young women, and not my own, to resonate at the end of these powerful stories. This is their chapter, their chance to share their understandings of their realities unencumbered by a so-called authoritative voice. Each young woman is the author of her own experience.

SAVANNAH

I met Savannah at the shelter several days after she had moved in. She was self-possessed and had a knack for storytelling, which she attributed to growing up in a storytelling culture. She spoke confidently and laughed easily. During her quiet moments she fought back tears and steadied herself by talking about her grandma, who she identified as her primary source of comfort. All of our interviews took place in the shelter; during the second meeting we were relocated to a room in the basement that was stocked with art supplies. What I remember most about her was how broadly she smiled when she realized that she was able to paint without cost while she lived at the shelter. On our third meeting, only two days later, she showed me the painting she was working on. It reflected her pride in her Aboriginal identity, her feelings of loss and renewal; above all, it was a testament to her determination to rise above adversity.

My name is Savannah. I'm not from Toronto. I just moved here in June. I moved cuz I was in an ugly relationship. He was controlling and he kept me from going to school and from trying actually to get a job. He would keep me from seeing friends and keep me from seeing family. My grandmother raised me my whole life. I talk to my mother at times, but our relationship is ugly too. My father's not involved in my life. I have seven brothers and two sisters, but we all have different mothers except for me and my one brother. He grew up with my mother. I grew up sometimes there and sometimes on the reserve with my grandma.

I guess I had an OK childhood. I didn't really do what children do. When I was three or four, I was molested by my own babysitter. It was a family member that my grandmother trusted. And, uh, going through all that, I was sexually active at a young age. I was doing stuff with boys my age when I was like seven or eight. Like, I didn't have sex or anything. I was just like doing stuff. I was confused.

My mother, uh, the reason that I went back and forth, back and forth, was because my mother was abusive to me. Like, if she couldn't find my brother to beat up she would attack me. And she would leave us home by ourselves when we were like seven years old. Like, we didn't know how to cook. We didn't know how to clean. We didn't know nothing. We would mess up the house cuz we were just young, right? And she wouldn't let us go outside because she didn't want anyone to see our faces, to see that we were alone.

I remember this one time she won money at bingo and I was shifting through my mother's stuff, cuz I was like bored. I found her little stash of money and I thought, "I'm hungry," cuz we didn't have no food. Nothing. I was like, "Are you hungry?" to my brother. He was like, "Yeah!" I was like, "OK, I'm going to steal a little bit of money then for bread and bologna." So I took like three bucks. It was enough to buy a little thing of bologna and bread. And we were sitting there eating and we didn't know what time my mom was going to come back. So we're just sitting there eating or whatever and she comes in the door. She sees bologna on the table. She's like, "Where'd this come from?" And then I got scared I was thinking like, "Oh my god, oh my god. She's going to hit me." I was like, "I took three dollars from your piggy bank." She ran to her room and she checked. I got scared and started getting up to hide. I was like just about to pass her room to go running to the closet. She grabbed me by the hair and dragged me into her room. And all I remember is she just threw me on the bed and she just put her hand around my neck and then started punching me in the face. I was scared shitless. I thought my mom was going to kill me. She was like, "Now you'll think again if you're going to take my stuff!" I was like, "I'm sorry! I'm sorry! We were hungry. There was no food!"

I was eight then. I moved back and forth between my mother's and my grandma's. When I was 13 that's when my friend, she introduced me to weed. I was hooked on weed till I was like 16. After school we would go and smoke it every day. And, like, my health was getting worse. I was having, like, memory loss. It was just really bad. And then when I was 14 that's when I finally, that's when I was sexually active. And that's when, ah, I started drinking heavily at age 13 too. And when I was 14, after all this had happened to me, I put myself in Children's Aid. I called in for my grandma's safety. I was concerned. I knew I was getting out of control. I didn't want my grandma to go through that, so I called Children's Aid and I put myself in it.

They put me in a foster home. I was 14. I was sharing a room and stayed with them for about two weeks. The reason why is because I got into a fight and I was uttering death threats. I did not know at the time that you can get charged for threatening someone. So they took me. I stayed with this nice elderly lady for a bit. She was so nice to me. I would have given up smoking just for her. She had a bunch of adopted kids there too. I told her about my life and my past and she understood my struggles and stuff. She gave me advice. Finally when a week passed the Children's Aid called and said they had a place for me. I was like, "Well, I'm staying here." And that foster mom she was upset cuz she was like, "Can't she stay here? I don't mind her being here. She's a nice girl." They said, "No, unfortunately she's an adolescent teen. She needs to be in a group home cuz she's out of control" or whatever. She was like, "She's fine here. She doesn't do nothing wrong." And, uh, anyway they had to take me and I got upset. I was crying. She was such a nice lady to me. But it didn't matter to them so I got sent to a group home. I'd been there for a month and that's when I went into depression. I was still 14. I went to the centre. It's like a mental centre. I went there when I was 14 because I was going through, like, really bad depression. And I was threatening to kill myself if I didn't go back to my grandma's. Well, what they did was I wasn't out of Children's Aid, but they let me go back to my grandmother's. So I went back to my grandma's and what I used to do was write down all my anger into a book. I didn't mean nothing. If I wrote a suicide note it didn't mean I was. I was trying to get it all out and onto paper. I didn't know that if you wrote something like that someone would like do something to stop you. My grandma found my diary and she read it. And she reported me.

So they took me to this place. It was like a place with … it was like a mental health hospital. I remember sitting in there in my robe or whatever. I refused to be taken to my room. So I sat on the couch all day and all night just thinking, "What is going on? Where the hell am I?" And I had no idea, but I was diagnosed with dysthymia. That is a rare, rare depression. I had no idea. And they put me on Celexa for a year, 16 months. They let me go after three weeks. Finally I left the hospital. And I went back to a group home because me and grandma got into an argument. When I was 14, around the time I was almost 15, I was stealing things from her. It got to the point where I would steal her bank card and go out and use that money to smoke weed. So she told Children's Aid on me. Children's Aid took me. Then I was going to leave the Children's Aid but I was too young.

That's when things got out of control again. That's when I was sexually abused in the group home. There was men working there too and, uh, I did not like that. I did not want that. But this guy he was kind of chubby or whatever. He was a guy who worked there and he would come into my room at night when my roommate was either gone on an overnight or, yeah, the only time he would come into my room was when they were gone on overnights. He would sit by my bed. He was like, "Oh, do you want me to massage your legs?" or "Let me massage your back." I was like, "I'm trying to sleep. Get the hell out of here." So he would leave, but then later I would wake up and he would be sitting on my bed playing with my feet. And then one time I was sleeping and I felt his hands on my legs. Like, under my nightgown. I was like, "What the hell!?" I was confused. I did not like him sexually. I did not like him touching me. But I knew in my mind that if I said anything something would happen to me. Nothing would happen to him, but something would with me. I was still 15. I was almost 16.

Right after that incident I got into a fight with this girl. Yeah, she was younger than me, but she had a mouth on her. She was talking real bad stuff about Native people. She was saying that we were dirty. And she was telling me that I was fat. I wasn't too worried about the name-calling. I'm not too … I'm not worried about that. If you say something about me, that's your opinion. But when she started talking about my race and being racist, I just snapped. That's when I just lost it. I remember she was standing outside on the porch and she said something from outside and I heard her. I got so mad. I went outside and I, like, clothes-lined her off the porch. And she was lying on the cement and her head was all bloody. And I got scared and I was like, "Oh my god. What did I do? Maybe I killed her. I don't know." So I ran inside, I called the ambulance and the cops, and I packed my bag for like two or three days, like all clothes, right? I took off.

So then I was a street kid for a bit. Then I met this man. He wasn't even close to my age. I never ever thought that I'd be attracted to an older man. Like, he was old. I was like 15 and he was like 40. He was all great at first. We went up to his place or whatever. He said, "Do you need a place to stay for the night?" I said, "Well, yeah I do cuz I'm a runaway." So I stayed at his place. I was trying to be nice so I tidied up his place a little bit. He came back with his sister and his brother and they were all older too. We started drinking and we were smoking weed or whatever. I started to be like, "I'm starting to be attracted to this guy." So we went to the kitchen. We were going to make a late dinner. I was leaning up against the counter or whatever. He started coming up to me and he was like, "You have beautiful eyes." I was like, "Aw, thank you." He was like smiling at me or whatever. I don't know why I did it, but I kissed him. I was like, "Oh my god. This is different." He was probably thinking, "Oh my god. She's so young. What am I doing?" But I lied to him about my age. I told him I was 19. He thought I was 19. So we didn't even have dinner. Like we were making out or whatever and we ended up sleeping together.

Around that time, I went back to the group home, like a week after that … right around that time, that's when I started self-abusing myself. I was cutting my arms and stuff. And the reason I did that was for attention and satisfaction. And, uh, I didn't do it to kill myself. I did it for satisfaction. It took away the pain. And it got worse. The cuts were getting deeper. And the blood was getting thicker. I remember every time I cut myself I would try to not let it bleed that much, but I was getting deeper and deeper. And then this one time I wouldn't stop bleeding and I was, the blood was just dripping from my hand. I remember going to the office and saying, "I'm sorry. I messed up again. I'm really bleeding. Can you guys help me out?" I did not want that guy who touched me at night helping me, but he did. I felt very uncomfortable. He was so rough with me because he knew that I didn't like him. He grabbed my arm. He grabbed the wound and just squeezed me. I was just in so much pain. He grabbed the bottle of stuff that's supposed to stop the bleeding and I thought he was going to dab it on me, but he put my arm over the sink and poured it all over me. I started screaming and I was so mad.

I was almost 16, so I went back to my old group home instead. We had my 16th birthday at my mom and her boyfriend's place. It was so nice. I felt like a kid. The family came up and saw me. I had attempted suicide four days after my birthday. Then on September 27 I went to jail for eight months for two assaults. I did eight months in a youth corrections place. When I got out I went to family court and I got myself out of Children's Aid. Finally. At 16 … I was almost 17. I moved back home with my grandma. I went to counselling. I got anger management. Oh, and the doctor took me off of the Celexa when I was in jail. He said that I was OK, that I didn't need it anymore. When I turned 17, I woke up one morning and told my grandma I was going to move to a bigger city on my own. I had my own place when I was 17. That's when all the drama started happening.

I was introduced to crack and crystal meth. I was binging on crystal meth for weeks at a time. I was living at my own apartment for eight months and then I got evicted. Before that though, I went to a shelter. I didn't know anything about, like, this was my first time going to a shelter by myself. I was in shelters with my mother when I was younger. So anyways, she dropped me off at the shelter and they … I didn't know you had to phone in before you came in, I just knew where the shelter was. So, I went there and they took me in. It was around the time, then … I don't know, that older guy from before was like … he hurt me, like sexually. I think he was just … I think he thought that I was being pleasured, but I wasn't. Like, I didn't know how to say stop or don't. The kind of person I was before was, I used to let everyone step on me, right? So, I ended up calling the cops on him. I told the cops, but that was a mistake.

They videotaped me in the office ... in the security guard's office. It was so uncomfortable cuz there was a man sitting there ... there was like three guy cops sitting there and then there was a main person writing down everything. And there was ... these things that you have here recording, they had, like, three of those and, like, two video cameras: one on the side, one in front. I'm sitting on a chair in like handcuffs and shackles cuz it's secure, right? Cuz when I told the cops, I got arrested for some other stuff I had done. And yeah, I had to tell them everything that happened and it was hard cuz I like broke down and I was scared. I felt uncomfortable. Like, they're all men, right?

He didn't even get charged. There was not enough evidence, they said. Well, um, we were like fooling around and whatever, but I was too high to do anything cuz I was trying to pass out. And, well, I guess it was rape, because he was forcing himself onto me. And I was ... I wanted to tell him to stop, but I couldn't cuz I was, like, really stoned and I didn't know if I said stop, if he would just like be even more like aggressive with me. So, I was just laying there crying, and then it just stopped and I fell asleep. And, in the morning, I told the staff about it. No, I didn't tell the staff about what happened, but I told them that, "I think I been raped," so they took me to the hospital emergency and I got checked out and everything. They told me that something has ... I guess I was ripped or something. It was really swollen and stuff down there, and I was like, "Oh, my god." Like, they hurt me at the hospital, cuz it was like really sore to pee and everything, and they had to put that thing in me and it was just ... it made me cry.

Well, anyway the cops, they were just like, when I was talking they were saying stuff like, "Well, why didn't you just say stop, you're hurting me?" And I was like, "It's hard, like you don't understand if you're a female it's hard ... you can't just say stop and like, why are you doing this. You can't because you're scared. It might be easy for you to say, but for us women, it's not." I don't know, like, it's stupid, friggin' things they say to me, cuz they don't understand and I don't think they really care. I thought they were just there for entertainment.

Anyway I got outta there. Then, around that time I met this girl, her name was Kris and we'd met in the past but we weren't friends. And she was living on the streets. And this is when it all started, cuz Kris buzzed my buzzer like at three in the morning, and she had all kinds of guys with her. She's like, "Oh, just want to come upstairs and smoke our stuff and we'll just leave." I said, "What kind of stuff is it, weed?" She's like, "No." I was like, "What is it?" She said, "It's crack." I was like, "I guess so, but just make it quick." That's when I smoked it. I got hooked. Anyways, for about ... it was about two months after ... no, about maybe two and a half months after I moved into my own apartment ... that's when I started smoking meth.

Kris moved in and we were like best friends and we would like smoke meth almost every week. It was just crazy, like it was getting to the point where I was selling my game systems and I was selling my old jewelry that my family bought me and I was pawning everything. I remember I would let the drug dealers come to my place with a girl, and they would do stuff with them in my bathroom, and they would say, "OK, well here's a piece of whatever for letting me use your washroom." I don't know. I know it's gross, but I didn't care at the time, cuz I just wanted my drugs. But I never performed any kind of sexual activity with anybody just for drugs. But, I remember my friend Kris did that, just to get me and her high. She wanted me to do it with her and the other guy. I said, "No." I'd rather go without drugs than get a friggin' STD or something, you know? And then it got so, like, gross to the part where like Kris was shooting it up. And like, at first, when I found this out, she went out to go see her son and I found her stuff. I told her to get out and she grabbed her stuff and left. I threw the bag of syringes at her.

And then, I finally decided I'm moving out. And, not only that, I got taken off welfare, cuz I wasn't going to school. And I got an eviction notice because like my windows were smashed and my balcony was full of like beer bottles and junk, and it was just really gross. So, I grabbed as much stuff as I could and took it back to my grandma's. That's when I went through the process of like cleansing myself finally.

I went to a New Year's Eve party the year I was 18 and I just kind of bumped into this guy. We started talking or whatever and then a couple months later ... we just kept being friends, right? But then he started telling me he had feelings for me. And he had a girlfriend at the time. She was older than him. And he said, he said he didn't really see it as a relationship because they were mostly drunk all the time. And, uh, I would come over and babysit and he would like pay me. Sometimes. And that's how we started talking, like after the party. He said, "oh well, I need a babysitter, so I'll give you my number." And that's what I like doing, like babysitting. And so there was a couple of times like where I would go over and babysit. He wouldn't leave. So I guess after a while

I guess he started having feelings for me. And I thought, well, I don't want to be a homewrecker or whatever, but if he's, I guess, not really into her, it's not my fault. So I said OK, whatever, might as well give it a shot. A few months later he told his girlfriend, "I don't want to be with you. I don't have feelings for you." She was like, "Oh? What are you doing? Screwing around with that babysitter of yours?" And anyways he was like, "Yeah. I have feelings for her." So anyways we started dating and I ended up moving in with him and stuff. Everything was OK at the beginning. He was being real nice to me. Like after a couple months passed living with him, everything just went downhill. He was playing with my head and he messed me up.

Yeah, he was, like, I started drinking heavily with him and we got into a fight a couple of times. He would pull my hair and he would grab my arm so hard that in the morning it would leave a bruise. Or he would grab my leg really hard, but I always had bruises on me. He wouldn't like hit me, but he would like just grab onto me and leave a bruise. And there were times when he would grab my hair if he didn't get what he wanted. We got into a couple of really big fights where he threw me off the porch. Once he did that, threw me right on my back on the ice. I dialed 9-1-1. He grabbed the phone and he threw it. And it was still on. I don't know how I did it, but I ended up crawling to my phone. Then the cops got there. The cops asked me what happened. I said, "Just take me. I don't want to be here. Please take me to my grandma's." They took me to the squad car and they were talking to him. The thing was they asked him if he wanted to charge me! I was like, "Oh my god! Are you flipping serious? Am I being punished for something? Because I thought I was the one who was a victim." They said, "Do you want her charged? Because we have her in the back of the car." I thought I was going to be sick. And I could hear them talking. He was sitting on the porch staring at me sitting in the car. And I just put my head down thinking, "Oh my god. This cannot be happening." I looked at him again and he shook his head no. I was just like, "Oh my god. Thank you so much." They took me to my grandma's.

Like, a week later I ended up feeling guilty. He did so much to get my attention. I started feeling guilty like it was all my fault. So I called him and said, "Can I see you?" "Yeah, I'll be over to pick you up." He came to pick me up. We started talking or whatever. He made me dinner. He was being all nice. So I was like, OK, I guess I'll move back in. Then the same thing started happening again. And I was just like, what the hell am I doing here?

Then me and my best friend went to a bar and that's when I decided, "You know what? I'm going to go back to Toronto with you." He said, "Yeah, you can. My roommate won't mind you staying with us for a bit." And I was like, this is it. I'm ready to do this now. I'm ready to leave and never come back. I'm ready to start a new life. I don't deserve to be treated like that. Like a piece of shit. That's how I got here.

When I first came to the shelter I couldn't even talk or socialize without feeling scared. Like, I felt like, "Oh, if I socialize like what's going to happen?" Cuz that's what I was thinking when I was with him. But he wouldn't let me socialize. He wouldn't let me talk on the cell phone. He wouldn't even let me see anyone. I had the opportunity to go to school and finish school and get a job or whatever. He wouldn't even let me do that. He said, "If you're going to live with me, you do your job to wash the dishes, make me dinner, do the laundry, and watch my son." And like I was in love with him, so I was like, "OK, I'll do that."

So anyway I came here. I've been here since June. I just sent my housing papers yesterday. Thank god. I have to wait till they call me back to tell me they've gone through. I went to a doctor and talked to her about it. So I have a doctor's note saying that I was in an abusive relationship. If that doesn't work, I'm going to call the Reserve police because they have records of the day the cops were called. I was thinking if they didn't go through I was just going to give up, but I'm not going to do that. I'm going to try again.

I'm excited because last night I went to an AA meeting with my friend. I felt so happy. I felt relieved. Because I'm actually doing something to help me. I'm planning on going again tonight. I think I am going to go. I'm looking forward to it. That's my plan. My plan is to like finish school and get my license. Then go to university. Get a degree in Hospitality. Or go to George Brown and do a course in like Culinary Arts. I enjoy cooking. Eventually have a family. My plan is to get my own apartment. Get a good job. Like, I wanted to go and travel. I want to go to Italy before I die. Yeah, I have a plan.

DANIKA

Danika was the first of the young women to approach me following my introduction to the residents at the shelter. She sat alone in the corner of the room and when I passed by she quietly told me that she would like to participate. Even though she was juggling work, school, and extra-curricular projects, she was the only one of the eight participants who showed up to every appointment that she scheduled. Soft-spoken and shy at first, she worried constantly that her responses were not clear or that she was not expressing herself properly. As time passed she became more and more comfortable, becoming excited and passionate when she spoke about the situations of young people in exceptional circumstances. She often struggled, both outwardly and inwardly, to make sense of her damaged, yet staunchly loyal, affection for her parents. The most introspective of the participants, she had an enormous degree of empathy for the other women living in the shelter, even those who bullied her incessantly. Although she was often demure and insecure, her determination to change her circumstances was fierce.

I'm Danika. I'm going into my last year of university. I'm in my fourth year of business management … um … I grew up in Canada. Toronto, Ontario. With my parents and I have a sister. I finished high school and decided to go off to university. I came to the shelter when I was 18. I'm 20 now. I just consider myself a young female. I don't really consider myself homeless. I have a home – it's just not traditional. I guess people label me that way. I live in a shelter for homeless youth. It's a mentality. Those words are so, I don't know, what's the word? Labelling or negative, like you're different, pigeonholing. Just cuz bad things happen to you, that's what we call you, you know? If you can't contribute, you stay over there. And they kind of mix all these services: they're like for homeless people. But you know, how am I different from someone who works and goes to university and lives in an apartment? Is that a normal person? I live in a shelter, and go to university and work while I'm going to school. Does that make me so different?

  I work at Starbucks. There's so much pressure. The job is, and I got, I've been getting acne too! I don't know if you can see it on my forehead, but it's because of the stress. Oh god! Did I tell you my work schedule? Nine in the morning until six at night. Then 5 a.m. to 2 p.m. Working these crazy hours on your feet after and before school, and, like, people, they just have no patience. I wake up so early in the morning. I try to be so quiet because no one is up except me at 4 a.m., and then I have to shower, and if I sleep in, I don't eat. I'm not back for lunch or snack so lots of days I don't eat until dinner. Then when you're there you just have to be so quick, quick, quick. Everything is like hurry up, hurry up. After work I come home and I'm sore. Working at Starbucks looks so easy, but it's not. It's so much work! And you do all this work and the next day it's the same thing! When I was new and training on bar, ah! I was just like, have patience please. And people just stand there and watch you make drinks. They're telling you to hurry up. Looking down on you like you're totally incompetent. Sometimes you just want to say, "Look, I'm going through some things. I'm trying really hard."

Then there's friends. The friendships I have at school are designed, well, they're more like business relationships. Like, we have meetings, and get work done, and create projects and it's strictly that. Any attempt they make to know more about me they get hit with a brick wall because I just can't share a lot of information, but if I did I think those relationships would be a lot more closer. Because they don't know I live in a shelter. They don't know, and I've been with them since first year. They don't know that my parents got evicted, or that I'm so poor right now, or that I still am struggling. Don't know the struggle that I had. Just during this time it's hard for me, I kind of took a step back from them because I was just worried that they would see the situation I was in and it would be so embarrassing and so bad. Afraid they wouldn't give me chance and just afraid of being so young and so broke. You know, and who wants to share that? You know? It's business school, most of those people are doing so well and their parents are business people and they don't have those problems.

I grew up in North Toronto, in that nicer area. And I lived there for 13 years and we had such a community because the same people I saw every day. It was a nice apartment. There was like my room, my parents' room, the living room. We were poor, or I guess a little above poor, but I was happy. The neighbourhood surrounding it, it had a little more money. It was kind of sheltered, I guess. I went to school. I had to make friends. It was all OK.

My childhood was very, very strict. I didn't get to go outside and play with friends. Because my parents were like, "There are bad people out there. We don't want you hanging around outside." They were strict with everything. They were always like, "What are you doing?" That's why I'm very close to my sister, because I couldn't go outside. Being at school was sort of like, "Look at this! I'm free from the apartment!" But you know they were good, they loved me, and we were close. There was a time when they won the lottery, but that didn't work out so well. My dad wanted to go home and he wanted to like help everyone in Guyana. My mom got really upset, but we didn't have it anymore. It was pretty sad. Uh. But my parents, and my childhood, it was like really, really close. Just my mom, my dad, my sister, and me. We have a lot of extended relatives, like a lot of Guyanese people stay on their own, they don't always stay with their relatives, but they're really close. But our little family was close and I think my parents tried to hide their struggles from people.

I felt forced to keep all these secrets. Don't tell so-and-so this and don't tell them that. Don't tell anyone about this. And it was like, "OK, OK." We lived without a roof for like two years and no one else really knew. And really just forging those kind of secrets made us really close. And you know, it made me be secretive with friends as well. You know? Because there is so much I couldn't share with them. You know, so people are like, "Hiiii!" And I'm like, "Hi, I'm evicted." You know? Their parents are like, "Oh, are you going to go home with that girl?" And I'm like, "Oh, I'm staying in a motel." You know, so I would have been forced to lie all the time. And I don't like lying. But I had to. Even now I think that most of the people I know are still with their parents. They still live at home and they still go to school and they still have parents paying. Yeah, most people when they hear that I'm a young person that lives independently, they're like, "Wow!" They don't know though, you know, there's so much they don't know. So you know, they think, "Oh, she's motivated and she's on the road." But I'm really private so I don't really talk about my situation.

What worries me most is not just school, but, um, money because as time goes by it's getting harder and harder to live here with all these women because although the shelter is free, I'm learning that there's no free lunch. Because when I first got here I was like, oh man, this is great. You know, I didn't have a place to live before and here they paid for your accommodations, they paid for your food, they like take care of you, but there's like a trade-off for that. So you have to like, well, the trade-off is your freedom. You're exposed to all these different things you don't want to be exposed to and you have to live and cooperate with like 54 other women on one floor. Some are in sex trade or on drugs or have severe mental health issues. People are in and out all the time. They fight so they're kicked out. And we have to share the washroom, the facilities, everything. So you can't lock yourself up, you can't avoid being around people, so that's a big trade off. We have curfew. We have to be home by like 12 o'clock. There's so many rules. Like you can't burn candles. You really can't do anything to your room because it's not your property. There's just a big cost that comes with living here. You can't invite people over cuz it's a shelter and it's so restrictive. It's your home, but sometimes it can't feel like your home. When you have hard times, though, you can't afford to be picky.

I've had some really hard times. I feel like I'm Oliver Twist, you know? I've lived a hard life. Like, all these obstacles, oh my god, you know, and all these other people are like, "Hehehe. I live with my parents. Hehehe. I live at home." You know? And for me, there have been times when I've had nothing to eat. I was going to school and I'd have to ask the bus driver if I can owe them the dollar today. All these embarrassing times. And in my program, I'm working like a mad person just trying to keep up. It's so hard for me. And I'm on a student group as well and I'm organizing extra-curriculars and activities. And in this group, they're really serious students and their expectations are so high. And sometimes I'm just like, Why am I here? I'm not doing anything or getting anything and I'm so tired. I'm just trying to survive. But that's the person I am, when I start doing something I have to finish. I can't just leave it. I've been doing this like this since, like, first year and now I'm graduating. It's just tiring sometimes.

In my second year, my parents had a lot of financial difficulties. The kind of jobs they had, it was really work as you go. Finding clients, selling insurance. In my second year, um, my parents, we got evicted from our house so we had to leave and we couldn't get anything, so you know I came home from school one day and thought I was going to go back to my house, but we had no place to live. So for a while we lived in their office and then, oh wait, actually that happened before. We lived in an apartment for 13 years and we got evicted the same way. So we started staying with a lady and we lived in different places, then we finally got this apartment and we slowly worked our way up to getting a house. This was from the house that we lived in that we got evicted. So my parents were left with nothing, so we lived in so many different places and it was in November of my second year that it just got horrible. And I was just like, "Oh my god. What am I going to do?" So I still carried on at school like everything was normal, but we still couldn't find a building so we were sleeping in the car and it was really crazy. Um, and that continued for about a year until I came to the shelter. So I moved here, living here and starting fresh again and trying to keep going on and continue with school. Because that's the kind of person I am. Once I'm finished nothing's going to be able to get in my way. So that's how things got bad and now here I am.

I was 18. Then the struggle happened earlier on in that year. It was in October and I was just like, "Oh god, how am I going to pay for all of these books?" School was so busy and I had so much homework to do. It was around midterm time and I had just bought the books and I was trying to cram and get OK marks. It was second year and things started out so well. I was excited about school and studying and I was living at home. It was when I got evicted in October and we were living in different people's houses. We lived in some man's house. It was OK, but that's when I saw my sister, you know, she got really upset, and, she … I don't really want to talk about her too much. I just really worry about her a lot. Anyway, so we lived in different people's houses for a while. That was until March. March things just started to go really bad. I was just really terrified. I finished second year on probation because my marks were so bad because I just didn't have that focus. I was doing really poorly in school. I then had to enrol in summer school to redo some courses. Around this time we simply did not have a place to live again. Um, we were living in hotels sometimes. My parents had their office, so we were living in their office all day. My parents worked, but they were so concerned about finding us a place to live. So every day we would go to the motel, go to a hotel, somewhere cheap, somewhere like under a hundred dollars. We would all share one room, and some were really bad. It was like a really bad place and really bad time for us.

Then what happened? Uhh. So there was this time we still had no place to live, at nights we slept in the car, all four of us. And I was still going to school. I had three courses at summer school. And sometimes I would show up to school and I didn't get to take a shower or do anything. I would just try to avoid people. I'd try to make myself less there, so that no one would notice me. I didn't spend much time with my friends. I'd say hello, but then I'd hide. I didn't want them to see my state. And yeah, that was the lowest, lowest point for me. Sleeping in cars and motels and worrying about whether we'd have a place to sleep at night. Still trying to redo courses to get my grades back up for fall. I passed those courses too: economics, microfinance, and stats.

I worked at my parents' office and I worked in the car a lot. They would drive around a lot and I would get to be with them. I would do my homework in the car. I was just trying to stay focused on doing well and passing. This is when I started looking for a shelter. Sleeping in the office, hotels, and in the car – that really caught up with me. And then one day, my parents told me, "Go to this hotel. We'll be there. We're going to be there. We'll find some money and then we're coming." And it was like 11 o'clock at night and I'm waiting at this hotel. So

I call them and my mom tells me to come back to the office because my dad couldn't find any money for the hotel, we have to sleep here again. And I just got so frustrated, and earlier on in the day I was thinking, you know, "I can't do this anymore. I'm going to go to a women's shelter. I'm going to a shelter. I'm going to find someplace else." I needed to focus on school and living with my parents was just crazy. My mom was so mad, but I was just gone.

I went to the Internet and started searching for women's shelters. I found one up at Kennedy and one here. I thought, "OK, this is good. It's close to school. I'll go there." I called and they were like, "We have one bed free. Would you like me to save you dinner?" And I was like, "Uh, dinner from a shelter? Um, sure!" I was so hungry at that time. Did I tell you? I didn't even eat during this month because we had no money for that either. No food. Things were so bad. It was so bad. I remember I'd be at school and I'd be hungry. I'd be so hungry and it was like, "Oh god, I'm going to go home and there's going to be no food." Sometimes we did have something like tuna or a chocolate bar, something ridiculously cheap like that could do the trick. But, um, that was the biggest of my struggles. All these things that are so basic. Things you need. You know, food, shelter, transportation. I didn't have it. And yeah, but anyways, um, yeah, um, the last night when they were like, "Oh, come to the office." I told them, "I'm not coming." I went straight to the shelter. I talked to the coordinator that night and since that night I never went back home. I couldn't do it. It was so traumatic. I wanted to be with my parents, but life was just so unbearable. It was so bad. And now I have so much freedom. School is so nearby. They give me [subway] tokens to go to school. If I need something they have it. And for the longest time during that year, I felt like if I needed something my parents couldn't do it: "Mom, can I have money to go to school?" It was always an if or a maybe. "Can you put like $10 in my account?" "Yeah, but, uh, the bank is closed. Sorry." Oh, man. God, I love them, but they just disappointed me so many times. It's so hard. It's so hard to deal with it. So hard to put your trust in them. But here, there's always something here for me, and that's why I'll stay. You know, because for me a family is something, a family should be able to provide, but if they can't …

At that point it was critical. You got to do what you got to do. I finished school. I finished the classes I had. The thing is that when I go home, when I leave school or work, I know that I'm going to have a place to sleep. I have a bed, the same bed, and it's free. It felt horrible before. And now I have a bed to sleep in and food to eat. It means so much to me. I'm so grateful for this. I am so grateful. I'm trying to stay strong. Stay focused. And trying not to let the situation kind of get me down. Don't get distracted. I have to keep focused on my goals.

ERIN

Erin was the first participant that I met who was living on the street. As she explained, keeping appointments is not the easiest of tasks when one is without a watch or a roof over one's head. As a result, Erin was the only "street kid" that I met with enough times to complete the entire interview guide. Erin was small but mighty, even abrasive at times. Out of earshot, though, her friends referred to her as "the mother hen." Once we took the subway together and she offered her seat to an elderly woman who was standing. Erin was a straight shooter who identified herself as her own hero. At 15, she was the youngest of the young women who worked with me. Her favourite response was to ask me if I was "really that naïve" or if I just wanted to hear her say the answer. When I told her both, she looked at me with eyes that patted me squarely on the top of the head. She referred to me as "kid" on multiple occasions. Understandably she had a complete mistrust of adults and signed her name illegibly. I am almost positive that I do not know her real name. She did not show up for our last appointment and I have not, despite many attempts, heard from her since.

Alright, so, you really wanna know about me? I dunno. I'm 15, almost 16. I'll be 16 in January. I'm, uh, I dunno, I'm living on the streets, but it's November now so I'm sort of looking for someplace warmer. I dunno what else to say. I'm stubborn and scrappy and smart. I'm kinda one of the guys out here I guess. I guess … I guess I take care of people a little. My teachers used to say that I have an attitude problem, but I don't think that's right. It's just cuz I had to deal with a lot and it's hard doing that when you're just a kid. Like my teachers would say that when I was in like Grade 4 even, but they didn't really know what it was like at my house and stuff.

I lived in a house. In a house that was like hell most of the time. Sometimes it was good, I guess. But my mom had me when she was young, like 15 or something. So when I was baby I lived with my mom and I guess with my grandma, and I think those were probably the happy times of my life, but I was too little to remember that. But when I was four or five my mom moved in with the asshole who was supposed to be my stepdad, but he was an asshole and he was really, really bad to me. We lived in an apartment in a small town. My mom is a bitch and I definitely don't talk to her. I don't really have any family around. I have lots of friends and stuff so that's who my family is mostly.

It's hard for sure and I don't like to talk about it, but I know that's like the whole point of this. First my stepdad, who I'm just gonna call Ed, was a child molester and my mom seems to think that's fuckin' OK or something. Uh, ya, so I guess … so I guess from the time I was like eight he was touching me or whatever. It wasn't as bad then as it was later, but whatever it still happened. I told my mom and she told me I was lying and slapped me around a bit. They drank and smoked pot all the time. Like, all the child government money went up in smoke and beer and whatever the fuck else they could get their hands on. Ya, they were drunks. Both of them.

I left there when I was 14, like almost two years ago now. Ya, Ed was out of fucking control by that point and my mom didn't want to do nothing about it and she was mad at me that he was doing it. Jealous or something screwed up like that. So yeah, he was full on me when I was 12 and I just couldn't take it no more. So I got the fuck outta there. My mom knew and didn't do anything about it. Who else was I gonna say anything to? The cops. I doubt it. The pigs aren't going to do anything about it. What will they do, arrest him? That guy pays the rent and for food and for everything. Then my mom is out on her ass too. Plus cops are assholes anyway they just want to use their power to show people how tough they are. Shit. You should see the way they treat us down here. They think that if they be the boss and hand out tickets and shit we're all gonna screw off. I'd be pretty tough too if I had a huge gun on my leg too. No, the best way to deal with this stuff is just get out. Like, I don't want to go through court and judges and asshole foster people who want to make everything all better for you. Good luck. Too late for that. No, I'm old enough to be here on my own and I'm making it work for me so that's what matters.

Well, I been around Toronto since then, two years now. Once I moved with this guy to Barrie for a few months but that was a dumbass move. Then I came back. When I got here, when I got here, I went to Covenant and know what they said, right? Not 16. They tried to send me back home, but I ran away from there and I was smart cuz I never use my real name so it's impossible really for them to do anything about it. I'm supposed to be in protected or whatever, but I met so many kids down here who was in those things and they sound like hell. So many kids down here ran away from Child's Aid or whatever. No, that stuff doesn't work. So anyway, I was lucky cuz it was summertime, so I went to Queen Street where MuchMusic is, ya know, cuz you see it on TV so it's something you know, and there were some other kids hanging out over there so I just went up and said hey to them. Well, at first it was just what's up and stuff, but then, yeah, they were homeless or whatever too it turned out and they were guys and I was a girl so I think that I was not scary or whatever so they helped me out. Like, they showed me food banks and places around here that you could stay where you weren't like totally out in the sidewalk. And they were my friends I guess. It's a lot like that Peter Pan movie in a way, these kids that don't have families and they just have other kids.

I bum money a lot during the day and I do the lost little girl routine and people eat that up, so I make decent money at it. I share it with the guys cuz that's how it works, like they make sure nothing happens to me and I pay for stuff like food or whatever. The first night here I slept in like a rooming house with these guys and a buncha other people. It was just like a big party in there, lots of drugs and stuff, but I found a spot and just curled up and slept, but didn't really sleep cuz, come on, I was kinda freaked out.

Now, I mean, it's just, uh, you can't always be around the same people all the time because people move and they find someone's couch to sleep on or whatever. But for me, it's like, sometimes a guy will let me sleep at his apartment if I blow him or whatever. It's totally not sex work! This is like, guys I know or friends of friends or whatever. No, not the same at all. I tried that once and it didn't work out for me, so I haven't had to do it again. But lots of girls down here do. Like either strip or sell sex or let people take pictures or whatever. I'm lucky not to have to do that. Really though it's amazing money, I just have kind of a thing with sex cuz of Ed and yeah, I just don't want to have sex if I don't have to. The once was like almost a year ago now. I was 15 already by then. Like, so this guy came by in his car and picked me up or whatever and we talked about my money. So he was actually going to pay me like $400 to spend the night with him. So I went back to his place and he had this nice huge apartment. Like, nice. He was a lawyer or a banker or something with a place like this. So we got inside and then he was kissing me and took my clothes off and all that shit. It was scary, but at the same time, I don't know, he seemed like an OK guy. But then I was almost totally buck naked and the guy asked me how old I was and I told him I was 18 and he looked at me and asked me again. I said 18. So this goes on and on for like ever and then he says, "I don't believe you." He says no matter what he's not going through with the sex and can he take me somewhere, whatever. And fuck, I'm all the way there and so I just want to get the money so I tried telling him I was 17 and he wasn't buyin' it at all. He seriously wouldn't even touch me even though I tried kissing him and jerking it and stuff. So we ended up back in his car and he dropped me off down by Harvey's and gave me $100 and took off. Well, I hope I never have to do it, but sometimes you don't got a choice right. When things get bad or whatever, you do whatever it takes.

Last winter was when I was in Barrie. It was hella cold so I basically just decided to girlfriend this guy we all knew and he was a dealer so he had some cash and an apartment up in Barrie. Um, what to say about him? Andy. Um, ya, so Andy's thing is drugs. He doesn't do them, but he deals them and he likes the people around him to do them so that they owe him money all the time and then they have to do him favours or whatever until they can pay him the money. So while I was up there I was doing a lot of drugs for one thing. So sometimes I guess I would be high or drunk or maybe both and then we would have sex without a hood and that was a problem because I got knocked up. Well, I wanted to keep it at first but then I looked around at my life and my mom and all her dumbass mistakes and thought, why the hell would I bring another person into that kinda life? Bad enough that I have to try to crawl outta this right? So I went and got an abortion. Lied about my age or maybe they just didn't care because I was almost 16 or something, but either way they gave me one. So, fuck, right? And that's that story. Don't see that guy no more.

Today I went and got lunch at a kitchen and then I sat around and panned by the McDonald's on Yonge Street. You know the one? Like, high up by the rich people places to shop on Bloor Street. Yeah, up there. Lots of rich people doing their Christmas shit, I guess, but so I made some money doing that. So I ate some McDonald's cuz some lady offered to buy me something to eat cuz they think you're gonna take their money and buy crack right? Whatever. I got to eat McDonald's today. Some days though, I'll go to a drop-in or to a library. You can sometimes, as long as you look not dirty or drunk or whatever, spend a lot of time in the library and they even have Internet and stuff there for free. So I can go online and check my emails and Google and go on MSN, you know? But then, I guess we would either see what was for eats at the apartment or go back to a kitchen. Some of the guys go dumpster diving and they get a lot of good shit. It's fucking insane what people throw out at restaurants and grocery stores and stuff. Like, it's not even disgusting, it's good. So sometimes I'll eat that. Sometimes though that's nasty ass shit and I wouldn't touch it. There are usually a couple picks, but then sometimes there ain't anything at all, so fuck dinner, ya know? Just depends on the day.

In January I'll actually be 16, which is the greatest thing ever. Because then I can get welfare and live in a shelter if I want to. And I don't. But it means I'll be a quote-unquote "actual adult" under the eyes of the law. It's so screwed up because I don't think I can be too much more adult than I am now, but I'm not 16, so I'm left to rot in the street, I guess. It's really shitty being under 16, people don't know. That's the other thing, no health card, no birth certificate, no nothin'. They don't like that over at the hospital that's for sure. And then of course you have to go through the whole long ass story of where you come from and where you're going and why you don't have a mommy and daddy. Everyone just thinks you do, right? But at one point I had some ID stuff, but shit gets stolen all the time. You can't keep stuff really.

I think it's that I am tough and I look out for me and I find other people to be around that look out for me and then I look out for them too. You find things and people that can help you. All over the place too, right. Like, sometimes you gotta figure out how to get to the other opposite side of the city to get something you need, but you figure that out, right. Like, you go look at a map for a while and then go down into the subway and stand beside that machine that gives tokens and wait till someone is getting a lot of them and then you just ask for one and they have so many that they feel bad not giving you one. That's a good way for getting places.

But the thing is, why can't I get any help because I'm 14 or 15. If you've already been on the streets for two years, a lot of stuff has happened to you and you know what? You probably want to stay there cuz you've got used to what it's like out here. I don't want to be taken by Child's Aid and I don't want to go to some gay-ass group house where I'm just gonna run away anyway. You know how many kids I talk to everyday, like every day, who took off from those places. They don't work. They work for kids that don't have any real problems. And that's not very many of us, I can say for sure. But man, like lots of kids out here need pills and need shrinks and need attention and no one can give them that or anything else at all. But that's a whole other thing. Kids my age have kids. Lots of them do. So how can you say they're not grown-ups when they've got a kid too. If you're old enough to have a baby, you're old enough to live on your own. We need help with that.

Um, no, I'm not a typical teenager. And yes, I am. We talked the other day on the way to the subway about being called "homeless," right? Like, that automatically makes you not on *The O.C.* or whatever, but at the same time I am still a 15-year-old chick. I'm figuring life out way, way, way faster than other chicks my age, but still, you know. I don't have time for all the bullshit and the shopping and the boy talk and the sleepovers or stuff, right? I wish my parents were normal and that I was normal and that we were all rich and everything was great and all. Of course I do that. But I don't got that. I got this. So like that chick there maybe gets a zit and her mom goes and buys her some stuff that they sell on TV. I get one and too bad for me, right? Like, I have a few other things that I need to take care of first.

JEAN

I met Jean entirely by mistake. I had a no-show appointment and went around to the outside patio to see if I could find the participant outside. She wasn't there, but Jean was. She was eating a chocolate bar that was melting faster than she could eat it and she asked me to sit down and eat it with her so it wouldn't go to waste. As we ate, she began telling me about her superpowers. When she looked at my hair, she said, she felt the colour red. Did I know what red felt like? The interviews with Jean proved to be some of the most challenging as her mental health issues made it exceptionally difficult to keep the interview on track. It would often take 15 minutes to get her to acknowledge that she had even heard my question. Staying the course with Jean, I was able to envision how difficult it must be for her to interact with social services and health professionals on a daily basis. One afternoon she asked if she could sing into the recorder. Figuring it might put the interview back on track afterward, I handed her the device. When she opened her mouth the voice that came out was powerful and pitch-perfect. Michael Jackson's "You Are Not Alone" never sounded so good. Afterward we went and ate hot dogs.

My mind can transmit radio signals. Isn't that weird? I have three powers really. The synaesthesia, which I don't really consider a power. Telepathy, and, um, uh, electronic voice phenomenon, which is also considered a form of psychokinesis. So I have really cool powers. Psychokinesis is anything that affects things out of time, matter, or space. So it's really weird how your mind can connect with an electrical object. Basically I stay away from microwaves, and, uh, anything like, um, radio towers and anything. And when I get really stressed out, and

I can't handle hearing people's thoughts, I make my own mind control–blocking device. It's called the thought-blocker, I call it. It's basically made of this tin foil and rubber tape. You put it on the inside of a hat and you just put it over your head and it blocks out thoughts. Or it makes it so that no more than one person at a time can hear your thoughts. It gets kind of annoying sometimes not having your own thoughts to yourself.

So I lived with my grandmother up until I was about five years old. And then from five to eight, I mean six to eight, I lived in Toronto. Like, I was born in Toronto and then I went to live with my grandmother out in a more rural area. And basically a lot of bad stuff happened to me, like abuse and stuff. With my grandmother's boyfriend and my mother's husband. So my stepdad, but he's not related to me. So that's where the mental health stuff starts. I'm diagnosed with synaesthesia, borderline personality disorder, and post, complex post-traumatic stress disorder.

I've had a lot of ... like, I've been through a lot. I've had a lot of abuse and neglect in my life. And embarrassment also. Like in a foster home. I've also had a lot of happy times too. Um, like I've even had times when I've been happy for longer than two years. I also used to have a problem, I probably shouldn't say this, but I used to have a bed-wetting problem until I was about 12 years old. And I used to get punished for that so ... I got that after I had been sexually abused. I started having that problem. Bedwetting.

I went to a shrink from the time I was really little. For some reason all of my psychiatrists have been male, but even my psychologist was a man, which kind of bothered me because I'm sort of afraid of men, but after I get to know them I'm OK with them. And um, my psychologist when I was little, I used to have a psychologist when I was about five years old that I went and saw and he said that I was very gifted. I was using bigger words than I would use now. Like I was using, say for example, words like, uh, spectrum. I was using those words. I started reading books when I was two or three. Sometimes I feel like I have to play dumb when I'm with other kids. Cuz one of my friends said, "Maybe you should get some smarter friends." Not that everyone I meet is dumb, I just feel like I have to not act like a genius. Not that I'm a genius. I'm just different.

I was in Children's Aid since I was about eight years old. Me, my brother, and sister. Or rather, my brother, sister, and I. My little brother is 16 now and my sister would be about 14 and a half. We all got taken away. I was eight years old at the time, my brother was five and my sister was three at the time we were taken away. And, uh, basically, I went to live in Children's Aid. My mom didn't take care of me. She neglected me. Like, left me in my diapers all day and night and stuff. Part of my memory between four and seven is blocked out because I can't remember it because those were the times when I was being abused. There's time I've blocked out that I don't remember. I'm sure if I remote view it I could probably remember, but that would probably be like pouring oil on a wound. Like pouring hot oil on an open wound. It would just make me worse.

But basically I was very mentally stimulated when I was living with my grandmother. I played with lots of stuff. I would try to leave school early and pretend I had the chicken pox and stuff so that I could get attention when I was little. And she would be like, "Oh my god, I'm so worried about you!" And then I could see how much I mean to her. I was attention seeking a lot when I was a kid. I would steal. One of my earliest memories is stealing cheese and Smarties from the fridge. I was very close to my grandmother. She's still alive. I don't see her anymore. She's in her 60s, but we don't really talk. I'm still mad at her. Because she let stuff happen. She knew what was going on. I do remember being taken away. And pushing my sister on a swing. I do remember being punished for so many reasons, like wetting the bed.

Um, what else? You want to hear what happened when I got taken away? This is a very interesting part of the story. It's also very bad too. My brother and sister and I were all at day care and they were checking for head lice and they found bruises on every one of us. So they called the police and the police came and they took us out to McDonald's. The police had all three of us little ones so they took us out to McDonald's. And um, I was sort of afraid of men, but he was sort of like our daddy. They were older guys and I looked up to them and thought they were cool. I always loved policeman when I was little. Actually my earliest ambition was I wanted to be a Power Ranger.

When I was about 13 or 14 I used to go to group therapy and I've also done a few self-harm programs. I was at a mental hospital with my first experience with mental health problems when I was about 14. I started having impulse problems … impulse control problems. Like trying to commit suicide, but not really having a plan before I did it. Like, just doing it. Like, not doing for attention, but just doing it kinda thing. And just like suicidal ideation, like researching about suicide and thinking about it. Cutting myself to see that I was real and that my skin was there. Stuff like that.

At 14 I had run away from a foster mom in Brampton and I, um, almost got pimped by a pimp or whatever. I was a lot skinnier and stuff. Like, this guy came up to me and started hitting on me and offered me $100 to have sex with him. Yeah, I was really afraid. And then I ended up calling the police. They arrested him for soliciting sex. And, uh, conspiracy to commit a crime with an underage. So with a minor. I knew him kind of. His nickname was T. I was walking down the street in high heels and jeans and I was dressed up and everything. I had just stolen someone's credit card, well, borrowed someone's credit card, and then I gave it back. I pretended that I didn't buy anything. So I didn't really steal it. But yeah, so I was walking on the street and he happened to stop me. And he offered me. He said, "If you," ... like this is kinda uncomfortable, kinda gross, but he said, "If you have sex with me, I will pay you $175." I said, "nope." That's why I eat a lot cuz I want to stay fat so that guys don't hit on me. My psychiatrist finally figured this out because I was eating a lot on purpose and drinking a lot of milk and pop and stuff. Stuff that would make me fat. At one point I was even drinking Ensures and protein bars so that I would get bigger. So I would get bigger and bigger. And I was also taking medication. So anyway I went to a shelter and said that I was looking for a place to stay and by law if you don't have any ID they can't refuse you. There's like a don't ask, don't tell policy. They can't discriminate against you if you don't have any place to stay. But I was in a tough situation. I'd run away. I ran away a few times to there. I was 14 but I had to say I was 16. I had to say that. I was forced to.

Two weeks later they called the cops. Or the cops sent out my picture because I was on the list for missing children. If you're zero to 18, you can be on the list for national runaways. Did you know that you can be zero years old? If you're not one yet, then you're zero. So, you know those pictures that offer a thousand dollar reward? It was like that except there wasn't a reward. They showed my picture to all the shelters and hospitals. And then the police came and picked me up like two weeks later. And like after they found me. Cuz like Toronto is a big city, it took a while to find me. Even if you're in a shelter cuz you have to get the picture all ready and everything. But they used my graduation picture for Grade 8. I was really pissed off about it. Like I have the hat on and everything. They took me I think to the hospital to get checked out because I had done some scratching and stuff on my arm. But, uh, um, the doctor thought it was just attention seeking. He said he thought I had borderline personality disorder because I was very impulsive. Moving around. Very impulsive about moving around and doing things. After that, that's when I overdosed and I ended up at another mental hospital. Mostly because I just … If things were going well, then I just wanted to ruin it, because I didn't want to get close to anyone. So it's what you call self-sabotage.

You know what's weird? Once when I inhaled the paint fumes. I woke up in the hospital after I passed out, the paramedics were asking me what happened. They were wondering and I heard them say something about radioactive isotopes. They said something about nuclear … they were talking, whispering. They said she was around nuclear waste so what's going to happen to her? And then they were whispering things a lot. And, um, I remembering thinking that my head hurt and that it was going to do something to my brain. I was thinking I'm going to be really different in a couple of months or a couple of weeks.

When I was like ten years old I was wondering why I got turned on by the girls and not the guys. And I asked my foster mom, "Am I supposed to like girls or guys?" She told me, "Guys, cuz it's the opposite sex." And I was like, "What's a sex?" And uh, basically, yeah. And then I noticed, like two years ago I basically realized I was gay. Gay doctors are the best. I had a gay psychiatrist once. He openly told me he was gay. He was the nicest guy in the world. It was like talking to a woman. I've had transsexual friends. I've never been against gay people. I love transsexual people. I don't find them attractive in that way, but they're cool. Not that non-gay people aren't cool. Just like non-super powers are cool.

I was sexually abused when I was five years old and eight years old and about 15 years old. So I was sexually assaulted three times. At 15, it was actually by a stranger at a house party. At my older foster sister's house party. We ran away for the night and we went to this house party. And I fell asleep and I think maybe someone put something in my drink, like in my juice. Because I wasn't even drinking alcohol, but we had been smoking weed. But someone put something in my drink so that I was walking around like a zombie. Like with my eyes rolling around in my head. I was really slow and then I couldn't remember anything the next day. I went to the hospital. Anyway, they did a rape kit on me and it tested positive. So someone had done that or whatever, but I'd never willfully had sex with anyone.

And then after that I stopped living in group homes and foster homes when I was 18 years old. I got my own apartment and it didn't work out because of some problems that I was having, like I was cutting my-self and stuff. And, uh, I very rarely wear T-shirts, but I was cutting myself and I, uh, I just wasn't stable, so they decided to send me to a shelter. And then I've been in and out of shelters and boarding homes for about two years. It's just shelters because I had no place to go, like I couldn't go to an apartment, and I couldn't go to a group home or a foster home because I was too old. For a while I slept down by the wa-terfront and I bummed money off people. Like, I think my net worth was about like 20 bucks a day. That was recently. For some days I lived on the street and I did my laundry at a drop-in and took a shower. But I slept outside with a sleeping bag. Basically I would just sit by the water and smoke cigarettes. Bum money off people. Look around in the mall. Walk around and have coffee. Go to the Internet. This summer, it was just a few weeks ago, about two weeks in total I did that. I didn't like it. It wasn't comfortable. Not like a bed or anything. No shelter would take me. I think there was a crisis in service where they have problems serving you because basically they have problems helping you because you have self-harm issues or you've been there tons of times and it doesn't work out, like you get kicked out or whatever. There's a lot of times when I feel unsafe. Like, um, from myself. Usually myself, not re-ally with other people. I wasn't really worried about other people. I had a creepy feeling sometimes when I was by the water of like murders. But not really. It would kind of creep you out though to live there. You think about water and dead bodies. But I also have a problem where I like to move a lot and I don't know why. I like to go from place to place. Like, I don't have trouble leaving a place.

I woke up in someone else's body once, and I was really freaked out. And then as soon as I thought, take me back to my own body. And then I ended up ... It was like two seconds later and I was like, "Please god, please god, let me go back to my own body." So I thought of myself as much as I could, every detail, my birthmarks, everything, and how itchy my mosquito bites were, and I said ... I lied down, I got out of my astral body and I tried to figure out who was in my body, and then it's in an-other shelter – it's like Covenant House – and I walked out of my body basically and I felt myself leaving the body and I went to the person who was a copy of my body, because I was saying, "What am I doing in this fat girl's body?" And they're like "Oh my god, I'm a girl, blah, blah, blah." And so I went up to him and I hopped in the body. And then I saw him jump out – like his astral body. And then it jolted right back into his body – it was lying on the couch. Then I was me again. Really weird.

Tuesday night I had jumped in the river. I wasn't trying to kill myself, but I was going for a swim. And they had to give me an IV right here because I had hypothermia, a mild hypothermia. But basically I had hypothermia. I was like shivering like this. And like I was really cold afterwards, like after you get out of the water you're really cold. The air mixed with the water makes you really freezing, but, uh, they had to give me an IV. They put something on my arm. It's sort of like a patch, but it's a really warm thing. It's something to like warm you up. It's like a heat …you know, like an ice pack? Except it's on fire. Then I came here. That's how I got here. Hopefully here I will be happy.

I'm happy around certain times, like for me to be happy, completely happy, I have to have the following things in my life: first one is lots of money; second one is constant music; third one is a TV, computers, and friends, and possibly video games like Nintendo or something. Then I'd be completely happy.

RADHA

Radha called me after seeing the flyer I had posted in the shelter and left me a remarkably articulate voice message. The astuteness she demonstrated throughout her interviews helped guide me through my analysis. Radha would not schedule appointments before two in the afternoon as she could never be sure how her mood would be first thing in the morning, plus she was struggling with a constant cold that she thought resulted from the poor air quality in the shelter. Her depression often stopped her from showing up to scheduled appointments, but eventually she told me to just walk upstairs and knock on her door until she woke up. Radha had as little contact as possible with both the staff and the residents at the shelter, often telling me that she wished she could write the shelter out of her narrative. An award-winning writer, she plans to write her own life story into a novel after she graduates from university.

My name is Radha. I'm going to university in the fall to study biochem. I'm a writer. I'm not that bad, which is a higher level of praise then I'll usually give myself. Five adjectives to describe myself: intelligent, creative, talkative, um, this is hard, witty, and sarcastic probably. I didn't have very good parents. They were both kind of abusive in their unique ways. I say kind of, but they pretty much are or I wouldn't be living where I am. So it would be the experiences of being raised by my parents. I guess not being white and going to schools that were predominantly white. It changed a little bit over the years, things became more multiracial, but I remember when I was in elementary school there were two Black kids, one Asian kid, and one other Indian girl. We were the token minorities in our all white school. Not that kids are overtly racist, but there are those undertones.

My family, well, Indian parents are strange, I will say that. They split up when I was young. I think my father loves me. I'm pretty sure he does. I think he cares about me, but his views on how to motivate me include just degrading me all the time. So it's really horrible because I'll just call him and it doesn't matter how much I succeed or any accomplishments I have – like I have a $12,000 scholarship to school, which I think is pretty impressive, but then he complains that it's not enough and this and that. My grandfather is a cruel, well, I don't know, I think it's an Indian thing that I just never got used to, you're not supposed to, you don't really treat kids like kids. You treat them like tiny adults. I distinctly remember my grandfather telling me when I was five and my little cousin was born that I wasn't the cute one anymore, so he was going to start paying more attention to the little one and I was going to stop getting gifts from him. Yeah, he was really mean. And my aunt has always hated me and hid like treats from me and when I was kid, which I didn't understand. My mom, she, I don't think she is well designed to live alone. She was always very lonely and that was hard for me because I was a kid and they were both pretty protective so I didn't have a lot of other friends. I went to the park on occasion with my mom, but I didn't really have a lot of other friends who visited. So I kind of became my mom's friend, but I didn't want to be because when I was seven I couldn't really deal with her talking to me about her not knowing the purpose of life. It really wasn't easy. And, uh, I used to have a lot of hatred for her because of it, because, you know, what could screw a kid up more than listening to your mother talk about suicide.

I started taking anti-depressants when I was 14 or 13. I can't remember. I think 14. I saw a psychiatrist, a child psychiatrist, when I was 11. I was just really depressed and no real further explanation for it. Um, I was having some difficulty at school, not in terms of education because that's always been pretty easy for me, but in terms of making friends. I don't know, I think my parents just thought it was typical childhood angst, but it wasn't. Um, I tried to kill myself. It wasn't very successful. It was just kind of like very surface wounds. People said it was a cry for attention. It was a very conscious cry for attention. I knew what I was doing, and I knew I wasn't getting the attention that I wanted. So I figured that was the quickest, easiest way to get it. So my parents drove me to a hospital and it was extremely strange because they never do anything together, ever. And they just sat there quietly until I saw a nurse and didn't seem upset. It was really weird. The next couple of days were really surreal, so I just kind of stayed there. Then I was transferred into this, I guess, pediatric psychiatric hospital. I stayed there for a month and, um, that was really hard as well because I was 15 at that point and I was still in school and it was very important for me to do well.

So I tried to keep up, but it was just a bad place for me because I think I was the oldest one there and everyone else had kind of a violent history, or a history of trauma and no one was really sad, everyone was angry. So I just, it's really bad when you don't fit in with a bunch of crazy people who have actually been like ostracized by society and they're like, no, we don't like you, go away. I tried a group therapy session once and someone just got mad at me so I just abandoned those. It was just horrible for a month. It was the worst kind of place. There were no windows, or no, there were windows but they were barred shut. There were no doors. And there was this real rule against physical contact. And you think that's fine, but if you go a month without skin on skin contact, you start to go crazy. Lunch was where my parents would come in and we would talk to the counsellor and they would say, "If you'd like you can go and have lunch for an hour." You know, just get out of the horrible place. I began to just look forward to these more than anything else because I hated being there so very, very much. One time when it was just my mother, she came in and they said we could go out and she said, "Well, don't you guys provide a lunch?" And they said they did, but you know I could go out and get one myself. And she said she didn't want to waste the money. And you know it was seven dollars. I begged her. I told her my dad would pay her back. I told her I would pay her back. I didn't have a job, but I would figure out a way. It just meant so much to me and because she's, her main mode of abuse is through money, she's, she's very, very, very frugal. But what it would have meant to me, I don't think she still understands.

So just recently with my psychiatrist there's been a new change. I started Zoloft, which has this problem where it always works for me in that I have like a negative spiral when it comes to how I think and it cuts me off at a certain point. Like I'll start thinking, oh god, this is horrible, so I start spiraling down, but with this I just can't. So it provides this block, but it also makes me feel really odd. I feel really like my emotions to everything are blunted. I'm not as happy when I'm happy,

I'm not as sad when I'm sad. It feels really weird. I guess mental health is the biggest thing because I can't predict anything about how I'll feel mentally. I'll either wake up and be OK or I'll wake up and feel horrible. That changes what I do. I have pretty frequent days where I'm too depressed to do anything. I'll just lie in bed crying or just have no energy. It scares me a lot because I don't really feel in control of things.

See, these are all the reasons I am definitely not a typical teenager. I'm so beyond teenagers actually. Like for example, this one guy I dated, his friends are all kind of jocks and teenage alpha male types. They're nice guys actually, but just ... So I always wondered what they thought of him dating me, because they always made fun of him for never dating anyone, so I wondered if they liked me or whatever. He said, they all predominantly liked white women, so he thought it was odd, but they made stupid, racist comments, like "Hey, J likes the curry." But it was just idiocy, it's kind of how they make fun of each other anyways. Like, I'm sure they mock the others based on their girls, or some aspect of their girlfriends anyways. And apparently ... And I asked him at one point, "So what do they think of me?" And then he said, "They're not particularly attracted to you and they don't see how I am, but they respect you as a human being. No one has ever degraded you; they know that you're really smart and no one's ever ... They just kind of don't understand what I see in you, but they think you're a good person." Only a teenage boy would tell you that to your face. It's just teenage bullshit.

My insecurity and my complete lack of confidence really don't work well with my sexuality cuz you have to have some liking of your body to want to get naked around another human being. So you know, I feel so bad when my boyfriend and I are together. I was like, "Well, your ass is skinnier than mine. Why are you attracted to me?" Although he specifically said that he likes my curves. I should have enjoyed it and I could have been enjoying it except that I was thinking about how I look and how I hate myself. And my depression relates to my fear of rejection, which relates to sexual things. With sex there's a huge risk of rejection. That's just how it works. So, horribly, there's this awful, frustrating feedback loop where I'm sexually frustrated and that makes me depressed, and being depressed makes me more sexually frustrated. Then I can't, you know, assuage that because there are no willing human males and I can't trust people and I'm afraid of being rejected.

That said, I think that I've just acknowledged that I'm a more sexual person than most. I lost my virginity slightly younger than average.

No, wait, the average is 17. I lost my virginity when I was 16, so that was slightly younger than average. This is stupid, but I've been struggling with this a lot, in a lot of ways I feel older than I am. Children of divorce are always older than they are, but it's just so many things. Having had to deal with moving out already and having to live alone. And being homeless, which ages you pretty quickly. Just taking school seriously, so, I don't know, I've always felt a lot older than I am. In my mind I'm like 23, so it's more acceptable. The value and the judgment around girls and sex are definitely a part of it. It also doesn't make sense to me because I've talked to my female friends and although they're ... I don't know. They're kind of on two sides. Half my friends are still very innocent and virginal and just not ready for anything and I respect that. Then half of them are kind of in my camp where they're frustrated, but they can't express it because it's "slutty" or they're "too young." It's just difficult.

As for being a parent, I don't want to, but I do. Like, I can't deal with certain things. I get frustrated very easily. And when I feel like a task is very simple and someone can't accomplish it I get really, really angry, which is something my mom used to do. I hate it. I realize that it's a negative quality that I have and I hate it so much. I don't particularly know how to change it. So I'm afraid on the one hand. I'm afraid of being like my mother, less so like being like my father because I'm just not repressive like he is. I'm afraid of having a horrible problem child who will just cause me intense misery. I'm afraid of a lot of things, but I just ... I don't know. I like children. Maybe I'll change my mind, but I don't think I'd be entirely happy without a family. No one will ever love you in the way that your parents did. And it's true. You don't get that anywhere else. So not having had the parental love expressed to me, the closest I could come would be the love I could give a child. I've considered adopting and a lot of other things because if there's one thing I've learned it's that family ties don't create closeness. I don't want to sound like the crazy person who wants to have a kid immediately. I want to be like 30 before I have kids. But I do see it as hopefully part of my life plan. Hopefully. Maybe it will be better for me not to. I don't know

This is weird, but what bothers me most about my living situation is that it ever happened and that I have to acknowledge it. I hate that. I hate that this has ever been a part of my life story. Now I have to deal with it. I have to deal with whether or not to tell people. I just never expected or wanted or had any plans to have this be a part of my life.

It hurts a lot that it is. I think that every time you tell a story you lose a part of it that's yours. It becomes other people's. Your telling becomes common knowledge. I tell people some things and I can try to be flippant about it so it doesn't hurt me, but it's hard to deal with it. It's just another layer of: what do I tell people? Where between the abuse and the shelter do I stop? I just can't even tell certain parts. Like living alone. I just kind of say I have roommates and that I share an apartment with them. That's as truthful as I can be. For my pride and for my ego and for a lot of reasons it's hard to deal with. I have no one to yell at me or be responsible for being my conscience or whatever. I get to be my own conscience, which is nice. But on the other hand, when I'm sick no one is feeding me soup. When I'm unhappy nobody's talking me out of it. On the one hand I feel like it's inevitable. I've always been older than I am. I need to be alone. I need to be able to deal with this or I'll never be able to deal with it. It's kind of a trial by fire. I hate that this is a part of my life. Because for whatever it is, stereotypes have their way ... I don't know, the fact that I'm not the average homeless teenager, it doesn't really make a difference. Just the majority of women who are here are here for reasons that are not very flattering to their personalities, so I don't want that to be me. I don't want to be associated with that.

The average person who lives here is non-white; probably below, under 25; irresponsible; lacking foresight and planning ability; and needing large amounts of guidance and support to complete basic ... I don't know, not basic ... any sort of self-improvement tasks, like encouragement to go to interviews or encouragement to continue one's education. I don't know – short fuse – there's a lot of temper issues. And very likely, there's some sort of history of family breakdown or abuse, because there's a lot of that as well. I wish my past was different. That my parents loved me the way that parents are supposed to. But they didn't. All I can do is make a better life for myself. No one can do that for me except me. So that's what I'm doing.

FAITH AND RAVEN

Faith and Raven agreed to be interviewed on the condition that they could tell their story together. Their living independently is entwined with their relationship, their sexuality, and their journey from Northern Ontario to Toronto. At 16 they have managed to navigate the social welfare system, the big city, and histories of violence to end up housed in an apartment of their own. We conducted the interviews in their apartment, which gave me a better sense of who they are. Later they invited me to follow them through their day-to-day lives as they attempted to sort out miles of paperwork, make friends, and rescue cats. They both struggle to stay in a mainstream school, preferring to play World of Warcraft and watch anime cartoons. Faith is responsible and reserved, handling the finances and the household chores, while Raven is energetic and bubbly. Both have colourful hair, many piercings, and matching tattoos, tributes to each other and to their favourite anime team. At times they talk over each other, completing one another's sentences or arguing about who said what and what happened when. Ultimately, though, a unified story comes through. It's their story – two threads woven into one life.

RAVEN: I'm 16. I come from Northern Ontario. I've been living on my own for six months now. Over six months, actually. I'm fully installed in an apartment, finally. I just finished my first month in my apartment. Very happy about it. I'm in Grade 9, again, for the third time.

When I was first born, I was born in British Columbia. My father wasn't around, cuz my mom had pretty much ran away to British Columbia to get away from my dad because he kept stealing money. He didn't want my mom to be pregnant and he tried to get her to get an abortion. But, she refused so she moved away to British Columbia where there was other family. So, I was born in British Columbia where my mother was a single mother and had my Nana, which is her mother, to help. We lived in a trailer park, lo and behold. And, I was raised by mostly, by Nana, for a good six, six and a half years of my life because my mom went to school, went to college, went to work 24 hours. Barely ever got to see her. That was pretty good. Like, went to school as a good little girl. Always came home dirty cuz I was a tomboy, but hey, that was me when I was younger.

Finally, at about seven, my mom started seeing a guy ... six or seven, my mom started seeing a guy. Everything was cool until he started becoming a trucker, then they just fell apart and became distant. Don't know why, but they did. Then finally, eight years old ... I'll never forget this year, cuz it was the day my stepdad came into the picture. That was hell. First year was great. He was nice, he was sweet, he was kind, all that good shebang that you wanna see in a stepdad, till the day they got married. Day after they got married, he yelled at my mom, punished me the wrong way. Since then, till the age of 13, he was abusive. I've never met my biological father. I only know his name, and that's it. But, anyway, my stepdad left, but then started going on about how he's changed, he's a different man now cuz he realized how much he lost everything and stuff like that. And for the first few months it was OK and stuff like that. But then he abused her. He started yelling again, he started fighting with my mom. And then, in my opinion, I was always ... I was always the little boy in the family cuz that's just the way it's always been. Like, my mom never had a husband and so I grew very protective. I was always trying to shield my mother, cuz in my eyes, it wasn't right for a single mom to go through that. So, I ended up throwing myself in the line of fire and took most of the hits. I was pretty much the only one he's ever hit.

I was in a psych hospital at 13 and then 14, and then 15 again. Yeah, 13 it was for ... they all thought I was on drugs, which I wasn't. My brain just kinda overdrived and it just went haywire and I lost it. This one night I came home and I was gibbering a mile per minute. Everything was interesting to me. I didn't want to talk to anyone, I was just gibbering out of nowhere. My mom thought I was on drugs, so she brought me to the hospital. Got screening done, they said I couldn't be on drugs and I was like, "Well, I'm not on drugs." And then they sent me to the mental hospital to get a huge like exam done. They just found out that my brain had completely farted, completely like broke down. And they diagnosed me as a mild sociopath because of all the damage emotionally that had been done to me over the few years. Didn't get any medication for it cuz I wasn't that bad, I was just on that borderline that like people who have trust issues are at. I was just on that border, border, borderline of sociopath. And then, a year later I went in for suicidal, having all that good stuff. And a year later was for another breakdown. So, 15 was my last one, was my big breakdown. Last year, I had just turned 15. Then in November, my mom finally kicked me out. Well, one, because I was dating Faith; and two, because she was just tired of plain gayness, apparently. I don't think gayness is a word. Apparently it is for my mom. I hated her for a while for it. She hated me. Life went on.

FAITH: I'm Faith. I'm 16 too. I've been in my own apartment for just over six months, well with Raven, and I'll be attending ... finally returning to school this September. I'll be in Grade 11.

When I was born, my father left my mother because he wasn't ready for a kid. And then when I was about two to three, she met my stepdad and she got together with him and he treated me like gold. Spoiled me rotten. I wouldn't go to bed until or take an afternoon nap until he came home from work to give me a kiss goodnight. And pretty uneventful life for the first little bit. Then I hit my teenage years, probably about

12, 13. Then my stepdad started with the verbal abuse about everything. Like, I'm fat, I'm ugly sort of deal, which killed my self-esteem. And it was right after I got through dealing with a lot of problems, cuz from the point of being ... yeah I was eight. Yeah, from eight to 13 I was dealing with sexual abuse outside of the family that I have been going to court about. A year after I told the police, they sent me to court. But apparently there isn't enough evidence, cuz my ex-best friend, whose dad it was that abused me, knew, but is saying that she didn't. Anyway the asshole pleaded guilty to a lesser charge of simple assault, as if he shook my hand too hard, and got parole. I went to court and poured my heart out while his lawyer called me a slut and said because I watch anime and I'm a lesbian, I'm oversexed and a liar. So, yeah, five years of sexual abuse that has scarred me forever and he gets a year of parole. So glad I told the cops.

So between getting over sexual abuse, being verbally abused at home, and then being picked on at school every day, I had a couple suicide attempts and the school decided that I needed a counsellor, though because it was such a small school, it was a voluntary counsellor that didn't know what he was doing. And, I was like, "I'm not talking to you" sorta deal. Especially cuz I didn't feel comfortable with older men. So I switched schools and I met Raven. So we started dating and things at home started to seem worse and worse, and my mom just hated the fact ... I had come out to my mother, but at the same time she said, "Oh, I accept it." But it was one of those, "Oh, I accept it, just don't do it." I eventually like ... I just couldn't stand my mom. She just kept doing all this stupid shit. And then she kicked me out, just before Raven got kicked out. We've been together now a year and three months.

After we left home at first we stayed with our friend who has two moms. Lesbian parents. And they were really nice to us. But we couldn't stay there forever. So we were renting a room in a house with access to bathroom, fridge, and stove, and washer and dryer. And we were told it was room and board when we went into the agreement, and that included food and what not. But that didn't actually happen.

RAVEN: Pretty much we were renting a room, which was a last resort, like I couldn't find anything else anywhere else. No one wanted to rent to us because we were too young. It was a rundown house, some of the walls were taken out, some of the walls were missing. You swear you'd fall through the floor any minute in some spots. You were like, "OK, I have to slowly creep over this part of the floor." Like, it was infested with mice at one point too and it was gross. And to top it off, the guy who owned the place, his wife was schizophrenic and bipolar, so she freaked every now and again. And then he decided that we were good meat to play with, and I was like, "No, no, no" cause Faith'd been sexually molested for years at this point. And I'm just one of those people, "Touch me and die," like I honestly snapped at him so many times. And so on December 24, I completely flipped the handle and they said that we were kicked out. And I was like, "Oh, happy Christmas."

FAITH: After that we moved in with her Nana for a month, but we weren't doing anything except eating and playing computer games, so it was time to go from there too. I got a job. I worked at Tim Hortons for all of three weeks before they fired, sorry, before I "quit" because they told me to go home cuz I dyed my hair blue. Nowhere in their code of conduct did it say I could not. Nowhere was I told I could not, but after I did it, it was wrong. Now, my supervisor ... I worked a shift three to eleven, five days a week – full time job. And, my supervisor had no problem with my hair being blue. She was like, "Whatever, who cares, it doesn't offend the customers." And, then, what's the issue? Like, you wear a hair net, who cares? Now, the thing with that is the day supervisor who's there ... like she's leaving as I start my shift and my supervisor is starting. She didn't like my hair, so she talked to the manager. I got told, "Go home until you dye your hair a different colour." And so, I was like, "Fine. Sorry." And so, I left and I couldn't dye my hair a different colour until I got my paycheque. So, when I went to get my paycheque, they gave me my record of employment, saying, "Bye." Never asked me to hand in my uniform. I still have a Tim Hortons uniform. And the record says that I quit.

RAVEN: We have no money now. So we moved in with these two guys we knew. They paid rent, we paid for groceries for four people. Makes sense, right? It's a fair deal in my opinion. Two people pay for rent; two people pay for groceries. So, we were keeping the fridge full, but I had to go for a tonsillectomy so Faith bought more expensive food that I could eat, like ice cream and stuff. When the one guy found out that there was food he couldn't touch he freaked out. His name was on the lease, ours wasn't. He didn't get what he wanted so ... "Get the fuck out." So we were kicked out on the street.

FAITH: And they couldn't give us that two weeks ... No, he was like, "You can go sleep on the streets right this second." And so he left in the morning and told us all our stuff had to be packed and out of there by the time he got home or he was calling the cops. And so we were forced to leave there. We went to Couch Hall. We were couch surfing. We couch surfed for like a month almost.

RAVEN: Then on the bus we met this guy. He lived like 40 minutes away, but he let us crash in his tent in his backyard for a bit. Eventually we migrated into the basement where no one was staying cuz his daughter had vacated her room because in the spring they get ants. But anyways, he let us move in and we were there for a month. Then it was June and it was warm so we stayed on the streets for six weeks. Then we decided to come here, to hitchhike to the city. When I left, every article that I was wearing, except for my boxers and bra, were from someone else, and my shoes. My shoes were mine, my boxers, my bra were mine.

FAITH: We each had a knife, cuz what we were doing is we were hitchhiking from Northern Ontario to Toronto because the youth shelter where we're from has 10 beds that are always full. And so they turned us away saying there was nothing they could do. They send us back to the adult shelter, which is also full. If we go to there, all they do is give us two blankets and say, "Good luck."

RAVEN: There's so many youth on the street, but they're doing jack shit about it. The point being is there are shelters in Toronto. We knew there were shelters in Toronto, and we knew we had a chance in Toronto because we could get into a shelter, which means we could have that time to get a job, get up on our feet, and everything else. So we hitchhiked. I've never been to Toronto, never. But we found the shelter and it had two beds. We were there an hour and a half later, cuz we got lost on the way. The subway is hard to figure for the first time!

FAITH: We stayed there for a few weeks and the shelter worker, lo and behold, actually got us on Ontario Works [social assistance], which we were denied up North. But we have an apartment now! Just the two of us. Our own place to sleep and be together.

RAVEN: Ontario Works is $550 a month each.

FAITH: No, we get $485.

RAVEN: Yeah, $485 is how much we get from welfare, each.

FAITH: Cuz we get $210 for basic needs and $275 for rent. So we have to change that so we get a little bit more, cuz our rent went up to $600, so we're each gonna get $300 for rent instead of $275. We're allotted up to $350 each for rent. And we're not offered anything for going back to school, because they stopped that just this year.

RAVEN: Yeah, they stopped awarding extra money for back-to-school supplies.

FAITH: And winter clothing allowance was taken away, too.

RAVEN: Yeah, and winter clothing was taken away, which is completely not right.

FAITH: It got put on baby bonus, but we don't get those. So we might be a little cold this winter, but at least it's warmer here than at home. This apartment is a basement shoebox, but we're not out on the street anymore, so we'll take it. And girls are at the shelter for years, and I just don't understand. The longer you're there … we found this out. The longer you're there, the less motivated you become. You just … it kills your mood, it kills everything. You just … give up. So we wanted to get out right away.

RAVEN: Now it's school that's the issue. Oh my god! We're trying to go to school and they made us come in for an interview where they asked a million questions about our situation and we had to fill out so much paper work. Then they want to call home. Who the hell are they going to talk to? What part of "I am on my own" do they not understand? We had our lease, we had our OW papers, we had everything, and still. Personally, I think it's because some adults just don't get the fact that we're living on our own. We're old enough to live on our own. Cuz just because …

FAITH: Like, everyone just assumes if you're 16, you're not old enough. You're supposed to be at home.

RAVEN: Age is not everything.

FAITH: It's really discriminatory or whatever that big word is.

RAVEN: Our age and being lesbian. Or whatever.

FAITH: I came out in Grade 9, and I came out as bisexual because I didn't know I was a lesbian. And then I said I was bisexual for maybe a couple months, and then I was, "No, I'm a lesbian." And so I had been a lesbian until I started dating her at the end of Grade 10. So, in the middle of Grade 9 till the end of Grade 10, I was a lesbian. And then, into our relationship, probably until the mid-Grade 11 area, I identified as a lesbian, so a good two years. Then she ruined it.

RAVEN: I'm technically considered transgender, kind of a deal, sort of, mostly, yeah. And to her, she never understood boys, she never understood like how they thought, how anything, right? Which is why she didn't date them. But, then she met me, and realized.

FAITH: It was confusing at the shelter cuz she was told to say that she's a girl. Like, "Shh, don't tell anyone."

RAVEN: When we came to Toronto, if I kept saying I was transgendered in the shelter I was in, because I was technically male, they would have shipped me off to a different shelter, cuz it was an all-female shelter, even though I looked female on the outside. You can look male on the outside and be identifying as female there. But not the other way around. So really, I have no label, cuz if I was female, I'd still go both ways, if I was male, I'd still go both ways. I only say one when I'm forced to or I'm not comfortable with having people knowing ... cuz I'm tired of being judged. I'm one of those people who hate being judged. But yeah, like I say, it's the fact that it's always been drilled and like hammered into my head, "You're a girl, you're a girl, you're a girl." I need to wrap my chest if I want to go out.

FAITH: It hurts her though.

RAVEN: It hurts. That's why I only do it only so often. I used to wrap my chest every second day. I'd go one day flat chest, one day boobs, one day flat chest, one day boobs. But they eventually started to hurt my ribcage and it started to shrink my ribcage. So, I stopped. I had to. But eventually I wanna be one of those dads that actually goes out and plays with their kids, like, "Look, hey, my dad's cool, yours isn't, ha ha." Like have one of those kids. Like they brag about their parents. I wanna be one of those parents.

FAITH: And I want to be an architect so I can work pretty much right after I pop the kid and still spend time with my kid working at home. And so it's ideal for having children, yet it still pulls in a lot of money to support your children. And so what I wanna do is like have kids and just be like the parent that can put their kids, like, if your kid's like, "Mom, I want a piano lesson," it would be like, "OK."

RAVEN: And, they'll want to understand people and like, they won't judge and I want them to be open-minded kids. And not turn into kids like me who check in to mental hospitals when they're kids.

FAITH: No cutting. She used to be a cutter too.

RAVEN: I hid them. I didn't do it sort of in places where people could see. It was just pretty much to know that I was still alive, to know that I was still me. I was still there. I wasn't just a shadow that everyone who could step on. I was just a doormat. I was pretty much stuck with my stepdad, stuck with my mom, and then school on top of that. It was bad enough that I'd leave a crappy home to go to a school where I was the odd ball. I got picked on, like it was hard, cuz there was no place really for me. That's how I felt. So, it was pretty hard. She used to too.

FAITH: My stepdad was really bad for the, "You're a fag, you're stupid," sort of deal. I was just like, cut. It is really common nowadays. You'd be surprised how many people are actually cutters. And on top of it during the time, I was being sexually molested, so it was just kind of everything gets thrown together into one big, happy bubble.

RAVEN: But neither of us do that now. We're stable. When we have jobs and money we'll have kids. A long time from now. Now we have to take care of each other. All this just makes you even closer in the end, cuz the more hardship you go through the closer you get.

FAITH: Though while it's happening, it doesn't seem like that.

RAVEN: Yeah. While it's happening you tend to fight, you get stressed out, you take it out on each other. Then in the end you realize, after all that, you actually, finally, when you're fully installed and you get your own apartment, you're like, "Hey, I can actually cuddle you, and look at what we've done. Look at how far we've made it after so long struggling." And it feels good. In the end, it just brought us closer.

ARIELLE

Arielle was invited to participate in the project by her social worker. A recent immigrant from the Democratic Republic of Congo, she spoke only French. The staff at the shelter told me early on that the refugee and immigrant population perspective needed to be engaged in the research. I agreed, seeking out translation services for the interview. Because my French is shaky at best and although the consent forms had been read to her in French, I was concerned that Arielle did not quite understand the project. When I began to ask her about her childhood she became angry and withdrawn. Because everything was mediated through a translator it was difficult to express my genuine concern and interest. At the end of the second interview, Arielle asked me what I did, how old I was, and what my motivations for the project had been. In very broken French, I told her. She sat quietly, thinking for a moment. Then she nodded her head and a single tear ran down her cheek. It was the only tear I saw her shed. The story she told was unimaginable.

Well, I am the way you see me. I came to Canada in 2006. I want to learn the language and help all those who are like me, who have the same kinds of problems and difficulties as I have. I live in the shelter. I want to help the people who are in pain and I want to talk with them. I want to speak English as much as possible. As I don't speak English well, I want to learn English. I want to learn all languages and talk with my friends so we get on well and I can help them.

My first problem is that I am here. OK, people here have different problems. There are people who've left their country. There are people who've left their parents' home where they had problems. It's like my parents ... Some parents don't want the children to do what the children want; of course, they want their children to do what the parents want. But children need to have the right to do what they want, you see, because, in the majority of people here, it is the children who are smart and who know very well. So, like me, they leave the house and the parents. Like, in my country, people ... children cannot wear miniskirts, they cannot wear tight pants. They must respect their parents and the people. There are rules in other countries as well, so with those rules, parents cannot ... for example, if the girl goes to another country, she is going to dress differently. She is going to dress like the girls in the other country, you see. And the parents don't want that. What's going to happen at home? The daughter is going to have a row with her father and she's going to leave. The father's going to say, "Leave my house. You are not my daughter anymore because you're not listening to anything." And now you are in trouble. So, where's the daughter going to go? She goes to the shelter.

So, that's why I want to help everybody. We must find a solution and decide how to react, how to keep on good terms with our parents and the others, what we are going to do later on in life … also, what advice we'll give our own children. People say that if you go to a new house where people walk on one foot only, you have to walk with one foot also. If they walk with two feet, then you must use two feet. So, if the person uses one foot only, do not try to use two feet or you're going to find yourself in trouble. I must be like the people here. People here dress correctly, so I must also dress correctly. But not like the people around me. I have to choose between correct and incorrect, you see. So I dress correctly, but I don't wear miniskirts. I dress with colours out of respect, you see. That's what my parents didn't understand about me.

I cannot tell you my story because it makes me cry. Listen, I come from my home country. My country was at war, OK? Congo. And it was really hard in my country. They say war is no good because … I don't know why people go to war, why they fight. But it's really very hard, what I suffered in my country. I think, I say, "Thank God, we are here together with you." I thank God for all that because I didn't know … It's good to tell all the stories and I want to tell everybody who does not know … But that, I don't want to explain because it makes me cry all the time. When I started going to school, the war was on. When I went on with my studies, the war was on. I came here with my mother and my twin sister and my brother. I'm 20 now, but I came here when I was 17.

My story is very hard. They killed people in the street. They really did. They cut the legs off children. They really did. All that was happening. I think that now we can believe they've changed. I don't know. When I talk, I see everything again. It's as if it was happening to me again. I said I have to forget all that. I must rub it all off but I can't. I can't. It's not easy. My story, it makes people cry, really. It's really hard. We are here together and I thank you, but you'll see it's not funny.

In my country, when the war started, the police would kill people. The army killed people together with the police. And they killed children and women and men. I had a friend, my friend there, with her mother she had fled to the village. They lived in the forest not to be caught by the police. Her mother was sick. Her mother had twins, two baby girl children, and a daughter, my friend there. The police came to the forest. The people who were there ran away. They left the mother and her children behind. The mother said, "I want to die. Go, go. Take the children. Bring the children with you." As soon as she said that, the police appeared and they pointed to the girl there. She said, "Mom, we're going to go." The mother used to work in a bank, she had a bit of money and she said, "Go, my daughter, go. This is the name of the person you must find. He's going to give you all I have and you're going to help your sisters."

The mother hadn't eaten. She couldn't eat sugar nor salt because there wasn't any during the war and there wasn't anybody to sell salt and sugar. And the Red Cross was also afraid to come because the Ninjas, the other Ninja police, they didn't get on and they killed people. And the feet of the mother were swollen because there was no salt. And her mother said, "Leave, go, go." As soon as she'd said that, they shot her mother. The grenade entered her other hand. And the girl took the twins. She kept just … she tried to hide in a tree which was very big. As soon as the police arrived, they saw the mother. They raped the mother in front of the girl. And the girl saw everything. And the police, they took their knives and they cut the hand of the mother. And they cut her breasts. The mother was saying, "Oh! I want to die, but my children, who's going to look after my children? Lord, protect my children when they go away to the cities." The police said, "Where are the children? We're going to kill the children." They went very close to the children but they didn't see them. It was a miracle from God. That's why I love God so much. And the mother died.

The police left with the mother's arm. In fact, they were children themselves. The girl came close to her mother. The mother said, "I want to die. You must leave this country. But I'll follow you where you're going. Tell your children, your sisters, not to cry. Where you're going, I'll keep you." The mother gave her the key. It was the key of her bedroom. In her room there was a trunk. She said, "There's money; there's stuff; there are very important papers. Take that." The girl said, "I don't know that village. I don't know how to get out of here." The girl took to the road. She buried her mother and she took her sisters with her. She told her sisters, "Don't cry. We're going to go away from here. Don't cry. If you cry, they'll kill us." And the girl walked with the two children. The distance was like from here to Montreal on foot. When she arrived in a village, the police caught up with her. One said, "You are our enemy. We're going to kill you." They took the girl to rape her and then, the girl, the baby, she peed. The police said, "Now, go to your mother. Your mother is over there." The baby girl said, "My mother is dead."

But he said, "Your mother is there. Go, go." For that he was stabbed himself and he died. The girl left the village in pain and the government found her. She explained her problems. Her mother had given her something and now she could take care of her little sisters. Now it's her who is the mother. I think she left the country. I don't know. Until now, it's her who's been looking after the children. The girl, the big sister of those kids. The girl who ran away with the twins. It's her who looks after them.

But the problems are very hard back home. That's why I say I cannot explain because it makes me cry. Because it happened to me also. During the war, I was under the bed with my brother. My mother was on the other side. I don't know where she was. The police, they killed people in each house. They went in and they killed people. On our lot, there were guards and as there was a president who lived not far away, they killed those guards. They came into the house, our house. They were seeking … they wanted to kill us. The police would shoot all over the house, all over.

As for my brother, a bullet just went through him from here to there. My brother was screaming. The police heard the voice. They entered our house. They took me. They told me, "We're going to kill you. Sing first and then you're going to die." The other one said, "But don't kill her, she's too young." And the other, "We'll kill her. She is the child of our enemies." One stabbed me here. Another … did that which makes me cry. They did that to me. Then the other pointed his arm at me. He wanted the bullet to come in here and go out there. The police said, "Leave her." I was crying and my brother too. He said, "We must kill them." The other said, "No, you can't kill them. I see the girl there. She's like my girl." Their chief came in. He saw me. He said, "What's your name?" I told him. He said, "I am sorry. I didn't want that to happen to you. I'm telling you to run away, to leave, or else my guards are going to kill you." He said, "Don't forget God, don't forget anything that may happen to you." And my foot was swollen. My brother wasn't speaking anymore. He was so much like that. I took my brother. The policeman got something together for my brother and one took me away gently. It was night. He took me. He guided me. He said, "Don't leave like that. You're going to go straight in front of you. Bring your brother. Go straight. If you see the police, say that you are the child of the lieutenant." I forget the name he said. As soon as he said that, the Ninjas, the other police killed him. The bullet entered the head of the lieutenant. And he was nearly dead. He said: "Go. Run … "

I ran with my brother. I put my brother in a wheelbarrow and I pushed him. I was running. But I couldn't make it. My foot where I was stabbed was so big. I kept saying: "Lord God, help me, help me, Lord." I ran with my brother. My brother wasn't saying anything. That was hard. He is really different from other people. That we were away was really a miracle from God. I thought I wanted to die because I wasn't myself any more. As soon as we arrived at the police, they took me as their maid, to work for them. I had to work. I told them, "I am the child of the lieutenant," and they said, "No, we don't believe you." And I had to run around for each one of them. There was one who said, "You girl, I know you from somewhere. What's your name?" I told him my name. He said, "It's a beautiful name. I want to help you run away from here." Then, my brother, he becomes so … like chalk. He becomes white. He becomes so white because of the bullet … it was the pain that was mounting. He seemed to want to die. He said, "I want to die. I want to die." I took him and I said, "OK, you're not going to die. We're going away from here." I took the wheelbarrow. We arrived at a place where there were people in a church. As soon as the people of the Red Cross saw me and my brother, they took my brother to a hospital. They also took me and they gave me a home. I lived where people lived.

All that time, I had not seen my parents. My father was not there. My father was here already. But, during all that time, I had not seen my mother and my sister. People told me they'd killed my mother and my brother and sister. I was so stressed. I thought I should go and kill the people who had killed my family. I decided to leave the place where I lived, where the Red Cross had placed me. I thought that I also should enter the army. I must go and kill those people. As soon as I arrived, they asked me, "What's your name? Why did you come here?" I said, "I must enter the army." They said, "No, you're very young and we don't want women." I said, "Listen, I am 25." "No, you're not even 25. You're very young." They said, "What's your name?" I told them. They said, "Don't you know it's the name of God? You must not go and hurt people. We'll look after you. Go, go and get on with your studies. War is going to end and you'll go to school." I said, "I don't see my mother." They said they would search for her. I gave a card with a photo to a policeman. Then the police really made an effort. They found my mother and they brought her to me. My mother was crying. During that time, my sister had lost her mind because they had been shooting just beside her and it made her crazy. They shot somebody and the bullet passed in front of her and then she couldn't see any more and then … she went mad. And the police, they brought my brother, my mother, and my sister. But my sister didn't know anybody anymore because she'd lost her head. It's hard.

But the policeman that had died. Before he could go, he said, "I want to give you something for my family." He gave me a card with a photo. He gave me addresses. He gave me the number of his bank. He said, "If I don't come back, you can give that back to my family. And this bank thing … You must look after yourself and your studies. Pray for me." And then the policeman left and he didn't come back. I asked his friends. They said, "No, he's not alive anymore." I looked for his family. We looked with my mother. We found his family, his wife and two children. And we gave them the keys and I said he'd given me the address of the bank. My mother said, "Don't give that." And I said, "It's not my money. Look at the woman there … this man left a wife and two children behind. This isn't my money. The money is for those children." And I gave it. His son said, "What's your name?" I told him. He said, "Can you be like my sister?" I said yes and he said, "Come and see me anytime." But that little boy died also. He died of sickness. I was 15.

And when finally we came to Canada instead of staying with my family, I am not with my family anymore. I am here. So what was the best thing about coming here? The best thing, I'll tell you. I came here because there was too much war. OK? Here children go to school. There's no war. Children are at peace. They are in good health. They get on well with their parents. The children in my country, they're not with their parents anymore. Their parents are not alive any more, OK? So why not leave my country to continue my studies? I have a dream that I want to realize. I want to be an architect. I have to leave my country, go to another country to study. Not … Not for my pleasure, just to study. Focus on my studies, pray, help everybody, advise everybody. Because of what I went through, I want to advise everybody and everybody is going to take my advice. And, as I was telling you, I think it's going to be good. You're going to understand certain things, what happens in other countries. That's why I like Canada so much. I want to be here. I want to look after myself and my studies. I must succeed. I want to be well. That's it. That's the reason I came here. That's it.

You're lucky I told you so much. In the Congo I gave everything I had to give. It's hard. It's very hard in other countries. There are people who cannot talk about the problems they've had in other countries. You can imagine the problems I have and what I went through and what continues until now. There's no end to problems. But they're going to end at some point. I am the child of God.

5 Sugar and Spice and Everything Nice: Age, Space, Place, Gender, and Health

[H]uman beings conceive of their lives in terms of moving-between – between identities, relations, people, things, groups, societies, cultures, environments, a dialectic between movements and fixity. It is in and through the continuity of movement that human beings continue to make themselves at home; seeing themselves continually in stories and continually telling the stories of their lives, people recount their lives to themselves and others as movement.

(Rapport & Dawson, 1998, p. 33)

Introduction

In analysing the young women's stories, it quickly became clear that I could not discuss health-seeking behaviours and access to health services without first delineating the social contexts in which these activities occur. The women repeatedly reported how their age, and discriminatory attitudes towards youth, had limited their movement, safety, and sense of belonging to a larger and more supportive community. Time and space, then, became the obvious starting points for narrating stories of youth homelessness. To fully grasp the impacts of homelessness on health and well-being, researchers must recognize that time and space are mutually constitutive (Dunn, 2000). Time, both as it is understood through aging and as it is understood as social and historical change, impacts on the ways in which spaces are defined and created. Spaces are produced by social structures and context specificity; they are dynamic and mean different things to different people depending on their access to resources within those settings. Discourses around age limit access to particular spaces and create barriers by setting different rules for different people according to their stage in life and their relation to centres of power. Young people's health and well-being is thus largely determined by the neoliberal rules and guidelines that determine the spaces in which they can and cannot live.

In this chapter, I explore the creation of identities that are intricately woven into the particular spaces and places – such as schools, group homes, shelters, streets, and psychiatric wards – within which, and in relation to which, young people live. I also look at how social locations, such as class and gender, interact with place to create opportunities and setbacks. As a result of their position within these physical and social spaces, homeless youth become visible as threats to the social order, but are also made invisible by their in-between child and adult status. Facing social exclusion, lacking state and personal supports, and confronting histories of poverty and abuse, these young women are charged with the difficult task of finding a place to feel at home both physically and emotionally.

The interface between storytelling, homemaking, movement, and identity is a crucial component in any individual's process of meaning-making; however, it manifests itself differently in the lives of people for whom stability is an uncommon occurrence. When one's life is in a constant state of flux, displacement and relocation act to create both physical and psychic homelessness. Although places are often thought of as fixed, they are in fact dynamic, containing different meanings at different times for different people in accordance with their access to power and resources (Dunn et al., 2007).

The unequal allocation of resources, due to class as well as gender, race, and age, means that spaces of inhabitation for homeless youth are often temporary, unstable, and public. The contexts and places that homeless young women find themselves within or without cannot be understood without reference to the social construction of age, which in many instances restricts access by the young. Such restrictions often lead to poorer health outcomes and social exclusion, itself a key determinant of the health of populations.

In most social science research, previously accepted behaviouralist conceptions that understand health as the outcome of individual responsibility have, for the most part, given way to perspectives that recognize that the most salient factors for good health are not necessarily individual behaviours, or even medical technologies, but rather social and economic factors (Evans et al., 1994; Frank, 1995). Following this line of argumentation, Dunn and colleagues (2007) note that changes in context could modify health outcomes for entire populations. In this project, contexts include discourses around age and protectionism, as well as the more obvious physical examples of streets and shelters. Political and economic forces that influence the distribution of wealth and power within Canada and other countries create health inequities (Coburn, 2004). Social geographers argue that place is germane to health outcomes because places "constitute as well as contain social relations and physical resources" (Cummins et al., 2007, p. 1825; see also Kearns & Joseph, 1993). Places, in their absence as well as their presence, have deep impacts on the health of homeless young people. Lack of secure shelter and length of time spent on the street, for example, are predictors of hunger (McCarthy & Hagan, 1992). In a 1999 study of Toronto's street youth, 43 per cent of respondents indicated that they had gone without food at least one day a week over the course of the previous month (Gaetz et al., 1999).

To fully grasp the impacts of homelessness on health and well-being, research must examine phenomena spatiality with the understanding that time and space are mutually constitutive (Dunn, 2000). Temporality, in this case, speaks to the passage of time by way of political and social change, but most importantly, it speaks to the significance of life-course phases in understanding the far-reaching consequences of social constructions of childhood. Time both as it is understood through aging and as it is understood as social and historical change, impacts on the ways in which spaces are defined and created.

Although I refer to the participants of this research as "youth," some of them are considered "children" in the eyes of the law because they are under the age of 18. Despite the fact that Ontario's department responsible for people under the age of majority is called the Ministry of Children and Youth Services, in children's rights legislation, such as the *United Nations Convention on the Rights of the Child* (1989), "youth" as a social and legal category is non-existent (James & James, 2008). The two terms are used selectively in political rhetoric depending on how much personal responsibility the speaker wishes to place on the individual under discussion: young people are children insofar as they are denied power and resources outside the family unit, but youth when they are involved in crime or are acting "inappropriately" (Kelly & Caputo, 2001). Children who are wards of the state when they are under 14 are, in some cases, eligible for support until they turn 21; however, there is almost no support for children who live independently but are over 14 and under 18 (Martin, 2002). When an individual over the age of

14 enters care for reasons of sexual abuse or violence, they are considered "adults" and are provided with little protection under child welfare legislation (ibid., p. 94). This political anxiety over youth being not quite child and not quite adult only acts to perpetuate the in-between status that youth feel in other areas of their lives, thus heightening feelings of exclusion. As Radha said, "Maybe it's the age thing, I dunno, but I feel like an outsider most all the time."

Childhood and the Life Course

In its beginnings, childhood studies was the exclusive domain of developmental psychology. James and James (2008) argue that psychology has had a greater impact on our thinking about, and attitudes towards, childhood than any other discipline; unsurprisingly, this has resulted in a highly medicalized view of what constitutes childhood. Medicalization can be understood as the expansion of the domain of medical jurisdiction into the lives of individuals, which eventually becomes a form of social control by which groups and individuals define their worlds in medical terms (Conrad & Schneider, 1980). As Foucault (1973) reminds us, medicalization as a form of social control is dependent on the social and political hierarchies that structure biomedical discourses. Children, who are particularly vulnerable to the control of adults, let alone medical professionals, have little or no say in the construction of these terms. Foucault (1975) also discusses the ways in which systems of surveillance have become omnipresent in the lives of individuals in contemporary Western societies. What is considered "normal," especially in terms of health and development, is often determined by accordance with age-based biological and mental criteria (Hockey & James, 2003, p. 14). Echoing feminist critiques of biomedical discourse, it is through these measurements that children are made objects rather than subjects. Dominant medical theorizing on child development has painted a picture of childhood that remains essentially protectionist in nature (Jenks, 2005). Recent developments in sociology, however, have begun to deconstruct medicalized notions of childhood, arguing instead that structural variations will produce health variations – no singular notion of childhood can encompass the diversity that exists within the category.

West and colleagues (2008) characterize the new paradigm of childhood studies in the following manner: childhood is a social construction, an interpretive frame for understanding the early years of human life; biological immaturity rather than childhood is universal and natural in human populations; childhood is a variable of social analysis which cannot be separated from other variables such as race, class, and gender; and, children must be seen as actively involved in the construction of their own lives (p. 268). Notably this characterization recognizes that childhood is infused with meaning depending upon the economic and political demands existent in particular societies at particular times (Hockey & James, 2003). This detail is particularly salient in light of continuously high levels of immigration and asylum seeking in Canada. Having arrived from the Democratic Republic of Congo, Arielle remarked on the ways in which children in Canada are unprepared for independent living, especially in contrast to those she grew up with: "In Africa, by the age of six you have learned how to get ready. You have been taught to wash the clothes. You've been taught to clean the house. You've been taught to shop for groceries. You must learn all this." Because she learned to be more independent at a young age, Arielle felt more competent and confident living away from her family in a shelter. To some people in Canada, however, a six-year-old girl managing household responsibilities might be considered to border on child abuse. In this case, cultural relativism and universalism are brought into relief; so too, however, are the ways in which childhood is a social construction that depends on time, place, culture, and context. Children are not adults-in-waiting, anticipating the birthday when they wake up legally competent, but rather social beings who influence and are influenced by the structures around them (West et al., 2008). However, children are so often seen as incompetent and are constrained in ways similar to society's other disadvantaged groups. As a result, young homeless women, who often belong to several of these groups, are multiply marginalized.

Childhood as it is conceived of in contemporary Western societies is a state of being characterized by innocence and immaturity, and so children require protection from the adults who imagine them in this way (Steedman, 1995). This sentiment carries over into the realm of public policy where children are not granted full citizenship and their dependency, particularly on parents and family, is presupposed and reinforced, as is evidenced by the lack of public support for independent people under the age of 18. Preserving childhood as an ideal that requires dependency on adults has meant that political and social institutions attempt to balance the care and control of children from inside family homes (Wyness, 2006). This leaves children who live outside of family homes virtually unsupported. As Erin said, "Why can't I get any help because I'm 14 or 15? If you've already been on the streets for two years, a lot of stuff has happened to you, and you know what? You probably want to stay there cuz you've got used to what it's like out here. You sure as hell aren't gonna go home." Teens that face age restrictions when trying to access resources – including looking up information online and in teen magazines – generally end up as far underground as possible and lack information and support when making decisions; sometimes preserving innocence also means preserving ignorance (Hockey & James, 2003; Scott et al., 1998).

In the case of homeless youth these false associations between childhood and familial dependency – both in terms of emotional and financial support – often negatively affect those living self-sufficiently. Although many young homeless women struggle to complete high school, there are also those who continue their education and advance through the post-secondary level. These highly motivated young people rely on government loans, such as the Ontario Student Assistance Program (OSAP), to pay high tuition fees and to purchase course materials; however, many of these loans assume that youth are dependent on their parents, as Danika found out:

> I don't think they think that anyone living in a shelter could also be going to university. I think the government just assumes, oh, OK she lives there, she has no family. But then on my OSAP application there's no way to indicate that I'm not living with my parents. I take care of myself. I need to get parents' signatures, but I'm supporting myself. There's no way I can communicate that to them.

Even when seeking basic necessities, homeless young women are discriminated against on the basis of both social and biological conceptions of age. When resources are scarce, competition between women becomes hierarchical and older women may use their age and circumstances as an excuse to horde precious resources. Erin often spoke about competing for food and sanitary supplies at drop-in centres: "So the older women take a look at you and they pull rank or whatever. 'You're just a kid. Go home to your parents. We actually need this stuff.' Yeah, right, and I don't. But the older ones can sometimes get really mean, and sometimes even gang up on you and stuff, so there's that too." Again, the assumption that young homeless people are better protected by the institutions of state and family than are adults is erroneous. The pervasive influence of medical discourse on conceptions of childhood often leads to a false correlation between youth and physical and mental immaturity. Similarly, at the Woodlawn shelter, a shared youth/adult facility, Radha was told that the physiological differences associated with age were a reason to prevent youth from using the building's newer showers: "Oh, the stupid adult-youth thing. I don't know. I asked what the concern was actually a while ago, and the only thing that I got was that some of the adult women are insecure when there's teenagers in their showers because our bodies are different, which I think is the most ridiculous, stupid thing in the universe." Prohibited from using the showers in which she felt comfortable, Radha opted not to shower for days at a time and at times risked being discharged from the shelter by sneaking into the off-access area. Radha also commented that the distinction between adult and youth bodies made her feel more uncomfortable about her body and contributed to a sense of age-based surveillance that many of the other participants spoke about as well.

Childhood is a product of discourse that does not adhere to any singular template and, as such, is a social identity better understood through standpoint (Wyness, 2006). The categories of youth and child do not exist independently of the individual, but rather become significant by way of particular individual responses (Hockey & James, 2003). So although two individuals may fit into the same category by virtue of their biological age, they may differ in their adoption or refusal of the label. All eight of the young women in this study discussed the ways in which they found it difficult to attach themselves to labels such as "teenager" because they believed there were typical characterizations of the category – such as "happy," "carefree," "playful," "irresponsible," "shoppers" – to which they could not relate. Hockey and James (2003) note, however, that personal agency, whether as a matter of choice or a matter of circumstance, can influence the trajectory of childhood. As Danika says, "When bad things happen to you it forces you to be mature. I would have never, ever thought I would be in this place. And when you deal with hardships and you see hardships it kinda makes you older." A "critical lack of fit" with the typical expectations of the label has the potential to change perceptions of a particular identity category (ibid., p. 202). Instead of considering these youth as outsiders, lost between identity categories, an understanding of homeless youth as representative of variations within the scope of childhood and youth identities would allow for a greater sense of inclusion and, perhaps, for greater awareness of their particularized needs.

For Archard (1993) the most salient feature of contemporary Western childhood is the concept that children are separate from adults –
they are separate in nature, in work, and in play, and they are separate
from the adult realms of law and politics. However, as Jenks (2005)
highlights, they remain subject to the legalities and policies of the adult
world. In Ontario, youth that are in the child welfare system, but are
not wards of the state, must leave the welfare system when they turn 18
and can choose to opt out of care at the age of 16 (Serge et al., 2002). A
Canadian study conducted in 2001 found that this gap in the child protection system is an important contributing factor to youth homelessness (Kraus et al., 2001). The study makes particular mention of youth
over 16 who are ineligible for protection services and of those who leave
care between the ages of 16 and 18, as both groups generally find themselves unprepared for the challenges of living independently (ibid.). Individuals under the age of 16 who are not in care are ineligible for most
services, including shelter. Shelter workers are required by law to validate the identification (which many street-involved youth do not have)
of those under the age of 18 (Novac et al., 2002). Erin best articulated
these gaps when she said:

> Well, in January I'll actually be 16, which is the greatest thing ever. Because
> then I can get welfare and live in a shelter if I want to. Which I don't. But it
> means I'll be a quote-unquote "actual adult" in the eyes of the law. It's so
> screwed up because I don't think I can be more adult than I am now, but
> I'm not 16, so I'm left to rot in the street.

Since the Harris government made cuts to social assistance in 1995,
16- and 17-year-olds who are able to receive Ontario Works financial assistance are unable to receive cheques directly; they must receive them
instead through a guardian or trustee, who is, in most cases, their social
worker (ibid.). In addition, these teenagers are entirely ineligible for
benefits if they are not enrolled in school or if they miss class repeatedly (ibid.). However, even enrolling in school is a significant challenge
for young people who are already trying to balance finding their own
housing and living on their own, supplying their own food, and taking
care of their health, often while dealing with the lasting effects of personal violence. Faith explained the challenges they faced: "We tried to
enrol in school [...] but they don't know. She [the school administrator]
had to talk to the principal and see what he said, and then he would
probably have to talk to the school board and see what they say and

then ... They're like all, 'Well, what went wrong? Why are you here?' Well, read the forms we had to fill out 80 times." For a 16-year-old who has just left some form of dependency, the task of living independently with few resources and fewer emotional supports can be daunting, to say the least.

This seemingly arbitrary age-defined line between childhood and adulthood differs between policies, reflecting the contradictory attitudes of policy-makers towards young people. When young people are penalized for their mistakes in courts of law they are seen as adults, whereas when they attempt to work full-time jobs they are seen as "students." Faced with these challenges, many young women end up homeless, whether invisibly – sleeping on couches or staying with older men – or visibly, on the streets. Here again, politically motivated language changes are worth noting. To say that an "advanced society" like Toronto faces a problem with street children would be intolerable to many, who see street children as an issue in developing nations, not here in Canada. Somehow, then, the language of homeless *youth* becomes more palatable, if still slightly distasteful. Images of children in adult spaces, especially public adult spaces, contradict idyllic notions of childhood (Kelly & Caputo, 2001). In the case of homeless youth, the separation between adults and children is visibly removed. In these situations, children seem out of adult control, which creates unease and, with it, discourses of risk and danger. Erin points to one of the most common stereotypes associated with the "risk" of homelessness: "So I ate some McDonald's cuz some lady offered to buy me something to eat. Cuz they think you're gonna take their money and buy crack, right?" Discourses of risk also tend to undermine the influence of the structural factors that contribute to homelessness and ill health in the first place. The label "at risk" often vilifies homeless youth, while simultaneously letting decision-makers and the public at large off the hook for providing young people with adequate social support. The social exclusion associated with taking an untraditional path away from family homes, or even state care, is often central to the ways in which youth become identified and defined both as children and as adults (Mallett, 2004; Wardhaugh, 1999).

In line with life course approaches to aging, the creation of social identities constitutes a process (Hockey & James, 2003). Life course approaches, as opposed to life cycle approaches, assume that stages in life are not linear or standardized (ibid.). Instead, ageing is seen as both a physical and social process characterized by variation and diversity (Featherstone & Wernick, 1995). As such, the life course of homeless young women need not be seen as unnatural or inherently dangerous, but rather as one possibility of many. Danika was quick to discuss the ways in which the label "homeless youth" automatically differentiates her from other people of her age: "It's like 'homeless youth,' like it's an endangered species or something. You know, 'We need to help the homeless.' Like that's all we are. We're people too. And there's youth on top of that." The double marginalization of homelessness and youth creates a feeling of double exclusion – a lack of fit into anything that might be considered "normal" by mainstream society. Intersecting marginalizations such as gender, race, and sexual orientation only further compound an already difficult situation. In the same way that it makes little sense to view "youth" or "homeless" as a single unified category, thinking about adulthood as a single stage in the life course is also problematic. Adults who have just had their first child will experience life differently from adults who have recently retired. Perhaps thinking of homeless youth as experiencing a particular phase in the adult life course offers the possibility for positive change and positive thinking.

Benoit and colleagues (2008) argue that as a result of social stratification, the life course of street youth is more productively understood as temporarily different from their more normative peers. The researchers' understanding of the non-normative life courses of homeless youth places homeless individuals not in the category of child or youth, but in the category of "emergent adulthood" (ibid., p. 326). Emergent adulthood is a stage of the life course when experimentation is necessary to adult identity formation (Arnett, 2005). For normative young people, behaviours such as drug use and sex with several partners are seen as part of the natural progression towards adulthood; however, when these same behaviours are discussed in relation to street youth they are often characterized as "risky" and linked to disease, addiction, and maladjustment (Benoit et al., 2008). Again, medicalized discourses that hold the measuring stick to child development and behaviour are quick to judge "abnormalities" without considering contextual factors such as socio-economic status. Youth who live without social support networks, who confront issues of violence or intolerance, and who spend shorter periods of time in the dependency phase are thrust into the emergent adult phase earlier than their better-supported peers. According to this characterization, homeless youth are not abnormal or deserving of stigma, they are simply in a more advanced phase of the life course owing to disadvantage and exclusion. As Erin said:

Like, [being homeless] automatically makes you not on *The O.C.* or whatever, but at the same time I am still a 15-year-old chick. I'm figuring life out way, way, way faster than other chicks my age, but still, you know. I don't have time for all the bullshit and the shopping and the boy talk and the sleepovers or stuff, right?

Resentful of the notion that she is somehow abnormal, Erin seeks to make clear that she is the same, but different. She would not have chosen to live the life she is living, but her so-called "risky behaviours" are often necessary to get by. As Benoit and colleagues (2008) conclude, "risky behaviours" cannot be evaluated independent of social conditions; they must be reconsidered with a view to structural causes. Decision-makers and the general public need to see that being young and homeless is just one of many ways that an individual life course can be rerouted and reimagined. Equipped with more support and a feeling of belonging, many of these emergent adults will continue their trajectory to stable and productive adulthoods.

Spaces and Places

I turn now to conceptions of social geography because, as Bondi and Rose (2003) assert, "the axes of identity [...] never operate aspatially but are bound up with particular spaces and places within which, and in relation to which, people live" (p. 232). Places and spaces exist in relation to the people who inhabit and move through them – some places are healthier than others and so are the people that live there. Because both spaces and identities only exist in relation to time, the phases of the life course, alongside social markers like class and gender, interact with place to determine spaces of access and spaces of constraint. As Cummins and colleagues (2007) suggest, an individual becomes relationally connected to multiple health-promoting and health-damaging spaces across the life course. These various relationships assist in determining the importance of place in the production and maintenance of health inequalities. For example, reports have shown that the stress associated with housing insecurity is significantly correlated with mental illness among low-income people (Dunn, 2000; Smith et al., 1993). Moreover, stable housing is a crucial component to forming a social identity and nurturing emotionally fortifying social relationships (Dunn, 2000).

Broadly, this project speaks to a wide array of journeys taken between rural and urban areas, across international borders, and from reservations to cities. More specifically, the geographical plane of this research is the urban space of the city of Toronto, Ontario. Toronto is Canada's largest city and home to one of the world's most diverse and multicultural populations – 49 per cent of Toronto's residents were born outside of Canada (Jacobson et al., 2009). Recent studies have shown an increase in poverty in the city as well as the concentration of poverty in particular neighbourhoods (Hulchanski, 2007; MacDonnell, 2007). Since the mid-1990s – when the provincial government downloaded many public services to the city and cut social assistance rates by 21.5 per cent – the municipal government has been unable to balance its budget (MacDonnell, 2007). In creating a struggle for basic resources, these deficits and their related cutbacks have changed the face of family homes, group homes, shelters, and state institutions across the province, all of which are significant and formational places for young women in exceptional circumstances. Homelessness is unquestionably a spatial condition. Wardhaugh (2000) writes that to be homeless is to "be a person without a place of one's own, to be someone who is displaced or out of place" (p. 111). While this may be true in the majority of cases, it is important to remember that some young people can be made to feel at home in non-traditional places that are inclusive, nurturing, and supportive of their needs, their histories, and their futures. Women's circumstances cannot be viewed atemporally – homelessness can be at one time debilitating, but at another time healing (CRISIS UK, 2007). Age and space matter in creating interventions to assist young women in exceptional circumstances. An important fact, which is often obscured by the label, is that homeless people live somewhere; although they are often forced to carry out daily functions in public places, they too negotiate space in order to live (Veness, 1993). Young people, and women especially, inhabit these spaces in ways that are unique to them. Perceived vulnerabilities to aggressive or violent men and adults, as well as law enforcement officials, require their creative use of bodies (often through clothing or tattoos) and of spaces (often those that are hidden). However, women, especially young women, have not been given much consideration in the literature on homelessness and space. Klodawsky (2006) cites a couple possible reasons for this omission: men are the more visible gender on the street, and homelessness is a levelling process that renders individual social identities unimportant, thus creating a singular focus on the overall condition of disadvantage. Other researchers have called for a moratorium on women's homelessness research, arguing that homeless women are fewer and have better and preferential access to services (Peressini, 2004; Passaro, 1996). Notably, several young women who were a part of this project agreed that they were advantaged by their gender in the search for services: Jean suggested that, "It's a lot easier for girls to find places to stay, like in shelters," while Erin found that, "Being a girl makes you definitely in a better spot. It's easier for me to make money panning because people feel more sorry for girls, especially young ones like me. I think it's easier for girls to get help, or maybe easier to ask for help sometimes." Both young women, however, neglected to mention their greater likelihood of being victimized by sexual violence or exploitation despite the fact that both had personally been targets of sexually abusive behaviour on the street.

The places in which homeless female youth interact are equally important as those in which they do not. The displacement that homeless youth often feel affects their sense of belonging and self-confidence and negatively influences the formation of skills and behaviours associated with healthy and meaningful social integration (Vandemark, 2007). All members of society experience parameters around their access to particular spaces and places: private homes, gated communities, and any number of places that are closed at night are off-limits to those who are uninvited. However, the spatial prohibitions placed on children are even more restrictive (Jenks, 2005). For girls these restrictions are even starker as they are thought to be particularly vulnerable and in need of protection, especially in public spaces (Katz, 1993). The repercussions of this social construction are far-reaching for homeless young women who have learned that they are unsafe and preyed upon when alone after dark in public spaces. This often leads young women to enter into sexual negotiations for a "safer place" with older men who are more securely housed. Danika saw this happen to another girl she knew: "[S]he moved into an apartment and the guy paid for it. She has everything she wants, but she doesn't care about him. You know, but she gives up certain things for that money, if you know what I mean. It's not for free." O'Grady and Gaetz (2004) argue that what sets young homeless women apart from their male counterparts is that on male-dominated streets, they are "alienated from more traditional environments for girls," such as family homes (p. 400). Although I disagree with the conflation of women and girls with the domestic and private realms of hearth and home, the stereotypical social constructions of girlhood and gender socialization are major contributors to the ways in which young women are treated and how they behave when faced with the prospect of living on the street.

While later sections of this chapter will speak to the places and spaces that young women inhabit, a discussion of the places and spaces where they are inhibited is equally necessary. One particularly stark and significant example extracted from the data is the space of traditional public schools. Childhood, as we now understand it in contemporary Western societies, was socially constructed in the second half of the nineteenth century; during this time, schooling became state-regulated and mandatory for children between 6 and 18 years old (Wyness, 2006). In most Canadian provinces today, all children are required to be in school (whether public, private, or home) until the age of 16; in Ontario, young people are threatened with the loss of their driver's licenses if they are not enrolled until the age of 18 (Justice for Children and Youth, 2006). Punitive measures such as this make life especially difficult for young people in exceptional circumstances who live in more rural areas, limiting their access to work and social opportunities. Because of their rules, regulations, and educational curricula, the structures of family and school are the most important forms of social control in the lives of children. For many homeless young women, however, schools are not seen as a safe place and their "outsider" status leaves them vulnerable to bullying and harassment. A Canadian study of homeless females between the ages of 18 and 25 showed that most of the participants had run away or left home between the ages of 13 and 15, and a full 50 per cent had not completed high school (Serge et al., 2002). When coping with the tumult of leaving home, living on the street, experiencing the loss of social and family networks, and coping with food and housing insecurities, young women are not well-positioned to attend school, study, or meet deadlines, as Jean expressed: "I dunno. I can't handle school right now. I'm so different than everyone else and I couldn't handle being made fun of, plus I can't do homework up in here. Some days I can hardly wake up cuz I'm having mental problems and that." Their inability to attend traditional schools removes young people from opportunities for recreation, socialization, and formal knowledge acquisition. Several participants commented that, once they found themselves on more stable ground, alternative school options such as Bridging Programs, which allow students to do course upgrades and access university programs, or online education would offer some flexibility for those living in untraditional environments. However, those living outside of the shelter system felt that the enrolment process for alternative education was too complicated or that any form of education was unmanageable in their current situation. In leaving school and home at a young age, homeless youth lose both of the structures that are most influential in traditional childhood development and in the creation of young people's support systems.

Questions about the spaces that homeless young people inhabit or avoid also draw attention to the complex dynamics between the visibility and invisibility of this diverse population. Wardhaugh (2000) suggests that homeless people are at once everywhere and nowhere, but that the general public does not really see them. In Toronto people look at homeless people on a daily basis. The very public nature of their lives means that the spaces most people pass through on their way between any two points are living spaces for homeless people. While they might look at and register the presence of "a homeless person," many people do not actually see the subject; this looking without seeing only serves to make homeless people feel more invisible. Only recently have social geographers begun to examine the roles that young women play in public (youth) cultures and the ways in which gender identities are both constructed and reconstructed in these spaces, thus creating a form of invisibility even within the research literature (O'Grady & Gaetz, 2004). Homeless female youth are also invisible in schools, invisible in child welfare legislation, and often invisibly homeless. In a seeming contradiction, however, homeless young women also report feeling overly and uncomfortably visible.

Lees (1986) posits that girls are subject to surveillance in the form of reputations that boys create and disseminate amongst one another. Teen sexuality is still dominated by gender ideals that suggest that boys are rewarded for their sexual prowess, while girls are punished and negatively labelled for theirs. I argue, however, that this surveillance is not just created by boys, but rather by a society that exploits female youth sexuality to sell everything from magazines to cars. The neophilia that permeates contemporary Western society encourages all people to worship at the fountain of youth, tells young women to look sexy, but not have sex, and marries youth with consumerism. Radha observed that, "like almost everything they sell is about youth sexuality, whether they want to admit that or not. Most of the women in these ads are 18 or under." As Pacom (2001) asserts, "the symbolic seductive power of youth is strong, but the real power is weak" (p. 90). Several of the young women in this study, including Danika, spoke about the ways in which adults seem to think that youth should be subject to scrutiny simply by virtue of being young:

People think that youth are like conflict or beauty. And they become such a spectacle: 'Look at them in their youth. Look at them in their most trying times. Let's look at them going through their drama.' I just don't like it. [...] It's just a feeling that people give to you, like, you know, 'Let's put you on a shelf.' Or, you know, just like, 'What are you doing?' So you're more in their eye. And all the pressure to look a certain way or be something they think you are. Youth really have a lot of pressure. It's true.

These surveillance practices have the effect of making young women feel self-conscious and insecure, particularly about their bodies and outward appearance. Many of the participants worried that their clothes or hairstyles were markers of their socio-economic status, signalling their difference from fashion-conscious youth and spectacle-gazing adults. Those who were visibly homeless and lived most of their lives on the street, such as Erin, felt this ocular intrusion even more acutely: "And you know when you're on the street all the time, people are always looking at you. Always. Even when I'm panning and they pretend not to be looking at me they are. So you live your life always being looked at. No privacy. No such thing for me." There are many reasons for young homeless women's attempts to remain unseen: avoiding stigma from normative populations, avoiding the risk of physical violence or property theft, or avoiding contact with police. In most cases this avoidance involves moving through and around central public spaces to more hidden locations, but as Wardhaugh (2000) remarks, it can also involve retreating into oneself or refusing to provide personal information. In the early 1990s Toronto experienced high numbers of visibly homeless youth (Novac et al., 2002). Strikingly, however, despite the concurrence of cuts to social assistance and social programming, the number of visibly homeless teens decreased in the mid- to late-1990s. Around this time the city implemented employment-training programs for youth, while the province introduced the *Safe Streets Act* (1999), which led to law enforcement officers performing sweeps of streets and parks and ticketing panhandlers and squeegee people with fines that ranged from $100 to $500 and up to six months of prison time for repeat offenders (ibid.). Ruddick (2002) has explored the ways in which these by-laws swayed potentially sympathetic members of the public by reframing youth homelessness as a threat to public safety. According to Erin, its other effect was to alienate youth from police officers, authorities that homeless young women should be able to rely on for assistance: "Plus cops are assholes anyway. They just want to use their power to show people how tough they are. Shit, you should see the way they treat us down here. They think that if they be the boss and hand out tickets and shit we're all gonna screw off. I'd be pretty tough too if I had a huge gun on my leg too."

Home

Conceptions of homelessness cannot exist without conceptions of home; thus, home seems like a natural starting point for the discussion of the spaces and places that homeless young women inhabit throughout their homelessness trajectories. Home is a varied but important signi-fier in almost every culture across the globe (Despres, 1991; Somerville, 1992). Inviting someone into our home is one of our primary modes of establishing, maintaining, and growing social bonds. Dunn (2000) draws the connection between housing stability and a sense of personal control, which workplace studies have shown to correlate significantly with positive health outcomes. Low degrees of control over one's envi-ronment, then, pose a risk to one's overall health and well-being. Home is not simply a place of shelter, but also a place of belonging, inclusion, and social support. House and home, therefore, are two separate con-cepts: the architectural structure of a building is but one component of the overall machinery of home, one that varies between societies, cul-tures, times, and places (Mallett, 2004). Several studies have observed, however, that Western countries like Canada have intentionally con-flated house, home, and family in order to serve "family values" agen-das that ultimately have economic "efficiency" as their root incentive (ibid.). Notably these same "family values," premised upon middle-class assumptions, put homeless youth in volatile situations by protect-ing the sanctity of family (read: dependent children), but not the needs of single women.

Feminist scholars have also interrogated understandings of home by problematizing the association between homes and discourses of pri-vacy that often define home as a feminized realm which is off-limits to public laws. As Savannah explained, many young women are left feel-ing homeless at home when confronted with violence or oppression within the family (Wardhaugh, 1999):

My mother, uh, the reason that I went back and forth, back and forth was because my mother was abusive to me. Like, if she couldn't find [my brother] to beat up she would attack me. And she would leave us home by ourselves when we were like seven years old. Like, we didn't know how to cook. We didn't know how to clean. We didn't know nothing. We would mess up the house cuz we were just young, right? And she wouldn't let us go outside because she didn't want anyone to see our faces. To see that we were alone.

Five of the other eight young women grew up in homes similar to Savannah's. In fact, women are more often assaulted, raped, and killed in their homes than in any other place (Goldsack, 1999). Too many young women can only experience safety outside of their houses and must work to create homes away from home. Robinson (2002) suggests that the opposite of homeless is not home, but homeness: a term that recognizes that home is an emotional as well as physical space and that allows for the possibility that homeless young women might be able to experience home within institutions associated with homelessness. As Danika said of the shelter, "I have a home. It's just not traditional." Following this line of thinking, a productive goal in the creation of state services for homeless youth, and homeless people across social identity categories, might be to create spaces of inclusion in which a person can develop a sense of homeness.

While home has meaning for all people, the meanings that children give to home and that homes give to children are unique. Mallett (2004) argues that "within households, gender and age are the key dimensions that differentiate household members' perceptions of the meaning of home" (p. 68). For children the house can sometimes offer little privacy or time away from parents, guardians, or siblings. Dunn (2000) posits that young people, and especially young girls, need a sense of control of private space, such as bedrooms, in order to maintain their health. Girls tend to spend more leisure time in their bedrooms than do boys, and are generally able to control access to, and the activities that occur within, that private space (James, 2001). For the homeless young women I interviewed, the idea of having private access to their living space is almost unheard of. Even in their original family homes, many of which were characterized by poverty, shared bedrooms were the norm; as in Erin's case, experiences of conflict and violence too frequently penetrated the entire home: "First, my stepdad [...] was a child molester and my mom seems to think that's fuckin' OK or something. Uh, ya, so I guess ... so I guess from the time I was like eight he was touching me or whatever." In addition to intra-family violence, growing up in poverty, whether homeless or housed, establishes a sense of exclusion at a phase in the life course when one is most impressionable (Leira & Saraceno, 2008). This is not to say, of course, that poverty and violence necessarily occur together. Research has shown that supportive relationships and family stability do combat the adverse social effects of poverty (Shanahan, 2000). At times, though, even loving families are not enough to combat the health-compromising effects of living without money, and young women are forced to fend for themselves. Danika comes from a close-knit family, but the hardships of poverty meant that she needed to make her own way in order to survive: "God, I love them, but they just disappointed me so many times. It's so hard to deal with it. So hard to put your trust in them. [...] You know, because for me a family is something, a family should be able to provide, but if they can't, sorry." Recognizing that her life chances were jeopardized by her family's lack of stable housing, Danika saw firsthand that home, house, and family cannot be conflated.

In Care

Canadian research on urban homelessness has shown that youth who have been involved with child welfare are over-represented in the overall homeless population (Serge et al., 2002). In 1999, 62,000 Canadian children received child welfare services outside their family homes, either in foster care, residential care, or in institutions such as psychiatric hospitals and youth criminal justice centres (ibid.; Tyyska, 2001). Foster care is family-based care for children who have been removed from their birth families, while residential care places children in group home facilities. Children are often placed in emergency foster care on a short-term basis until a longer-term placement is assigned or available (Serge et al., 2002). Children are not able to stay in care after they turn 18 and often find themselves in homeless shelters shortly thereafter. In fact, in the later 1990s, 48 per cent of youth who sought post-transition services at Toronto's Covenant House – Canada's largest youth shelter – were former children in care (George, 2005). Leslie and Hare (2000) have commented on the insensitivity of Ontario's current child welfare system, citing in particular its inability to prepare youth for independent living and the overcrowding of shelters. In Toronto alone there are approximately 3,000 children in care and every year 600 youth over the age of 16 are released from the child welfare system (Serge et al., 2002). Startlingly, there is no tracking system to follow the trajectories of young people once they leave their care situations, although there is clearly a substantial link between being in care and ending up young and homeless.

Serge and colleagues (2002) attribute this link to a system failure insofar as child welfare does not help children cope with the issues that have catalysed their removal from the family home in the first place. Their critical lack of trust in figures of authority and in family has considerable ramifications for the future relationships of these youth. A number of studies have found evidence of re-victimization during care, which only intensifies initial traumas (ibid.). Unfortunately, my research provides no exception. After having been sexually abused multiple times as a child, Savannah was again assaulted by a worker at the group home in which she lived:

> And then one time I was sleeping and I felt his hands on my legs. Like, under my nightgown. I was like, "What the hell!?" I was confused. I did not like him sexually. I did not like him touching me. But I knew in my mind that if I said anything, something would happen to me. Nothing would happen to him, but something with me. I was still 15.

Savannah never told anyone about these incidents, which occurred repeatedly over the eight months she spent there. Her understandable mistrust of authority and her fear of rejection eventually led to her taking her frustrations out by assaulting another resident who was hospitalized after the assault. After being charged for this incident Savannah found herself in jail for the first time. The worker who repeatedly assaulted her kept his job. Three-quarters of the 60 young homeless respondents in Poirier and colleagues' (1999) study indicated that their experience with the child welfare system was negative or catastrophic. Forty-one per cent reported severe punishment, abuse, intimidation, or rape. It is unsurprising, then, that youth who have left care and eventually become homeless typically have lower educational attainment and are over-represented in the criminal justice system (Mann-Feder & White, 1999).

Another link between being in care and being homeless is incompatible or unstable placements characterized by multiple moves between care placements (Serge et al., 2002). Jean typifies this connection: "The longest I ever stayed in one place in care was about four years. I'm what they call a frequent flyer. A frequent flyer is someone who goes to the hospital a lot and they have like legitimate reasons to be there a lot. Just like an airline." When I asked her why she moved around so much, she explained, "[It was] mostly because I just ... If things were going well, then I just wanted to ruin it because I didn't want to get close to anyone. So it's what you call self-sabotage." When I spoke with her, Jean was attending therapy on a regular basis and was able to use the language of psychotherapy to explain her behaviours; she was still unable, however, to stay in one place for long. Over the course of the month that I spoke with her she switched shelters twice.

A review of the international literature on outcomes for youth leaving child welfare systems shows dismal results (George, 2005). Generally, when youth leave care they are afforded a single chance to make their new housing situation work; should a young person be unable to manage on her first attempt she is prohibited from re-entering the system (Aldridge, 1996). Again, these policies signal the failure not of the 16-year-old youth, but of a system that creates and perpetuates dependency on adults and that "leave[s] children without resources when those adult protections are withdrawn" (Lansdown, 2006, p. 147). Even those programs that exist to assist youth with their transition from dependence to independence concentrate on "life skills" such as doing laundry, making meals, and finding employment. Nothing prepares young people for the stigma, exclusion, discrimination, and poverty they will face (Fitzpatrick, 2000). Furthermore, because of their differing funding and accountability mechanisms there is no collaborative strategy in place to share information or provide continuity of care between child welfare services and the youth shelter system (Serge et al., 2002). More accountability about the efficacy of these systems is owed both to the young people who are ostensibly protected by the systems and those who foot the bills.

On the Street

The streets of urban centres are pivotal in the discussion of homeless youth and health, as street-involved young people occupy them for the purposes of socializing, working, and sleeping (O'Grady & Gaetz, 2004). This is especially true during the day when the young people who live in shelters are prohibited from being in their rooms and must vacate for the day. Although many of the homeless young people in Toronto's downtown core do not sleep on the street, they do occupy that space, experiencing the perils and possibilities of street culture. The false dichotomy between private and public becomes apparent relatively quickly to those who inhabit the streets as they are forbidden from entering most private spaces and many public spaces as well (Wardhaugh, 2000). As they are confronted with both subtle and overt signs that they are not allowed in stores unless they are making a purchase, not allowed in restrooms unless they are customers, and not allowed to stand in the street asking for money unless they work for a registered charity, young homeless people come to understand that they are not welcome anywhere. In addition, street-involved youth are confronted with what Davis (1992) calls the "strategic armoury of the city against the poor": hyper-vigilant policing, street furniture engineered to make sleeping uncomfortable if not impossible, and strategically timed sprinkler systems that ensure stairwell sleepers are awake well before the start of the business day (p. 160). In order to avoid these inconveniences, youth migrate outside the busier areas of the city and into more secluded locations. For a young woman this change of location can be particularly precarious as it moves her away from street lights and the public eye which, although stigmatizing, can also provide protection. Savannah explained that as a young woman, she has more safety concerns than men on the street:

> First of all I have to worry about being safe more than the boys do. Being a girl you aren't as strong and you're on your own and there are a lot of crazy people way out here, I mean really crazy, like mental, you know? Mentally deranged or whatever. And being a girl what you have is sex. And that can be tough because guys want that and sometimes they just aren't afraid to take it or at least try to take it.

Under these conditions it becomes difficult for homeless young women to protect themselves and their property.

Gaetz (2004) demonstrates the ways in which the incessant media spotlight on youth criminality obscures the fact that many homeless youth are more likely to be the victims rather than the perpetrators of crime. Indeed, street youth are among the most victimized populations in the country (ibid.). Leading a public life exposes young people to strangers, including those who are desperate for resources and those who have histories of poor mental health and substance misuse. Theft is a particularly big problem for those living on the street. Due to frequent relocation and shared accommodations, keeping anything of value, including identification or health cards, becomes a struggle. As Erin said, "At one point I had some ID stuff, but shit gets stolen all the time. You can't keep stuff really." Being without belongings in a place where one feels that they do not belong only exacerbates feelings of isolation, not to mention the multitude of problems that result from not possessing any form of identification. Alienation from police and figures of authority, especially if one is already involved in criminal activity, provides street-involved youth with little recourse when they are victimized.

Gender is another key determinant of whose body is allowed where and, once there, how one experiences a given environment. Women's perceptions and experiences of safety influence their opportunities for mobility, income generation, and shelter (O'Grady & Gaetz, 2004). When surviving on streets that are dominated by masculine power and control, women are more likely to lead even more marginalized existences, disappearing into shadows and attempting to attract as little attention as possible. The exception to this is street sex work, although tactics in this case are complicated as the same invisibility rules do apply. Wardhaugh (1999, 2000) states that women who are more visible on the streets tend to be accompanied or protected by men – their pimp, their son, or any other relative or acquaintance. For street-involved young women under the age of 16, invisibility is necessary for safety, but it is also imperative to avoiding apprehension by law enforcement or child welfare services – a key fear for many street-involved young people, including Erin: "I don't want to be taken by Child's Aid and I don't want to go to some gay-ass group home where I'm just gonna run away anyway. You know how many kids I talk to everyday, like every day, who took off from those places? They don't work." This particular population of women is difficult to find and, in my experience, will withhold personal information such as birth names and addresses in order to stay as anonymous as possible. The implications of this are clear: avoidance of any type of professional authority, be it social workers or doctors, means that mental and physical health problems go unreported and untreated.

Performances of gender also become integral to survival and safety for young women living on the street. Huey and Berndt (2008) refer to two such performances as the "femininity simulacrum and masculinity simulacrum" (p. 187). The two most common strategies for young women surviving in male-dominated public spaces are to adopt hyper-feminine behaviours or hyper-masculine behaviours. In the former example, women who are usually, but not always, heterosexual, use displays of traditional and even stereotypical femininity to help them seek a male protector or compete with other women for the affections of particularly powerful men (ibid.). Developing a formal relationship with a man decreases the likelihood of victimization by others, but often involves the exchange of sexual or domestic services. In Erin's situation her gender performance is attached to her femininity as well as to her age. At 15, she lamented her boyish body as it makes it difficult to play the hyper-feminine role in seeking protection: "I'm a scrawn, like sometimes I can even pass for one of the guys cuz I have no boobs. And boobs get you a lot when you're a chick. Guys love boobs. We all know that." In the same sentence, however, she commented on how those same physical characteristics allow her to perform gender in a more masculine way, passing as "one of the guys." When generating income through panhandling, Erin uses the social constructions of age, gender, and childhood to her advantage: "I panhandle a lot during the day and I do the lost little girl routine and people eat that up, so I make decent money at it." Tactics such as these enable young women to make creative and positive use of the constraints that hinder their access to resources in every other facet of their lives. This creativity, resourcefulness, and resistance is typical of young people on the street who manage to create spaces of agency in the midst of hardship. Of course the performance of a hyper-femininity that involves provocative dress and damsel-in-distress routines can be dangerous in and of itself. Would-be-victimizers are more likely to seek out easy targets, making the interim between the initial performance and the procurement of a protector a particularly precarious time (Huey & Berndt, 2008). Hyper-masculinity, on the other hand, signals a denial of the feminine, but provides greater security and self-sufficiency for young women. Performance of this gender role mainly involves gaining weight and dressing in larger clothing to hide the shape of the body and in drab colours so as to not draw attention to oneself. Jean exemplified this performance: "I almost got pimped by a pimp or whatever. I was a lot skinnier and stuff. That's why I eat a lot cuz I want to stay fat so that guys don't hit on me [...] and big clothes are good for that too." Recognizing the risk posed by femininity, many young women eschew it altogether changing body shape and size as much as possible to adopt a more masculinized persona.

Invisible Homelessness

Living on the streets is usually interspersed with periods of invisible homelessness: living in places that are unstable, unseen, and impermanent. Invisible homelessness means having a roof overhead, but lacking support and resources; many women in these situations report feeling intense isolation and loneliness even when living with other people (Sistering Toronto, 2002). Smith and Gilford (1998) report that invisible homelessness is more likely to be experienced by women than men, who are more likely to be visibly homeless. Because of the unique challenges that women face on the street, the relationships they create in order to live under a roof are often problematic, exploitative, and hazardous to their health and well-being (May et al., 2007; Maher et al., 1996). As Raven described it, the house that she and Faith first lived in together was an example of invisible homelessness:

> It was a rundown house, some of the walls were taken out, some of the walls were missing. You swear you'd fall through the floor any minute in some spots. You were like, "OK, I have to slowly creep over this part of the floor." Like, it was infested with mice at one point too, and it was gross. And to top it off, the guy who owned the place, his wife was schizophrenic and bipolar, so she freaked every now and again. And then he decided that we were good meat to play with, and I was like, "No, no, no."

In Raven and Faith's case, their youth and sexuality also contributed to their precarious living situation. They often faced discrimination from landlords who refused to rent to young people, especially those who were lesbian – a fact that Raven and Faith stopped mentioning in order to find the place they describe above. Young women also employ informal tactics, such as couch surfing and car camping, in order to avoid streets, shelters, or drop-in centres. As Danika shared, families often rely on these same tactics to avoid stigma and shame from other family and peers: "My parents had their office, so we were living in their office all day. [...] So every day we would go to the motel, go to a hotel, some were cheap, some were like under a hundred dollars. We would all share one room, and some were really bad. So there was this time we still had no place to live, at nights we slept in the car, all four of us." Attempting to continue her university studies while living in a car with little food eventually pushed Danika into the shelter system and away from her family.

Although poverty is a major contributor, young women become homeless from any number of family housing situations marked by instability, abusive behaviours, or a combination thereof. After leaving or being pushed out of home or care situations, young women usually find themselves in a temporary arrangement with friends or family (CRISIS

UK, 2007). After these arrangements break down, many young women attach themselves to older, more financially secure men for whom they may provide domestic, drug, and sexual services, sacrificing their autonomy to "boyfriends" who often control their activities and interactions (Maher et al., 1996; O'Grady & Gaetz, 2004). Not infrequently these men will offer "protection" to several girls at once, creating a kind of harem for himself. Erin described one such man: "I been sleeping at a friend's place lots of nights. He's got an apartment that he gets from welfare and stuff and so lots of us will go there when it gets cold. Then we do stuff for him. Like, clean the house or go to the foodie or give him splits of panning money. I dunno, sometimes give him a blow or whatever, like I said." As it happens, Erin's "friend" was 30, while she was still 15. Erin is aware that this sexual relationship is illegal under age of consent statutes and is a clear case of exploitation, as she refused to provide names, details, or locations. As she said, "I could do this by my choice with one guy or with force with who knows how many other ones." Lacking the resources to support themselves independently, many young women, especially and perhaps most worryingly, those under 16, "choose" the lesser of two evils.

Shelter

Shelter data for Toronto shows that almost a quarter of new admissions are people between the ages of 15 and 24 (Callaghan et al., 2002). As Raven and Faith's invisible housing experience demonstrates, young women are virtually disqualified from rental housing as they are unable to provide evidence of credit or long-term employment records, often leaving them at the whims of unscrupulous landlords. In 1999, 2,150 single female youth resided in Toronto shelters, representing dramatic increases in shelter use by Aboriginal, sexually diverse, and black women (Callaghan et al., 2002; Novac et al., 2002). Youth homelessness is most apparent in the downtown core, where the majority of non-residential services for youth are found. Although many health, social, and legal services are located in these high-traffic areas, only one youth shelter – the largest in the country – is located in the core (Novac et al., 2002). Other residential services are located outside of the downtown area – an intentional choice by policy-makers who sought to ensure that young people were able to maintain ties to their home communities and that they stayed away from other homeless individuals downtown who were, in their eyes, more likely to be involved in risky behaviours (ibid.). However, young homeless people seeking access to services outside of shelters are obliged to travel to the core to fulfil their needs. Perceptions of the downtown core as a high-risk area obscure the fact that violent crime and poorer health outcomes tend to spike in lower-income neighbourhoods like the East end or areas of North York (Hou et al., 2003).

Shelter culture varies between shelters that provide services exclusively to women and those that cater to men or both genders insofar as men's and co-ed shelters are more commonly associated with violence and criminal activity. Women are generally more satisfied than men with the services provided by Toronto's shelters, which may be linked to the feminist organizing of the 1960s and 1970s that demanded women's shelters be built, organized, and managed in women-friendly ways (Fournier & Mercier, 1996; Novac et al., 1996). Research has proven, however, that living in the comparatively safe space of women's shelters involves more personal trade-offs in the name of social control, which occurs through strict rules and regulations, greater domestication, chores, and expectations of "proper" behaviour (Novac et al., 1996). Neal (2004) suggests that these trade-offs often mean that the oppressive conditions women have fled are reproduced in women's shelter environments. Danika's description of the shelter as a highly regimented environment demonstrates this:

> You know I didn't have a place to live before and here they paid for your accommodations, they paid for your food, they like take care of you, but there's like a trade-off for that. So you have to like, well, the trade-off is your freedom. You're exposed to all these different things you don't want to be exposed to and you have to live and cooperate with like 54 other women on one floor. And we have to share the washroom, the facilities, everything. So you can't lock yourself up, you can't avoid being around people, so that's a big trade off. We have curfew. We have to be home by like 12 o'clock. There's so many rules. Like, you can't burn candles. You really can't do anything because it's not your property. There's just a big cost that comes with living here. You can't invite people over cuz it's a shelter and it's so restrictive. It's your home, but sometimes it can't feel like your home.

These aspects of control, including the fact that shelters close during the day, create a sense of spatial anxiety that diminishes the ability of young people to experience homeness and belonging in the building in which they live (Vandemark, 2007).

In a study of the role that bedrooms play in the lives and development of adolescent girls and young women, James (2001) discovered that the control they exercised over their rooms correlated to their sense of self-efficacy and general well-being. She asserts that the decor of one's room – from posters to candles – provides a young woman with a sense of security, while Steele and Brown (1995) claim that the decor of a teenager's bedroom reflects her emergent adult identity and self-representation. At the shelter, young women are not allowed to decorate the walls or make the room unique in any way; the space is a place to sleep – a house, but not a home. Many young women in James' study also saw their bedrooms as "a refuge from the critical gaze of others" (p. 87). For a population concerned with constant surveillance and lacking any form of private space, young homeless women would certainly benefit from one space on a floor with tens of other women to which they could escape from prying eyes. The greatest obstacle to private bedrooms is the simple fact that the space does not exist – shelters are oversubscribed on a regular basis with three or four young women sharing any given room. Under these conditions developing a private sense of self away from the stigmatizing gaze of others is difficult if not impossible.

Many of the young women associated living in the shelter with infantilization or criminalization as they had to ask for and justify everything they needed from shelter staff. As Danika said, "You even have to justify your use of tokens [for public transportation]. Transportation is essential! We're in Toronto! If you need to get to work or need some extra tokens, staff are like, 'Sign here to say you took them.' Oh my god! You feel like a criminal." Several of the young women participating in this study also mentioned that they had been expelled from several women's-only shelters because of zero-tolerance policies on violence and substance misuse, which forced them to rely on mixed-gender adult shelters where they felt uncomfortable and unsafe. While these rules are clearly and necessarily in place to protect residents, punitive measures may not be the best option for curtailing violent outbursts between young women who are themselves products of violent environments. In contrast, for some women, such as Arielle, these controls substitute for the rules of the absent parent: "I love all the staff here. They are so nice. I say they are really different from my parents. When I see them, I don't worry about my parents because they give me advice. They like me very much. I laugh with them." Arielle's response may be attributable to the fact that she was raised in a culture in which children are taught to revere adults, and parents especially, but even so, the point remains that for some young people, guidance and rules provide the structure necessary for them to remain motivated and focused. The rule-based culture of youth and women's shelters, then, is not straightforwardly positive or negative, but rather one unit of shelter culture that could be examined to ascertain which rules are in place because they are necessary and which rules are in place because they are traditional or have "always been that way." Those rules that are seen as unnecessarily oppressive could be adjusted or removed in favour of ones that would create a more confidence-inducing environment for residents.

Women living in shelters also detailed concerns about nutrition and cleanliness within shelters: Radha spoke about allergies due to poor air quality; Danika spoke about the high-carb meals with low nutritional value; and every shelter resident I spoke to commented on the filthiness of showers that at various points contained bloody pads, vomit, feces, and open condoms. Further, the stigma that accompanies shelter use follows young women on their way in and out of the building and is at times perpetuated by shelter residents themselves, as Radha demonstrated: "[W]hat bothers me most about my living situation is that it ever happened and that I have to acknowledge it. I hate that. I hate that this has ever been a part of my life story. Now I have to deal with it. The majority of women who are here are here for reasons that are not very flattering to their personalities, so I don't want that to be me." The need to differentiate oneself from one's homeless peers often leads to conflict within the shelter, creates hierarchies, and enhances feelings of marginality and exclusion in those who become disenfranchised, even by the disenfranchised. In addition, shelter is not a universally appropriate solution; some young women do well living in service-led environments while others face personal challenges such as addictions or mental illnesses that make shelters unsuitable to their needs (CRISIS UK, 2007). As Sistering Toronto's (2002) report on homelessness and women's health concludes, group living environments are neither "ideal nor desirable living situations," but they are "a necessary part of the health care system" (p. 9). Furthermore, it is worth repeating that the critical lack of resources – both human and financial – faced by overworked shelter staff provides them with little opportunity to look beyond the current, barely manageable situation.

Own Place

It is not unusual for homeless young women to be independently housed at one or several points in their homelessness trajectories. Although young women can apply for Ontario Works benefits to help them cover necessities such as housing, the application process is long and complicated and many women do not qualify for various reasons. When they do receive such benefits, social assistance rates for sheltering a single person are $372 a month (Ontario Ministry of Community and Social Services, 2011). In Toronto, one could never afford a private apartment on such a small amount which means that young women are left to rent rooms, share apartments, or live in substandard housing, usually in areas of active drug trade (Novac et al., 2002). Savannah provided a prime example of the effect this type of housing can have: "I had my own place when I was 17. That's when all the drama started happening. I never really knew it was a crack building, I thought it was just a building where some people got their stuff. I was introduced to crack and crystal meth. I was binging on crystal meth for weeks at a time. I was living at my own apartment for eight months and then I got evicted." Savannah's situation is not atypical of young people who are living on their own for the first time. In the research literature young people speak to difficulties in maintaining housing tenure due to previous experiences of trauma, mental illness, and violence and a lack of basic life skills (Robinson, 2005). These inadequate living situations often have negative consequences for young people's sense of control and self-efficacy – not to mention the physical health impacts of drug use and the rodent and insect infestations that are common in the marginal housing market.

Raven and Faith, on the other hand, provide a positive example of young people's experiences with the housing market. Although they had several destructive relationships with unscrupulous landlords in the past, they eventually managed to secure an apartment on the outskirts of the downtown core. Raven explained the benefits they are now enjoying: "Then in the end you realize, after all that, finally, when you're fully installed and you get your own apartment, you're like, 'Hey, I can actually cuddle you, and look at what we've done. Look at how far we've made it after so long struggling.'" Their situation varies from the one described by Savannah in several ways. First, the stability and comfort of their intimate relationship creates a built-in support network – the two young women care deeply for one another and are there to encourage the other when hope begins to fade. Further, they are able to pool their social assistance money to afford a basement bachelor apartment that, although tiny, is completely their own. This is not to say that their situation has been easy; on the contrary, they often face sexual discrimination and spent months sleeping on couches, in basements, in mice-infested rooms, and on the street. Their story does, however, speak to the power of feeling included and supported – both emotionally and financially.

State Institutions

Different forms of institutions, such as psychiatric units and correctional facilities, become stops along the way of many homelessness journeys. (CRISIS UK, 2007; Neal, 2004). Histories of growing up in the child welfare system are strongly predictive of mental illness and substance misuse (Serge et al., 2002). Kearns and Smith (1994) argue that people who suffer from pre-existing mental health conditions which are left untreated are more likely to end up in low-quality housing or in one of many homeless conditions, most likely ending up on the streets after being unable to cope with the effects of their illness in shelters. Smith (1990) has written about this trend as the "health selection process," which posits that the sicker the person is, the less likely she will be able to negotiate the housing system, therefore becoming sicker and continuing the downward spiral into homelessness. In Ontario, the deinstitutionalization that occurred in the mid-1990s has resulted in increased numbers of mentally ill people living on the streets or in precarious housing (Sealy & Whitehead, 2006).

Three of the young women I spoke with had been placed in psychiatric units on more than one occasion, usually following suicide attempts or suicidal ideation. Many people have negative associations with mental health institutions, resulting largely from historical conceptions of "insane asylums" and depictions in movies and on television, such as *One Flew over the Cuckoo's Nest*. Notably, however, both Savannah and Raven refer to their time in psychiatric hospitals as times of respite and reflection which they desperately needed. For Raven, "They just gave me time to cool down, have time to think, and gave me a place where I could at least jot all my ideas, try and solve things, and my brain cooled down and I was fine." Or as Savannah said, "Yeah, the hospital, it was a vacation for me because you were only allowed to wear like a gown and when you went outside you could wear your normal clothes or whatever. [...] They give you snacks, we did crafts, and they let us go to school. I don't know. I just felt like I was a kid again." The stay at the psychiatric hospital that Savannah refers to occurred when she was 14. At the hospital, she was granted a few weeks in which to experience the carefree childhood she never had, which allowed her to feel protected and cared for, bolstering her mental health and enabling her to move forward. The lives of homeless young women are often chaotic and unpredictable. Spending time in an institution away from the stressors of family conflict, group homes, or difficult decisions in general, allows young people to slow down and to talk to mental health professionals who are trained to guide them through their times of crisis.

Of the eight young women, Savannah was the only one who had served time in a correctional facility. After going to the police to report being raped, she was arrested on an outstanding assault warrant and taken into custody. Once she was in restraints she was interviewed about the circumstances surrounding her assault:

> They videotaped me in the office ... in the security guard's office. It was so uncomfortable cuz there was a man sitting there ... there was like three guys sitting there and then there was a main person writing down every-thing. I'm sitting on a chair in like handcuffs and shackles cuz it's secure, right? And yeah, I had to tell them everything that happened and it was hard cuz I like broke down and I was scared. I felt uncomfortable. Like, they're all men, right? Well, they were just like, um, when I was talking they were saying stuff like, "Well, why didn't you just say 'stop, you're hurting me.'" And I was like, "It's hard, like you don't understand if you're a female it's hard ... you can't just say 'stop' and like, 'why are you doing this?' You can't because you're scared. It might be easy for you to say, but for us women, it's not." I don't know, like, it's stupid, friggin' things they say to me, cuz they don't understand and I don't think they really care. I thought they were just there for entertainment.

Savannah's story is not representative of the entire correctional system, but this particular incident obviously raises concerns about the treatment of young women under detention. The insensitivity displayed by the individual law enforcement officers and the system failure that allowed a bound 19-year-old woman to be interviewed about a rape by four male officers without any female accompaniment speaks volumes to the tremendous gaps in protection for incarcerated young women.

Migration

Forced to leave her original home due to violence, Arielle's story, although not representative of all immigrant or refugee stories, paints a picture of a set of circumstances that merit individual discussion in the connection between age, place, and health. In the Democratic Republic of Congo, millions of civilians have been raped, murdered, and forced to flee the devastating effects of war. During times of conflict properties are destroyed or stolen, schools closed, and hospitals ransacked; the scale and force of conflict has a "totalizing effect on all citizens" and seeking refuge is the most difficult for women (Schafer, 2002, p. 29). Congolese women bear the burden of securing family, filing paperwork, and avoiding violence both in refugee camps and from those who might attack them in their own homes (ibid.). Many families, like Arielle's, were forced to separate and flee their attackers, running through thick rainforest and, if they were lucky, escaping to neighbouring countries where customs and languages were often entirely different than the ones they knew (ibid.). Many East African women suffer from severe trauma manifest by systemic rape, the violent deaths of loved ones and children, and humiliation; Arielle and her family managed not only to survive, but also to find asylum in Canada, demonstrating incredible fortitude and determination. To then leave her family to begin a life of independence in a new country is remarkable, to say the least.

Approximately 50 per cent of refugees and 30 per cent of immigrants who reside in Canada live in Toronto (Novac et al., 2002). In 1999, 16 per cent of female youth living in Canadian shelters were immigrants or refugees (ibid.) Given the continuation of civil unrest in conflict zones around the world, and Canada's need to grow its population through immigration, these numbers are likely higher today. Many young refugees find themselves homeless after sponsorship breakdown or internal conflict within families in which individuals have spent long periods of time apart (ibid.). Arielle's father, for instance, was already in Canada attempting to procure the proper paperwork to secure his family's passage when the militia attacked her, her mother, and siblings. Between his departure and his family's arrival in Canada three years later, Arielle had lived in chaos, survived rape and torture, rescued her brother from near death by gunshot wound, become displaced, and had lost and been reunited with her mother and twin sister. Christopoulou and de Leeuw (2008) argue that the trajectory of migration commonly begins as a result of a threat to family homes and the parents' ability to provide for and protect their children. In their earlier work, Christopoulou and de Leeuw (2005) assert that every migrant family is a broken family: spatial displacement automatically disrupts social networks, such as extended family and, in turn, deeply influences experiences of belonging.

Of the myriad experiences that immigration and asylum-seeking entail, their common denominator is leaving one's homeland and reconstructing life in an international destination. Homelands, in the words of Mallett (2004), are "possessed spaces or territories with defined, though not always visible, boundaries that must be observed and respected by those not from there" (p. 73). Those boundaries must also be respected and negotiated by those who are simultaneously attempting to reconceptualize those home boundaries while learning about and adapting to the boundaries of the reception country, as Arielle experienced: "People say that if you go to a new house where people walk on one foot only, you have to walk with one foot also. If they walk with two feet, then you must use two feet. So, if the person uses one foot only, do not try to use two feet or you're going to find yourself in the dump. I must be like the people here." As Arielle found, even speaking in parables can be problematic in Canada where most people are unaccustomed to that form of speech and often ask her to repeat her point. Migrant children face a dual challenge: attempting to retain family values and traditions in unfamiliar environments, and learning and teaching the values and traditions of the reception country to their family members (Christopoulou & de Leeuw, 2008). Bhabha (1994) has referred to this phenomenon as the creation of a "third space," which he views as a liberating communication between cultures that allows an individual to subvert and create new meanings out of the blend of old and new. In speaking with Arielle, however, it was clear that the inhabitation of the "third space" was double-edged: while she could create a new life for herself, being culturally in-between also created substantial problems in the re-definition of familial, generational, and social roles:

> Like, in my country, people ... children cannot wear miniskirts, they cannot wear tight pants. They must respect their parents and the people. There are rules in other countries as well, so, with those rules, parents cannot ... for example, if the girl goes to another country, she is going to dress differently. She is going to dress like the girls in the other country, you see.

And the parents don't want that. What's going to happen at home? The daughter is going to have a row with her father and she's going to leave.

Arielle's desire to adopt the cultural codes of her new home became irreconcilable with her father's demand that she retain those of their homeland. Kilbride and colleagues (2000) found that these intergenerational tensions often become significant challenges to youth resettlement. Alongside the post-traumatic stress that Arielle suffers, she also feels a great deal of guilt for leaving her parents' home – although she believes that it was her only option if she is to thrive in her Canadian life. As Klodawsky (2006) notes, the health repercussions of resettlement are problematic in that the federal government oversees matters of immigration and transitional support, while health care is the jurisdiction of the province. The newcomer settlement services provided by the Canadian government are temporary and finite, whereas ensuring the well-being of newcomers is a long-term project. Without a link between federal immigration and provincial health and welfare, many young people are falling into this service gap.

Migration does not always involve movement across international borders; those who run away from or are pushed out of their original homes are also migrants (West et al., 2008). Gender, race, age, sexuality, ability, and class impact who moves where, and why they do so. Martin (1987) refers to young people who flee from abusive homes or overcrowded spaces as "domestic refugees" (p. 93), such as Raven and Faith: "Then we each had a knife, cuz what we were doing is we were hitchhiking from home in [Northern Ontario] to Toronto because [the city in Northern Ontario's] youth shelter has 10 beds that are always full." Clearly the differences between domestic refugees and individuals in situations like Arielle's are stark, but some similarities do exist between the two situations. Of the eight young women interviewed, six were born outside the Greater Toronto Area. Koskela (1997) maintains that the feeling and reality of homeness is related to women's sense of security in the cities in which they live – being at home in the city means having roots there and taking possession of one's surroundings. In the case of homeless youth from rural areas, feeling at home in the city can take months as one learns to locate and access transportation, safe havens, and resources. Raven and Faith's journey from Northern Ontario to Toronto brought them to unfamiliar territory that they had to learn to navigate quickly. Raven had never been to Toronto before, and

Faith's experience in the city was limited: "I've only ever been in here for layovers for a bus, because my aunt lives [in Southern Ontario]. We were [downtown from Yorkdale] in an hour, an hour and a half later, cuz we got lost on the way. The subway is hard your first time. Toronto is like humongous for us."

Feeling lost in physical or social surroundings is a key contributor to feelings of displacement. Losing one's place in the world destabilizes one's sense of self and belonging, which in turn can lead to anxiety and depression and compromise one's ability to live a healthy life (Robinson, 2003; Ryan et al., 2006; Vandemark, 2007). Homelessness is not simply the state of being without private shelter; it is the absence of social networks and the lack of resources; the inability to feel secure and self-effective; the related toll on physical and mental health; and the lack of the feeling and reality of belonging.

Belonging

Belonging is critical to social inclusion, self-efficacy, control, and, therefore, to health. As Somerville (1992) suggests, perhaps one of our greatest social problems, for housed and homeless people alike, is the lack of this feeling of belonging in and to particular places – a rootlessness that creates a sense of emptiness and fuels consumption in the search for fulfilment. Interviews by Serge and colleagues (2002), as well as my own experience, reveal that the issues faced by homeless youth cannot be resolved through housing alone. The impact on Jean of her constant relocation and disconnection from her foster family signals the importance of belonging to people and places: "I had run away one time and I had said to the police that I wanted a family and I started crying. And then my foster mom said, 'Don't worry sweetie, we're going to find you a family.' [...] I went to Toronto. And then next I think was the overdose." As long as homeless youth face constant social exclusion by virtue of their separation from supports, low socio-economic status, and lack of formal education, they are unable to feel "at home" anywhere.

Changing this requires changes in attitude and public policy. As Jackson (1995) attests, "we often feel at home in the world when what we do has some effect and what we say carries some weight" (p. 123). If power is exercised through the control of space, the realm of public policy belongs to those who are most able to insert themselves into high-level discussions: the wealthy, the well-connected, and the well-educated.

Lacking a voice and citizenship rights, homeless youth are defined and labelled by distant others and have limited, if any, opportunities to be heard. As Danika expressed, before they are given a chance to define themselves, they are told by social discourse who and what they are: "I guess people label me as a homeless youth. I live in a shelter for homeless youth. It's a mentality. Those words are so, I don't know, what's the word? Labelling or negative. Like you're different, pigeonholing. Just cuz bad things happen to you that's what we call you. You know? If you can't contribute, you stay over there." Danika's sentiments echo those of a number of the young women involved in this project. Moving beyond a label that is imposed by virtue of circumstance is an obstacle to seeing oneself as an individual with the capacity to contribute and create one's own understanding of her surroundings.

A productive, if lofty, goal for researchers and decision-makers at all levels would be to create interventions that reposition youth away from a culture of exclusion and towards a culture of inclusion. For most homeless youth, their first feelings of social exclusion occur in schools and at home where they are teased by peers and mistreated by family members. In a study in which children living in low-income families were asked about the hardships of poverty, most indicated that the social exclusion inherent in not fitting in with other kids felt worse than the physical deprivation they experienced (James & James, 2008). The processes of social exclusion intensify as youth enter the spaces of homelessness and are denied access to resources and public spaces, stigmatized, infantilized, and criminalized (Gaetz, 2004). Creating inclusive environments in shelters and at points of service is as beneficial to social economics as it is to homeless youth, as research has shown that there is a positive correlation between homeless accommodations in which people are content and included and personal development in other areas of their lives, such as school attendance and employment (CRISIS UK, 2007). As Savannah found, feeling "at home" in Toronto presents new opportunities for those who have spent most of their lives in more rural areas: "[Kids in Toronto] have more opportunities to do something with their life and to like meet new people and not be like racist and it's just [...] you can socialize, you can meet new people and it's like multicultural. It's big, just a lot of things, you can get a job here." Associating your city with opportunity instead of oppression goes a long way in creating the sense of belonging necessary for young women to grieve, heal, and move forward.

Conclusion

The construction of childhood envelops many competing interests, contains many contradictions, and serves different interests in different times and spaces. Above all, it is not solely about young people – it is a social construction that is the measuring stick for the condition and direction of a given society (Hollands, 2001). Phrases like "The kids these days!" or "As the kids say...," signal the ways in which the health and social situation of young people drives change and reflects social values. Living in various homeless places and spaces, and by virtue of their age and gender, young homeless women face unique risks which often send them underground and out of sight. Out-of-sight, out-of-mind policies enforced by punitive measures and discourses of safety that privilege the security of "the public," of which young homeless people are apparently not a part, only serve to further alienate and exclude youth in exceptional circumstances. However, just as youth are more than homeless, they are also more than victims. Young homeless people negotiate space and restrictions in creative ways, displaying a resilience and fortitude that flies in the face of discourses of young people's innate need of family protection. Having been through such an arduous journey, some homeless youth may also "come equipped with a heightened sense of survival and sense of accomplishment" (Christopoulou & de Leeuw, 2008, p. 261). Nonetheless, when children and young people are compelled to leave homes and to inhabit public space, at the risk of being punished by the state that should be in place to protect them, society has a crisis to resolve. The health of societies and of youth are in jeopardy when a young person's vital sense of inclusion is bartered for ineffective rhetorical language and alarmist discourses of risky children. The experiences of adolescent girls lay the foundation for their futures and have a substantial influence on the overall health of the societies in which they live (Petchesky & Judd, 1998).

The stories that inform this analysis of youth and place converge and diverge in interesting ways at both expected and unexpected junctures. In light of an often-oppressive set of social circumstances, the role of subjectivity cannot be understated in these discussions. One woman's journey from civil war to a downtown Toronto shelter raises a different set of questions than does the journey that starts in suburban Toronto. Nonetheless, the shared circumstances of living in shelters, living in care, or surfing from couch to couch provide points of contact to illustrate that place matters in critical ways. Undoubtedly young homeless women's choice is constrained, but they do make decisions in directing their own lives and in creating opportunities, no matter how limited.

This chapter has sought to connect time and space in order to demonstrate that life course stages, constructions of childhood, and histories of violence, politics, and social change, are integrally and necessarily tied to spaces of access and spaces of constraint. Creating places in which young people can feel safe and build bridges over fundamental gaps in trust is a crucial exercise in helping homeless youth achieve their goals. Criminalization and punitive measures to keep young people out of public spaces and under control in shelters and group homes only facilitate retreat into spaces of fear. Treating young people in exceptional circumstances as emergent adults provides them with one tool in moving towards spaces of care.

6 Seen and Not Heard: Negotiating Health and Wellness

The value of compassion cannot be over-emphasized. Anyone can criticize. It takes a true believer to be compassionate. No greater burden can be borne by an individual than to know no one cares or understands.

Arthur H. Stainback

Introduction

In this chapter, I begin to analyse the health concerns that participants indicated were the most important to them. In doing so, it is difficult to separate the treatment of health concerns from issues of access. While definitions of health vary from young woman to young woman, most indicated that they were only concerned about their health when they were in pain or when a health condition affected their normal routine. When they discussed their visits to clinics, hospitals, or community services, women also spoke to those issues that prevented them from returning or that confirmed their belief that providers were unable to understand and respect their particularized needs. This section of the project aims to illustrate the ways in which treating people the same is not synonymous with treating people equitably. Impacting holistically on psychological, emotional, physical, and spiritual health, homelessness is in and of itself a serious women's health issue. Focusing on mental health and sexual and reproductive health, this analysis seeks to underscore those issues that are most commonly faced by this particular group of young women. Depression and anxiety – often related to past or present abuse, but always correlated with poverty and powerlessness – were present to varying degrees in each of the young women. In a community research study of homeless women organized by Sistering Toronto (2002), 93 per cent of the women interviewed indicated that they suffered from some form of mental health complication arising from their current living situation. Analysis of sexual and reproductive health shows that young women are in need of sexual education and sexual health services that are attuned to their particular concerns and contexts – services that treat women holistically, not only as receptacles of sexually transmitted infections or bearers of children, but also as sexual beings with unique desires and concerns. Once again the heterogeneity within the population raises important points of contrast between women, but also demonstrates that services that are youth-centric and culturally competent are most likely to be accessed by homeless young women and trans people. Identifying the health issues that young people themselves are most concerned about, and asking them how best to help them seek help, provides critical insight into creating truly equitable health services.

Overview

Canada's public health system is often cited as a definitive aspect of Canadian identity; maintaining public, equal, and universal access to basic health and medical services consistently ranks as an issue of chief importance to the Canadian public (Mendelsohn, 2002). The *Canada Health Act* (CHA) (1984) is a federal act that was adopted in order to create a set of criteria to which the provinces and territories must adhere if they are to receive transfer payments for health from the federal government (Health Canada, 2004). These criteria include public administration, comprehensiveness, universality, portability, and accessibility. Under the CHA insured persons are promised universal coverage for medically necessary hospital and physician services; however, as care becomes increasingly devolved into homes and communities, it moves beyond the stated provisions of the act. The scope of insured services that are seen as medically necessary to insured persons within the realm of clinical practice, then, becomes an area of concern for those who fall outside the typical patient profile. Importantly, too, immigrants to Canada may be subject to a waiting period of up to three months before they can be considered insured persons under provincial legislation (ibid.). Despite its claims to universality and accessibility, then, the implementation of the CHA can create barriers for homeless people who require services that are not administered in hospitals or by physicians, and discriminates against newcomers who may require care, especially if they are young and homeless in an entirely new place.

The reality is that homeless individuals, who are arguably most in need of medical services, do not, in fact, have equal access to the services they need. Treating each person the same does not mean that people are being treated equitably. Health services delivery that is truly equitable requires an approach that recognizes the differences between the health of men and women, adolescents and adults, those who are housed and those who are not, and those who hunger and those who are fed. From this research, and that of others, it is clear that homeless youth access services differently than other groups. They are not well-served by models of care that treat symptoms as individual or solely biomedical, nor do they have access to the supports that are available to most young people to maintain good health. Inequitable funding, delivery, and organization of care often lead to differences in health status between income groups. As Braveman (2006) argues, "these differences systematically place socially disadvantaged groups at further disadvantage in health" (p. 180). Truly valuing the tenets of the *Canada Health Act* first requires the recognition that it – via those responsible for its impartial execution – is not currently upholding its promises of equal access for all.

The particular health conditions that homeless young women face demand particular responses from the health care system to ensure that they are well served and that their health is as optimal as possible. Homeless youth face a disproportionate number of health problems when compared to their more typical counterparts, but research has shown that homeless youth remain medically underserved; they do not visit clinics or access services as much as their housed peers (Barry et al., 2002). Structural barriers include the social, economic, political, and cultural circumstances that privilege some while marginalizing others (Daly et al., 2008). Barriers to access are entrenched in the funding, delivery, and organization of health care – from individual physicians to provincial legislation. It is debatable whether the current systems of care are solving or perpetuating the existing disconnect between homeless young people and health services, which systems require greater support and which require an overhaul.

Another key barrier to access is a lack of services that recognize and respond to population diversity within the category of homeless youth. For example, Aboriginal people make up three per cent of Toronto's overall population, but comprise 25 per cent of its homeless population

(Du Mont & Miller, 2000). Fifteen per cent of Toronto's shelter users are immigrants or refugees (ibid.). Cultural and linguistic inequities in health care have been linked to an increase in medical errors, prolonged hospital stays, hospital re-admissions, and the over- and underuse of certain medical procedures (Centre for Research on Inner City Health, 2009). The social determinants of health, like age and housing status, are crucial to understanding the health experiences of homeless people; however, the social determinants alone are not enough to provide the whole picture. As Graham (2004) highlights, "the social factors promoting and undermining the health of individuals and populations should not be confused with the social processes underlying their unequal distribution. This distinction is important because, despite better health and improvement in health determinants, social disparities persist" (p. 101). In effect, the social determinants of health and one's social locations are co-constitutive when looking at health outcomes. Diversity issues must be addressed at the micro, meso, and macro levels in both programming and policy. Programs that aim to close the inequity gap must understand diversity to include race, culture, religion, and sexuality as well as socio-economic status and life course stage (Daly et al., 2008). Facilitators that foster self-esteem, trusting relationships, and social support, too, must be recognized and integrated into programming.

Before considering how young women living in exceptional circumstances can attain equity in health service encounters, we must first understand the multitude of health issues by which they are affected. To say that the health inequalities faced by homeless female and trans youth are the result of homelessness writ large is to oversimplify a complex group of circumstances. Rather, the vulnerabilities they face often begin in early childhood or infancy due to poverty, abuse, and neglect and continue through their life course trajectories (Benoit et al., 2007). That said, once homeless, especially street homeless, the likelihood of being exposed to further vulnerability increases rapidly. Mortality rates for street youth are as much as 40 times that of the typical youth population, with suicide and drug overdoses appearing as the chief causes of death (Kidd & Shahar, 2008; Roy et al., 2004; Shaw & Dorling, 1998). To date, the majority of research on the health of homeless youth has focused on their particular health conditions and susceptibilities, relying on quantitative measures and statistics-based evidence. Qualitative researchers have described how little is known about the ways in which young people themselves make sense of and define their health

universes (Ensign, 2001; Reid et al., 2005). Ensign (2001, 2004) has gone
a long way to achieving these qualitative research goals in her work
with homeless young women in the United States, and her research has
provided great insight into the work of foregrounding the lived experiences of young people, both complementing and complicating research
in the Canadian context. Those who have begun this work in Canada
have shown that life stories are full of inconsistencies and seeming
contradictions, which are reflections on the complex circumstances in
which homeless young people live (Reid et al., 2005).

International and domestic research has shown that traditional models of medical care do not respond well to the needs of socially disadvantaged groups (Daly et al., 2008; O'Connell, 2004). Because meeting
the daily necessities of life, such as shelter and food, must necessarily
take priority in the lives of homeless individuals, addressing health issues tends to fall off the list of priorities, which often leads to an increase in emergency room or crisis visits when their health conditions
become too severe to ignore. Moreover, in a recent Toronto study of the
impact of gender on survival activities among street homeless youth,
O'Grady and Gaetz (2004) report that females are more likely than their
male peers to describe their health status as unhealthy, to report feelings of depression on a regular basis, and to report going without food
for a day one or more times per week. They go on to emphasize the negative effects that these conditions – and others, including lack of sleep,
lack of proper nutrition, and an inability to maintain proper hygiene
– have on the young women's employability and general functioning
(ibid.). Erin touches on challenges of nutrition and hygiene when she
explains how some of her friends go dumpster diving: " … [T]hey get
a lot of good shit. It's fucking insane what people throw out at restaurants and grocery stores and stuff. Like it's not even disgusting, it's
good. So sometimes I'll eat that. Sometimes though that's nasty ass shit
and I wouldn't touch it, so I just don't eat." Concerns about nutrition,
cleanliness, and safety are also prevalent in the shelter and emergency
hostel system, with studies showing that nutritional deficiencies are
more common among homeless women than they are among homeless
men (Novac et al., 1996; Sistering Toronto, 2002).

Although I have defined health broadly and kept a close eye on all the
ways in which social structures and positioning affect women's health,
I have chosen to focus particular attention on the areas of health most
commonly discussed by the research participants: mental health and
sexual and reproductive health. Mental health and sexual health are not

exclusive categories, but rather overlap and become co-constitutive. In a list of health complaints gathered by Sistering Toronto (2002), homeless women reported that "unrelenting, debilitating stress and anxiety" were the greatest sources of health concern (p. 5). While these depressive conditions are consistent with my sample, mental health concerns also extended and overlapped to cover issues of violence (both past and present) and, importantly for young female populations, cutting or self-harm. Of course these situations are not unique to homeless young women, but they are often intensified by a lack of stability and support. Likewise, the physical transformations of adolescence and the tendency in this period to identify more with peers than family, creates a self-consciousness related to appearance and anxious self-questioning as to whether their development process is "normal" (Ensign, 2001). For homeless youth, body image perceptions are complicated by the stigma of homelessness and by their inability, or at least limited ability, to join a consumer society that constantly sends social messages about fashion and teenage identity whereby one's social worth is defined by how much you have.

The majority of youth homelessness research tends to treat sexual health and reproductive health as one and the same, focusing solely on reproductive health issues such as pregnancy, sexually transmitted infections, and "risky" behaviours (Ensign, 2001). By virtue of being biologically female or transgendered, these traditional reproductive health concerns are important topics for discussion, especially since so many young women discussed their terrible experiences with Pap smears (Jean, Savannah, Erin, Danika, Faith, and Raven). However, these reproductive health issues are not the sole concern of young people, nor are they written about in ways that are conducive to understanding health as homeless youth understand it. Sexual health, on the other hand, is a more controversial topic as it covers issues of sexual pleasure, healthy relationships, and sexuality. Sex education, where it does exist, will sometimes refer, whether overtly or subtly, to adolescent male desire, but often frames female sexuality as dangerous or easily victimized (Impett & Tolman, 2006). In adult women, sexual satisfaction is linked with positive self-concept and sexual motives such as caring and intimacy (ibid.). Research suggests that this trajectory begins in adolescence when sexuality is an integral part of girls' lives, when it is at best not often discussed and at worst labelled as "slutty" or "promiscuous" behaviour. The young people involved in this research participated in a range of sexual activity, from abstinence to sexual monogamy to sex with multiple partners concurrently, yet because of their fear of being labelled or judged, they did not ask the questions to which they needed answers. Although adults might not care to discuss teenage sexuality, young people need more information in order to make smart and informed decisions about sexual behaviours based on their own preferences and desires.

Mental Health

Any number of social, psychological, and contextual factors can impact a person's mental health; however, evidence has repeatedly demonstrated that poverty and its associated pressures are highly likely to have a negative effect on mental health and well-being (World Health Organization, 2007). According to the World Health Organization (WHO), "Mental health is not just the absence of mental disorder. It is defined as a state of well-being in which every individual realizes his or her own potential, can cope with the normal stresses of life, can work productively and fruitfully, and is able to make a contribution to her or his community" (ibid). Like physical health, the social determinants of mental health are critical to health outcomes: stress, social exclusion, discrimination, violence, and their interrelationships are all predictors of poor mental health. This definition of mental health will be relied upon throughout these chapters as it signals the fact that mental health supersedes individual factors and is not simply the existence of a disorder in the brain. As Astbury (1999) highlights, however, the WHO definition fails to identify gender, which is crucial in analysing individuals' capacities to attain good mental health and equitable treatment.

As in the case of physical health and well-being, the intersections of gender, race, class, immigration status, sexuality, and any other range of social locations are primary factors in the determination of mental health status; however, studies have also shown that these intersectional dynamics also impact upon the way services and treatments are accessed and administered (Bondi & Burman, 2001). Feminists have long criticized the psy-establishment for its inequitable treatment of women, which is especially prevalent in situations where women lack autonomy, social capital, income, power, and control (Ostlin et al., 2001). The systemic discrimination in psychology and psychotherapy is inherent to the andro- and ethno-centric, heterosexist, and elitist foundations of professions that function, ultimately, to naturalize women's social subordination (Bondi & Burman, 2001).

Traditionally, the health professions have tended to focus mental health therapies on illness rather than health, on the individual rather than the social, and on top-down rather than bottom-up solutions (Weare, 2000). Foucault's theorizing around medicalization, and its extensions by feminists, has demonstrated the ways in which the psy-professions have been integral in controlling, establishing, and maintaining inequalities in society. "Expert" opinions and diagnoses are often based on normative conceptions of gender, sexuality, class, and race that tend to control and constrict women's treatment options. The following discussions of mental health, then, attempt to expose these vulnerabilities and critique the psy-professions that continue to deny the agency and experience of the young women under their care.

Those with mental health problems are often not well-served by the health care system and this is particularly the case for the young and homeless. Precarious housing and social exclusion can have a double-edged impact on young women who may or may not seek medical treatment. Those who have weak or no ties to social services often go untreated, exacerbating conditions that remain with them into adulthood. On the other hand, sometimes a psy-diagnosis is adopted as a tactic for gaining access to resources that may only be available to those who assume a particular label, whether the young woman feels comfortable with that label or not. In addition, it is important to note that what is often easily brushed aside as a disorder can, and often should, be understood as a rational response to irrational or pathological social environments. Thus, it is vitally important to remember the mantra of homeless advocates: "a diagnosis is not an indictment" (Novac et al., 1996).

Mental health workers who work at the Woodlawn shelter often counsel youth who are staying there; however, this population of youth is transient and often have long and violent histories of maltreatment that require therapies that are long-term and sustainable. All eight of the participants experienced mental health issues of various kinds and in varying degrees. At times mental health issues occurred in conjunction with, or were exacerbated by, addictions. In a recent study of 226 homeless shelter youth between the ages of 13 and 17, 60 per cent met the criteria for dual or multiple mental health diagnoses (Zerger et al., 2008). Dissociative symptoms, conduct disorder, disengaging coping styles, depression, suicidal ideation, post-traumatic stress disorder, cutting, and a range of other diagnoses are frequently attached to young homeless women – and this study is no exception (Booth & Zhang, 1997; Tyler et al.,

2003; Tyler et al., 2004; Votta & Manion, 2004). Many feminist researchers have signalled the ways in which these labels are ineffectual and, in fact, act to further stigmatize and devalue women's own experiences and legitimate frustrations (Burstow, 2005; Caplan, 1987; Caplan & Cosgrove, 2004; Ehrenreich & English, 1978). The major impacts of homelessness include depression and despair, which intensify existing mental health and substance use issues. With each diagnosis and set of symptoms, young women become less and less able to access appropriate services (Sistering Toronto, 2002).

As many studies fail to point out, the reasons for this inability are manifold. The most obvious reason for this lack of access is that mental illnesses such as depression often cause lethargy and debilitating sadness, or, in the case of more complex diagnoses, lead to unpredictable behaviours and mental confusion. Multiple diagnoses often mean multiple care providers, which mean that one must visit multiple clinic locations in order to receive treatment and care. Without support, a stable living situation, or the resources or ability to keep track of dates and times, navigating a complex health care system becomes virtually impossible for many young homeless women. Furthermore, with each successive diagnosis, the stigma faced by an individual also becomes compounded; labels like "homeless" only serve to further marginalize the individual. According to the participants in this study, many homeless young people choose not to engage with the system in order to preserve their dignity.

Research has shown that suicide is the number one cause of death among youth homeless populations, with suicide attempt rates ranging from between 20 to 40 per cent (Roy et al., 2004). Five of the eight participants in this work had attempted suicide two or more times. Suicidal behaviours have been linked to a number of life history factors: history of sexual, physical, and emotional abuse; substance abuse within families; suicide attempts among friends; and social stigma (Greene & Ringwalt, 1996; Kidd, 2004; Yoder, 1999). As Faith explains, incessant abuse and bullying, compounded with ineffective health services responses, creates a fertile environment for suicidal thoughts and behaviours:

> I wasn't into that crowd, so if you're not in their crowd, you're the opposite and they just don't stop, they go at you like nothing. So, between getting over sexual abuse, being verbally abused at home, and then being picked on at school every day, I had a couple suicide attempts and the school decided that I needed a counsellor. Though because it was such a

small school, it was a voluntary counsellor that didn't know what he was doing. And, I was like, "I'm not talking to you," sorta deal. Especially cuz I didn't feel comfortable with older men.

Faith's story draws attention to several key factors in appropriately attending to the mental health of young women, especially the need for multi-level, multi-sectoral attention to the issue. The problems she faced began at home, but extended into the school system as well. Her experience speaks to a critical lack of mental health services in rural and Northern Ontario; Faith's "voluntary counsellor" was not a social worker or a mental heath practitioner, but a caring member of the town. Although the voluntary counsellor may have had good intentions, the lack of a qualified professional exemplifies the problems in downloading health services onto the community. Moreover, her history of sexual abuse created an understandable unease around men, and her experience demonstrates the importance of ensuring that the context of young women's lives are taken into consideration when delivering health services. While the school system and the health care system are treated as silos in the creation and implementation of policy, some cross-coordination would facilitate important and necessary adjustments.

Another important but less explored mental illness common to homeless youth is post-traumatic stress disorder (PTSD), from which recent studies have found that 33 per cent of young homeless people suffer (Kidd, 2007). Herman's (1997) chart overviewing the effects of PTSD provides valuable insight into the ways in which many of the young women's stories and behaviours align with this condition (Table 2). When reading this chart, it becomes clear that many of the young women participating in this research fit the criteria for a condition that indicates exposure to trauma. According to Whitbeck and colleagues (2007), "besides living in a war zone, the vulnerability posed by running away and the experiences associated with being homeless and alone may pose the greatest risk for post-traumatic stress disorder among adolescents" (p. 721). Researchers exploring the health of Canada's Aboriginal peoples have also identified the traumatic effects of colonization and European contact as a form of complex or cultural post-traumatic stress disorder (Wesley-Esquimaux, 2007). The groups of people that are most commonly discussed in the PTSD literature, however, include soldiers and those involved in civil wars or genocides. In this respect Arielle's PTSD could be said to have a double causal relationship: her experiences in the Congo and her homeless status in Toronto.

Table 2. Complex Post-Traumatic Stress Disorder Overview

1	*A history of subjugation* to totalitarian control over a prolonged period [of time] (months to years). Examples include hostages, prisoners of war, concentration camp survivors, and survivors of some religious cults. Examples also include those subjected to totalitarian systems in sexual and domestic life, including survivors of domestic battering, childhood physical or sexual abuse, and organized sexual exploitation.
2	*Alterations in affect regulation,* including: persistent dysphoria; chronic suicidal preoccupation; self-injury; explosive or extremely inhibited anger (may alternate); compulsive or extremely inhibited sexuality (may alternate).
3	*Alterations in consciousness,* including: amnesia or hyperamnesia for traumatic events; transient dissociative episodes; depersonalization; derealization; reliving experiences, either in the form of intrusive post-traumatic stress disorder symptoms or in the form of ruminative preoccupation.
4	*Alterations in self-perception,* including: sense of helplessness or paralysis of initiative; shame, guilt, and self-blame; sense of defilement or stigma; sense of complete difference from others (may include sense of specialness, utter aloneness, belief no other person can understand, or non-human identity).
5	*Alterations in perception of perpetrator,* including: preoccupation with relationship with perpetrator (includes preoccupation with revenge); unrealistic attribution of total power to perpetrator (caution: victim's assessment of power realities may be more realistic than clinician's); idealization; sense of special or supernatural relationship; acceptance of belief system or rationalizations of perpetrator.
6	*Alterations in relations with others,* including: isolation and withdrawal; disruption in intimate relationships; repeated search for rescuer (may alternate with isolation and withdrawal); persistent distrust; repeated failures of self-protection.
7	*Alterations in systems of meaning,* including: loss of sustaining faith; sense of hopelessness and despair.

From: Herman, J.L. (1997). *Trauma and Recovery: The aftermath of violence – From domestic violence to political terror*, p. 121. New York, NY: Basic Books.

Again, physical, emotional, and sexual violence destabilizes children's lives, resulting in psychosocial damage that also weakens their ability to trust in parents and other adults. Sexual attacks like those experienced by Arielle are increasingly recognized as belonging to a set of military tactics wherein rape becomes a weapon of war (Hick, 2001). The main perpetrators of this type of attack are soldiers from military, rebel, and paramilitary groups, although it is not unheard of for civilians to partake in this type of action in shows of solidarity with their group (ibid.). In the eastern Congo, between 1990 and 2000, 80 per cent of the fistula cases reported were diagnosed to be the result of sex crimes, demonstrating the violent and brutalizing nature of these attacks (ibid.).

Arielle describes the manifestation of her PTSD in the following way: "When I talk, I see everything again. It's as if it was happening to me again. I said I have to forget all that. I must rub it all off, but I can't. I can't. It's not easy." In Canada she has been hospitalized several times as a result of the stress she feels in recalling the trauma she faced: "Stress makes me sick. What kind of sickness? My eyes hurt. My body also. Everywhere. I don't feel well any more. I also get a fever with stress. And when I go to hospital, the doctor tells me that I think too much. I have to stop thinking. It's stress. You're not sick. So, I don't take medication if I am not sick." Arielle's response to her doctor is indicative of differing cultural perspectives on health and wellness. When the doctor tells her that her sickness is psychosomatic, Arielle understands this to mean that because her body is not truly physically ailing she is not sick; thus, she does not take medications even though the physician has prescribed them. The cultural and linguistic differences that exist between Arielle and her physician require further exploration. Without speaking to her physician it is impossible to say whether the physician is aware of the ways in which Arielle is interpreting her medical advice; however, an unfilled prescription seems to indicate that the doctor may be missing something resulting from issues of cultural competency.

To cope with her symptoms, Arielle attempts to shift her thought patterns and stays focused on her spirituality and her future potential by connecting with shelter staff. In fact, she points to the attention shown to her by shelter staff as the primary reason she is able to cope with her stress. Different research investigating these coping strategies would respond differently: those who advocate pharmacological intervention might say that Arielle is refusing to help herself; however, those who believe in an approach characterized by social support and care would be more likely to support her decision. Regardless, this is Arielle's choice to make and she manages remarkably well in light of her history of violence. This example, however, is reflective of the fact that when homeless young women are receiving care, they may be receiving care that is inappropriate to their needs. The goal then is not just access to care, but access to those services and clinics that provide good, culturally appropriate care.

PTSD, whether the result of historic or contemporary factors, affects one's ability to positively value oneself and to find order and meaning in daily experience (Herman, 1997). In Herman's (1997) study of 428 homeless adolescents, PTSD occurred alongside depression and addiction approximately 50 per cent of the time, and was highly likely to occur concurrently with a diagnosis of conduct disorder. Often, a young person's "bad behaviours" are the outward manifestation of the impact of trauma, which is important to note when considering youth involvement with the criminal justice or child welfare systems. When young people lack the mechanisms and resources to deal with early and ongoing trauma, behavioural issues continue to contribute to stigma, incarceration, and amplified mental health problems. PTSD sufferers typically have more chronic health concerns and more challenging relationships with health care practitioners (Novac, 2006). The conclusion of Whitbeck and colleagues' (2007) study indicates that the most likely candidate to suffer from PTSD is an older female adolescent (approximately 19 years old) who has experienced abuse at the hands of a caretaker and then been subsequently victimized after becoming independent. Savannah is a textbook case for Whitbeck's findings. She is 20 years old, was physically and sexually abused throughout her childhood, and was incarcerated for violent behaviours on three separate occasions; now, she may be falling through the cracks as a result of a lack of trauma treatment. Savannah was first incarcerated after an altercation with a worker in a group home: "[The group home worker] told me to get out of his way, but I wouldn't. You know what he did to me? He pushed up against me with his penis. He just kept pushing into me. I didn't even care at that point. I used both my fists and I punched him. He went flying to the floor. I went to my room and packed my stuff." Having never been to therapy or seen a counsellor, Savannah's immediate reaction is to fight for her safety – a behaviour she learned at a very early age due to physical attacks from her mother and sexual attacks from caretakers. Sadly, the abusive group home worker charged her with assault and she spent months in detention. In cases like Savannah's, imprisonment is not as effective in stemming unwanted behaviours as programs such as anger management or rehabilitative counselling or, better still, serious and sustained political attention to continuing structural violence would be.

Violence

More than 20 years ago, Walby (1990) claimed that violence against women is "sufficiently common and repetitive, with routinized consequences for women and routinized modes of processing by judicial agencies, to constitute a social structure" (p. 143). In this light, the far-reaching implications of that violence should come as no surprise. A multitude of studies have shown exceptionally high rates of violence in the families of homeless women and girls (Du Mont & Miller, 2000; Klodawsky et al., 2006; Novac, 2006; Yoder, 1999). These women often suffer the physical and psychological impacts of that abuse for the duration of their lives. Novac and colleagues (2002) have registered these impacts on homeless youth, citing alienation, lack of trust, and isolation as responses to legacies of violence – all of which are major contributors to PTSD and depression. Other startling correlations between childhood sexual abuse and adolescent behaviours include a greater likelihood to have been in the care system; to engage in sexual intercourse before the age of 13; to engage in sexual bartering practices; to develop addictions; and to attempt suicide (ibid.). Each of the participants in this study engaged in at least one of these behaviours over their life histories; seven of the eight were survivors of abuse. Another salient effect of violence, especially for this research, is a mistrust of adults, including health care professionals. As Erin says, "I'm not crazy. I'm sure I'm fucked right up cuz I was an abused child or whatever, but I don't need pills or a shrink or nothing like that. I get depressed. Of course. But I'm not going to see some doctor. You can't trust 'em." Treating the effects of abuse necessitates cultural competency on the part of care providers, continued judicial enforcement of the laws of protection, decreased glorification of violence in the construction of masculinity, increased recognition that intimate partner violence occurs in both heterosexual and lesbian relationships, and early education in schools so that young men and women know from an early age that violence is unacceptable.

All the participants said that their increased susceptibility to violence was the number one issue for young homeless women. For Savannah, "It's hard, cuz like people take advantage of you because women are weak in like ... physically we're weak but emotionally we're strong;" in Arielle's experience, "It's more difficult because of what I went through with the men." Erin agreed that, "Being a girl you aren't as strong and you're on your own and there are a lot of crazy people out here, I mean really crazy, like mental, you know? Mentally deranged or whatever. And being a girl what you have is sex." Despite their decisive answers, however, very few young women disclosed their fear of abuse or their past abuse to their health care providers, partially due to stigma and partially because they did not see violence as the domain of health services. The latter reason also prevents some service providers from addressing issues of violence with their clients. Service providers at community agencies have expressed frustration with the federal government, which provides funds only for issues that deal directly with settlement (usually in terms of employability); violence or the prevention thereof are not viewed as settlement issues (Sistering Toronto, 2002). Similarly, public health units are not provided with funds specifically targeted at violence prevention campaigns and resources (ibid.). Another major policy concern that directly impacts young women's safety is the prevalence of mixed-gender shelters and the dearth of those providing services exclusively to young women and trans people. Novac (2006) has shown that young heterosexual women living in co-ed shelters are subject to sexual exploitation and dating violence during their tenures. All of the young women who were currently residing in the YWCA shelter indicated that their choice of accommodation was a conscious decision based on the fact that they would not have to live with young men. In Danika's words, "Yeah, I don't want to live with guys. I don't know. I just wouldn't be comfortable." This is not to say that all homeless young women would prefer to live in single gender shelters, or that this type of shelter set-up does not create difficulties for trans people; but, given the prevalence of violence in most homeless young women's lives, and according to the young women working with this study, more women's-only shelters for youth would be well-received by their clients (Goering et al., 1990).

Cutting

Self-harm is defined by Laye-Gindhu and Schonert-Reichl (2005) as "deliberate and voluntary physical self-injury that is not life-threatening and is without any conscious suicidal intent" (p. 447). Youth make clear distinctions between these self-harm practices and suicidal behaviours, demonstrating that the two issues need to be explored independent of one another. This phenomenon, commonly referred to by the participants as cutting, has drawn the attention of teenagers, physicians, and the popular media alike, with some media outlets referring to self-harm as this generation's anorexia (Finlay, 2000). Researchers and clinicians have noted that self-harm is increasingly prevalent, with more and more young people presenting with the cuts and scars of self-harm (Klonsky et al., 2003). As Raven said, "It is really common nowadays. You'd be surprised how many people are actually cutters out of the teen society. There's people who actually do and you'd never guess. You'd watch them change during gym and you'd never see them. Like, you'd never guess." Studies that have explored young people's motivations to self-harm have found that the two most common explanations are cutting to manage overwhelming emotions and cutting to "feel something" (Horne & Csipke, 2009). Although these two reasons – that individuals cut when they feel too much *and* when they feel too little – appear paradoxical, it is clear that this phenomenon is a physical manifestation of mental anguish. Characterized as a mental health issue, cutting obviously has very real physical expression, thus demonstrating the necessity of treating mind and body not as a dichotomy, but as vitally linked. Other research views self-harm as an addictive behaviour: when the body is cut it responds by releasing endorphins that also assist in anesthetizing emotional pain by producing a temporary "up," which increases the likelihood that cutting will continue when the individual seeks that fleeting relief (Ellis, 2002). Savannah explained her cutting in the following way: "I did it for satisfaction. It took away the pain. And it got worse. The cuts were getting deeper. And the blood was getting thicker. I remember every time I cut myself I would try to not let it bleed that much, but I was getting deeper and deeper." Similar to substance use, the more cutting one does, the more accustomed the body grows, therefore becoming less responsive. Inevitably the cuts must become deeper and more frequent in order to produce the same physiological response.

Given these addiction-like characteristics, which would indicate that self-harm could continue over the course of many years, and the fact that self-harming behaviours usually appear in adolescence, it is critical to acquire an understanding of cutting from the perspective of adolescents themselves (Laye-Gindhu & Schonert-Reichl, 2005). The first research to be conducted in Canada on the links between homelessness, youth, and self-harm began in 2003, and very little has been done to advance these findings in subsequent years. As is the case with other mental health conditions, self-harm is more prevalent among homeless youth than among their housed counterparts – 69 per cent of a 428-person sample of homeless youth reported engaging in self-harm activities at least once, with cutting appearing as the most commonly used approach (Tyler et al., 2003). Unsurprisingly, early childhood violence, traumatic activity, and depression are positively correlated with the tendency to self-harm (ibid.). Horne and Csipke (2009) agree that cutting is most often used as a method of expressing or releasing anguish, preventing traumatic memories, or distancing oneself from overwhelming emotions. Five of the eight young women involved in this research had either a history of or a current issue with cutting. For Raven cutting was, "just to know that I was still alive, to know that I was still me. I wasn't just a shadow for everyone to step on." For Faith cutting helped deal with her step-father's verbal abuse, while for Jean self-harm meant, "cutting myself to see that I was real and that my skin was still there."

While cutting is widely viewed as an adolescent issue it is also, like anorexia, seen as a women's issue. Research varies in its conclusions on this issue: one study notes that women comprise 97 per cent of those who cut themselves; however, other studies, though much fewer in number, have suggested the number of men who self-harm is on the rise (Briere & Gil, 1998; Favazza & Conterio, 1989; McLane, 1996; Suyemoto, 1998). The women who lend their voices to this research thought that cutting was significantly more common among young women and girls, which led me to question the ways in which social constructions of gender might impact upon the tendency to self-harm. One of the earliest clinical researchers on self-harm, Pao (1969), originally labelled these self-mutilating behaviours, "Delicate Self-Cutting Syndrome." Pao was convinced that this phenomenon was unique not only to young women, but also to those who were especially attractive. Brickman (2004) duly notes that the addition of the adjective "delicate" to Pao's diagnostic label connotes "frailty, daintiness and fragility," and she wonders if the term "'mutilation' would be used so readily to describe wounded skin on a less appealing body" (p. 97–8). Pao's sampling techniques, which focused exclusively on what he considered to be attractive women, led to a more general consensus in the 1960s and 1970s that cutting was, indeed, a female phenomenon. The alarm bells of medicalized, not to mention sexualized, female bodies immediately sound in light of these constructions, as discourses such as these constitute forms of social control. A more socio-cultural reading of self-harm behaviours might take under consideration research that has shown that girls are more likely to internalize their emotions, while boys tend to turn to external outlets like punching walls or yelling (Leadbeater et al., 1995). In a society that encourages passivity and restraint in girls, perhaps it is less surprising that girls hurt themselves in lieu of voicing the emotions that, from an early age, they are told are unacceptable (Shaw, 2002). For young women who internalize these gender norms, it is possible that cutting is another form of self-regulation (Ellis, 2002). Interestingly, borderline personality disorder (BPD) is the only mental illness for which self-harm is a major diagnostic criterion (Brickman, 2004). As such, many young women who self-harm may be further stigmatized by psychiatric discourse which often assumes that BPD patients are uncooperative and confrontational – attributes which are particularly unattractive in women (Nehls, 2000). Of course, the diagnosis of BPD itself is often questioned by feminist scholars who see the label as another way of containing and denying women the right to express anger or frustration at unjust social circumstances, or to act outside the limiting set of gender norms.

Levenkron (1998) claims that self-harm is an "individual psychopathology" whereby those who self-harm act outside the norms of Western culture by allowing themselves to be overwhelmed by their compulsions (p. 23). Although cutting and suicide are two distinct phenomena, some researchers focus on the assertion that the shame and guilt that follow a self-harm incident can, over time, compound, creating a total inability to control escalating negative emotions, which may in turn lead to an actual suicide attempt (Laye-Gindhu & Schonert-Reichl, 2005). Much of the clinical research on self-harm employs biomedical or psychiatric discourses that often amount to victim blaming and concentrate primarily on individual pathologies. The language of "risk," "unorthodoxy," and "abnormality" is common in the attempt to ascertain clinical explanations that often hold the individual solely accountable for her behaviour. This focus on the context-free individual fails to recognize that cutting may, in fact, be a response to the unworkable social expectations set out for girls and young women. Cutting does not occur in a vacuum. The social factors that contribute to mental illness are often disregarded in the attempt to treat the patient's physiological symptoms (Ellis, 2002). While it is uncritically accepted that self-harming behaviours are usually employed as coping responses to overwhelming emotional pain, the roots of these emotions require further exploration and more holistic forms of therapy. As the participants' life stories attest, women who cut experience a host of other complications in their lives: addiction, abuse, and food and housing insecurity to name but a few.

Another common misconception about people who self-harm is that cutting is an attention-seeking behaviour. Jean recalled several occasions on which she was told by health care practitioners that she was cutting for the attention: "They took me, I think, to SickKids to get checked out because I had done some scratching and stuff on my arm. But, uh, um, the doctor thought it was just attention seeking. He said he thought I had borderline personality disorder because I was very impulsive." She went on to describe another similar situation with an emergency room nurse: "She said to me 'Oh, you know what, I think you're doing this for attention.' Who would take the trouble like to go to the hospital just for attention? That's what I said to her. And then I told her she was a B with an itch." Young women who cut as a response to feelings of helplessness are left feeling even more so when their serious and legitimate issues are pawned off as "attention seeking" – another individual pathology. In Jean's case, instead of doing a thorough social life history check, the doctor automatically attributed her cutting to BPD and impulsivity, again removing the social context in favour of psychiatric labelling. The fact that cutting almost always occurs privately does not provide evidence to support the claim that self-harm is a manipulative behaviour. Moreover, the women in this and other studies detail the strategies they use to hide the evidence of their cutting. Raven said, "I hid them. I didn't do it, sort of, in places where you could see. Places that you could easily cover with clothes or long shirts." As Ellis (2002) asserts, hiding the evidence reveals young women's attentiveness to the social stigma attached to their behaviour. Several health researchers working directly with young women have suggested that the first step in treating and preventing self-harm should be to teach young women less injurious, more constructive coping strategies (Ellis, 2002; Laye-Gindhu & Schonert- Reichl, 2005; Ussher, 1992). Schoppmann and colleagues (2007) found that caring touches between self-harmers and the trusted people in their lives constituted a valuable intervention. This finding proves especially noteworthy for the clinicians, therapists, and social workers who work with young homeless people who cut.

Body Image

When health is assessed against traditional measures of morbidity and mortality, youth, even youth in exceptional circumstances, fare much better than their older and younger counterparts (Ensign, 2001). As UNICEF (1997, 1999) has highlighted, however, if one measures health in terms of indicators such as social and emotional health, young women tend to fare poorly; this seems especially so for young women living in poverty. As gender roles become more sharply defined during this stage of the life course, young women are also faced with increased social pressures and sexually maturing bodies; the effect of this phenomenon on young women is generally associated with lowered levels of self-esteem (Pipher, 1994). As their biological age begins to align with the age of the young women they see on TV and in advertising, many young women begin to compare themselves to an unattainable ideal. As Danika expressed, the drive to be thin is common among young women: "I just, I don't want to be fat. I'm so exposed to like YouTube and Facebook and TV. And I'm seeing all these things. You feel like you need to replicate those bodies, you know? Like, follow that. I feel if I'm not small like that I'm not accepted or I'm not the norm." This is not to say that young women are not aware of the damaging impacts caused by media representations of young women. On the contrary, they are quite media savvy, as Radha demonstrated: "I've talked to another friend, when we were watching TV, I just laughed off something and he said, 'Yeah, it's not real, but doesn't it look good?' That kind of made me sad, but the thing is most people understand that real human beings don't look like TV human beings." Nonetheless, knowing does not always alleviate the pressure to conform to the celebrity-culture standard of feminine beauty, and opinions like the one expressed by Radha's friend do not make life any easier for young women. As Radha further demonstrated, these conflicting feelings also affect young women's abilities to enjoy their early sexual experiences: "My insecurity and my complete lack of confidence really don't work well with my sexuality cuz you have to have some liking of your body to want to get naked around another human being." Radha's feelings concur with Impett and Tolman's (2006) research, which demonstrates that young women's concern with their physical appearance interferes with sexual pleasure and satisfaction.

For homeless young women these pressures are felt even more acutely, especially when advertising tells them that the key to beauty is buying products and clothing that make one look a certain way (Wolf, 1991). Confronted with poverty, insecure housing, and a lack of adequate nutrition, buying into the latest fads is impossible, but the expectations still exist. When living on the street the comparison point is not only those in the media, but also well-to-do peers at school or in public places. As Erin said, looking across the street at a young woman shopping with her mother, "She can pay for beautiful clothes and hair dye and, fuck, she probably goes to the gym or tanning beds every day or something, which we sure don't do. Right? Like, how can you even compare?" Society's standard of beauty is doubly unattainable for women who compare themselves not only to celebrities, but also to real women their age who have advantages they do not. Several of the young women, including Jean, also indicated that the verbal abuse they faced in childhood and early adolescence often took the form of insults against their physical form: "I had a couple people tell me in my life, 'Well, if you weren't so fat you would be pretty.'" The internalization of these criticisms made young women believe that other people viewed them in much the same way. In the participants' narratives, body image issues were related to depression, low self-esteem, social withdrawal, and self-isolation. Every participant identified at least one aspect of their physical appearance as the cause of distress and anxiety.

Stigma

According to Link and Phelan (2001), "stigmatization is entirely contingent on access to social, economic and political power that allows the identification of differentness, the construction of stereotypes, the separation of labeled people into distinct categories, and the full execution of disapproval, rejection, exclusion and discrimination" (p. 367). The multitude of labels that are attached to young people – "at risk," "homeless," "delinquent," and "non-compliant," to name but a few – act to further distance those at the margins from those at the centre. Stigma is a vitally important feature in the study of the lives of homeless youth because it reveals that the unequal distribution of resources is not the sole factor in the production and reproduction of health inequities. As Courtwright (2009) asserts, addressing health disparities requires the exploration of those factors that are not considered typical within the discourse of distributive justice. Even the term "homeless," which I attempt to employ as sensitively as possible throughout this work, is rife with stigmatizing assumptions that serve to enhance young people's already acute feelings of exclusion. This term is, of course, a catch-22 of language. One requires a means of discussing the situations of youth in exceptional circumstances, but does not wish to further marginalize those whose diversity the label homogenizes. Perhaps, then, a step in the right direction is to change the negative and inaccurate associations many people attach to the term.

Kidd's (2007) study of youth homelessness and social stigma determined that being the object of negative stereotypes is related to feelings of worthlessness, loneliness, and isolation. These feelings only increase when one is discriminated against based on multiple subject positions such as age, sexuality, race, ability, and health status. Further, stigmatization tends to be internalized even within members of the same group. Devaluing a trait in oneself leads to devaluing that characteristic in others as well, thus creating a need to make others feel a similar sense of shame (Courtwright, 2009). Radha, for example, was keen to divorce herself from the homeless label, which she managed by drawing on a stereotype of others in her situation and demonstrating the ways in which she was not like them: "Just the majority of women who are here are here for reasons that are not very flattering to their personalities, so I don't want that to be me." Of course, as the narratives of the other shelter residents evince, all of the young women who in some way fit conceptions of homelessness are so much more multi-dimensional than the stereotype allows. A variation on the internalization of stigma occurs when young people become self-defeatist, believing that what other people say about them is true. Jean recounted a particularly troubling story when I asked her why she was not wearing shoes although she was standing outside: "I had been walking around in bare feet. I thought that I didn't deserve to wear shoes, so I put my shoes in my backpack." Some people would attribute this behaviour to the severity of Jean's mental health conditions, but the possibility remains that this perception of her worthiness stems from her internalization of the negative comments and judgment directed at her by others. The combination of childhood abuse and blatantly racist and discriminatory comments leveled at her illustrates the import of recognizing stigma as a key issue in assisting young people and in bolstering their confidence and self-esteem.

As this evidence demonstrates, stigma in the lives of homeless youth occurs constantly and with far-reaching consequences. The discrimination against them happens on both an individual level and, perhaps more disconcertingly, an institutionalized level that builds inequality into the foundations of social, political, and economic structures. Homelessness and stigma are structural components that shape young people's relationship to the world around them – both hinder the accumulation of resources and challenge one's ability to conform to mainstream social expectations (Roschelle & Kaufman, 2004). The signifiers of success in Western culture – wealth, consumption, education, and power – are ubiquitous and difficult to ignore or reject (Kidd, 2007). As Danika asserted:

> I just don't like the way people look at other people who are struggling, like there's something wrong with them. Homeless people, it's the same way, they're not treated, they're not treated with respect. Treated like they're inferior people. You know, they may have the same capacity as people who have more money, they just don't have money. You know, they could be very smart, very articulate, very aware of themselves, but at that point in time they just don't have money. It's not fair to treat them with less respect than someone who does have more money.

Among the eight young women I interviewed, the most commonly cited strategy for dealing with potential stigmatization was to try to pass as someone who was not struggling to make ends meet. At times this approach only served to further entrench feelings of marginality as emulating the behaviours of "normal kids" while retaining some identifiers of their lower socio-economic status magnified the differences between them. One particularly stark example involved a pair of lululemon-brand pants that Jean found in a give-away box at the shelter. When she wore them to the mall, other young people hassled her, suggesting that she must have stolen the pants because she would have been unable to pay for them. Her position in the social hierarchy was made clear to her as she became aware that symbols are interpreted differently depending on one's position relative to the epicentre of power.

The pervasive nature of stigma clearly has implications for the delivery of health care and for the health-seeking behaviours of homeless young women. In fact, this study and others indicate that the past stigmatization young women have experienced from health care practitioners is significant enough to stop them from seeking care (Gelberg et al., 2004). Erin explained that seeking care in the past was damaging to her self-esteem: "I don't want to go. I guess that's how it is. They either hate you for being 'not normal' or they feel sorry for you and make you feel like shit. Like, treat me like you would any other person." Stigmatization, then, undermines health in two significant ways: by deterring young women from seeking health care services, and through a decrease in self-confidence and an increase in feelings of worthlessness and anxiety (Courtwright, 2009). Those who work and engage with people living in exceptional circumstances must create environments that promote dignity and self-respect for all, so that marginalized individuals feel like they belong, not just among their peers but also as equals in society (Hoffman & Coffey, 2008). For this to happen, health care service providers must make changes, such as improving interpersonal communication by having welcoming administrative staff and clinicians, eliminating discriminatory policies such as requiring payment for missed appointments, and even reconsidering the built environments to create private check-in areas in clinics. Those who have the most experience with these situations are in the best position to offer their expertise on this point. Having looked at the situation from both a homeless and a housed perspective, Danika shared her thoughts on health service spaces: "You shouldn't be able to tell that, oh, this is a place for homeless. You know I just see things. I spend a lot of time watching things and thinking about them. You just kind of go, 'hmmm.' I've seen this and I've seen that. I've been on both sides. ... Why is this so different?"

Sexual and Reproductive Health

The field of reproductive and sexual health includes the health conditions and health services that have traditionally and more conservatively been defined as women's health: control and protection of fertility. These health issues are well-studied and well-supported from both a financial and a public health perspective, predominantly because of their association with particular representations of femininity. In order to capture the less traditional, more controversial side of reproductive health, I spoke to the young women about their sexual health and sexual health service needs, because sexual health is also about pleasure, satisfaction, protection, and partnerships. Importantly, sexual health begins with ensuring that young women have positive self-conceptions and that they feel comfortable and confident in negotiating their sexual relationships (Jones-Johnson et al., 2006). Positive sexual health outcomes among homeless youth are associated with sex education, an orientation towards the future rather than the present, and the ability to assert one's wishes to one's partners (Rew et al., 2002a). However, the ways in which young women themselves understand their reproductive and sexual health-seeking habits are astonishingly absent from most of the Canadian research literature (Ensign & Panke, 2002). In light of the ways in which adolescent female sexuality is both glamourized and maligned in Western culture, it is vital to understand the sense-making activities of the young people who embody this paradox. The vast amount of money that is funneled into public health campaigns aimed at preventing teenage pregnancy and sexually transmitted infections (STIs) also contributes to the long-standing dichotomy between the "virgin" and the "whore," allowing very little space between those two positions.

Many of the young women involved in this research cited the Gardasil human papillomavirus (HPV) vaccine advertisements that were ubiquitous on Toronto public transit in 2009 as an example of their confusion over sexual health messaging. Through posters on almost every bus and streetcar and at bus stops across the city, young women were told that they should protect themselves from potentially fatal forms of HPV that are linked to reproductive cancers and that are communicated through sexual contact. Six of the eight young women had no idea what HPV was or that the posters were advertising a vaccination against a sexually transmitted infection. Savannah explained that although she saw the posters repeatedly, she didn't realize what they were advertising: "And, I didn't know like all the effects and stuff like that would happen to you. Finally I read about it in a pamphlet and it said something like, I think, discolour and warts and stuff, and I was like, 'Oh, my god. Is that what those ads are about?'" The advertisements – featuring racialized poster teens who proclaim that "smart" girls do "everything they can" to protect themselves – are so vague that sex is entirely removed from the equation. However, the Gardasil campaign *does* announce that the vaccination is recommended for girls as young as 11 years old, which seems to make a significant yet unstated message about the sexual practices of young people. At present, the Ontario government pays for the vaccine only for female students enrolled in Grade 8; for others, this "life-saving" vaccination costs $360 – more than Ontario Works offers as a monthly shelter allowance, as Danika observed: "I think you have to pay money for some kind of vaccine. I think that could definitely be a barrier for people getting it who don't have the money. Like, I can't afford my rent so why would I pay for my health." Here again is another chink in the armour of a supposedly universal health care system. Those women who can afford it can choose to have the protection of the vaccine. Offering the vaccination for free to low-income women, or providing the vaccine for free in shelters or at health clinics for homeless youth, would at least give homeless young women more options in deciding whether or not they want to be vaccinated.

Girls' sexual ideas and identities are not formed in a bubble, but are impacted upon by a plethora of social and cultural messages (Impett & Tolman, 2006). Current research has shown that young women continue to face sexual double standards which encourage, at worst, total denial of sexual desire and, at best, containing those desires within a monogamous sexual relationship (Tolman et al., 2006). Given the long-standing predominance of these messages, it should not be surprising that young women are not forthcoming about the sexual behaviours they are or are not engaging in. Young women are aware of the double standard and hyper-vigilant surveillance that falls on them as the result of their biological role in the reproductive process and, as Danika explained, they feel the effects of this scrutiny very acutely:

> It almost makes me being a girl feel like more sleazy. Or like, how come there's all these things I need to know, but it's not shared. Because there's like that gender gap, boys feel like, oh I don't have to deal with that, that's a girl's issue. Almost like brings shame to it, or makes it seem embarrassing or something you can't say without getting a disapproving look, but you know, people are people. Not just women are doing these things. That's the way human beings are. Why should people come out with this "ew, that's gross"? Why are we girls faced with so much shame? That makes me annoyed.

This feeling of shame was a decisive factor in many young women's decisions not to speak to adults about their sexual behaviours and curiosities. This barrier is especially significant in light of evidence that some young people lack information about safe conduct in less normative sexual situations: three of the young women had engaged in group sex; three had been involved in open relationships; two engaged in anal intercourse; two had been involved in sex work or sexual bartering; and four identified as lesbian or bisexual. The picture painted here is a far cry from abstinence or heterosexual monogamy. When I showed concern for her safety after Raven told me about a time she engaged in unprotected group sex, she told me that they were not worried about STIs because the other partner "[only] slept with like people I knew and most of the time the people I know are normally, like I talk with them, so I know, so I knew they were clean, which means that [the other partner] was clean, which means, hey, he was safe to have sex with." Clearly several assumptions were made in this situation, with the young women trusting word of mouth rather than practicing safe sex. When I brought this to their attention, they tried to placate my concerns by telling me about another incident in which one man engaged in group sex with four young women. Faith assured me that in that instance, "the dude wore a condom."

"One condom?" I asked. I was then met with bewildered looks, followed by, "How many did you want him to wear?" When I suggested that the man should change condoms between partners, both young women scoffed at the idea as such a process would surely "kill the mood." No amount of abstinence education is going to prevent some youth from experimenting. What youth need is a safe environment where they can learn and ask questions about sex that fall beyond basic anatomy and diagrams of reproduction without being judged.

For homeless youth, sexual and reproductive health concerns take on different dimensions depending on the individual's context. A number of studies have shown that homeless youth are more likely than their typical peers to be sexually active, and generally engage in intercourse two to three years earlier than other adolescents (Ensign & Santelli, 1997; Rew et al., 2002b; Walters, 1999). Survival sex – when individuals trade sex in exchange for shelter or food – is also common among homeless youth. Sex trade participation creates a greater vulnerability to STIs, HIV, and unintended pregnancies, as negotiating condom use often becomes difficult (Reid et al., 2005). Erin's experiences speak to these contextual issues, "I think it's up to me to make sure a guy wears a condom or whatever so that I don't get knocked up or get AIDS or something. That's a worry more for girls, I think. Sometimes it can be hard to make a guy do that if he's all horny and stuff or all horny and high or drunk, ya know?"

Adult homeless women report more gynaecological symptoms than do those who are securely housed (Gelberg et al., 2004). While the evidence is less clear in the case of younger homeless women, each of the women who participated in this research reported at least one, and sometimes several of the following conditions: yeast infections, pelvic pain, ovarian cysts, abnormal or painful periods, and STIs. In Toronto, since 2001, rates of chlamydia, syphilis, and gonorrhoea have increased among the general youth population and the city also reports higher rates of sexually transmitted infections than anywhere else in Canada (Flicker et al., 2009). For young women who live on the street, birth control, including condoms, are difficult to hold on to due to theft by others or loss due to constant relocation.

Menstruating while living on the street also poses unique challenges for women who often have difficulty accessing menstrual supplies or finding suitable, private locations in which to properly clean themselves and change pads or tampons. Often, as Erin explained, this combination of factors forces women to engage in petty theft to meet their needs:

> Tampons you can get sometimes at drop-ins, but not always. Lots of times I just go and steal them. I know that's not right, but you have to do something. You can't just bleed all over the fucking place, right? Condom's a hard one too. You can go to pretty much any clinic and get free ones, but that means you have to go walk in there and embarrass yourself grabbing a handful of condoms. And everyone looking at you like you're selling it, right? Then there's the other thing that even if you do go in there and get condoms, they're the cheap kind and guys don't like wearing them cuz they're too tight or not comfortable or whatever so you have to try to convince them that you didn't just get them for free or you have to steal some of the good ones from Shopper's.

Erin's take on the women-specific difficulties of protecting and caring for oneself while living on the street also speaks to the sometimes-blurry lines between stigma, health, crime, and physical necessity.

Rew and colleagues (2002b) found that homeless youth possessed knowledge about the symptoms, transmission, and prevention of STIs, but knew little about the longer-term consequences of leaving such an infection untreated. On the other hand, Gelberg and colleagues (2004) found that homeless young women were ill-informed about contraception and general issues concerning their reproductive health. Likewise, the recent Toronto Teen Survey out of Planned Parenthood Toronto, which employed peer researchers to interview other youth about their sexual health, indicates that the general youth population lacks the knowledge necessary to make informed decisions about their sexual health (Flicker et al., 2009). Although knowledge varied from person to person, this research supports that of others who have found that youth need better and less stigmatizing access to sexual information. When I asked the five participants who were currently sexually active about condom use, the responses were consistent: "Not really. Kind of, sometimes, sometimes not" (Faith and Raven); "Sometimes I'll do it without a hood" (Erin); "I'm pretty good about condoms; I've forgotten, but I just take the morning-after pill" (Radha); "Sometimes I'll use them, usually" (Savannah). Each of these young women indicated that condom use was primarily tied to pregnancy prevention rather than as a barrier against STIs. When Faith and Raven were informed that a former sex partner was infected with chlamydia, they ranked getting tested as a low priority because, as they said, "We've already come to the conclusion that if one of has it, we both have it. If it was something really dangerous, we would go." Simultaneously echoing and challenging Rew and colleagues' (2002b) findings, Faith and Raven were ill-informed about the potential long-term sequelae of chlamydia, and appeared equally in the dark about its prevention, treatment, and symptomology. In Flicker and colleagues' (2009) research, young people were asked to list the top three health topics that they wanted to learn more about. Healthy relationships, HIV/AIDS, and sexual pleasure – the latter of which not one participant had learned about in a formal setting – topped the list (ibid.). Among the eight young women whose voices inform this research, top considerations included: sexual pleasure, negotiation of sexual control, and an outlet for their concerns about "normal" sexual functioning. Radha's experience with her most recent sexual partner summarized these needs for more information: "I gave in every once in a while because I couldn't deal with his complaining and I wanted him to shut the hell up. It was like ... I can't say it felt like being raped because I've never been raped, but I just, it was just spectacularly painful. I had no desire to be there whatsoever. I was just kind of closing my eyes and crying and waiting for him to finish."

The amalgamation of these diverse factors signals a critical need to reconfigure sexual education and sexual health services in ways that are sensitive to the particular concerns and preferences of young people. An alarming 83 per cent of the young people surveyed in the Toronto Teen Survey indicated that they had never seen a health care provider regarding a sexual-health related issue (Flicker et al., 2009). Data from my research suggests that feelings of embarrassment or shame or the fear of being judged prevents young women from talking to health care providers about their sexual health. As Danika said, "Sexual health is way up there, but it's embarrassing ... It's just not like a regular conversation. People feel much more comfortable saying, 'I have the stomach flu.' But, oh, 'I think I'm pregnant!' Or 'I think I have gonorrhoea!' It's just ... It's different. But I mean, it's really important because people do it all the time." Notably, in their research in the United States, Ensign and Panke (2002) found that one important undermining factor exists for homeless young women who are not currently, or who have never been, sexually active: health care providers assume that they are sexually active and do not believe them when they insist that they are not. The non-sexually active women partaking in these interviews – including Jean, whose experiences are discussed in the next section – also raised this concern. Danika was not sexually active, yet as her remarks above demonstrate, she still felt hesitant and embarrassed at the thought of talking to a physician about sexual health-related matters. In addition, the social stigmas attached to lesbianism, transsexuality, and sex work also create barriers for populations who are arguably most in need of sexual advice as they rarely see themselves reflected in any form of traditional sexual education. Health care providers and educators alike need to adopt constructive, non-judgmental attitudes when dealing with the sexual health of diverse groups of young women, recognizing that some young people are engaged in the same array of sexual behaviours experienced by adults, while others are not sexually active at all.

Pelvic Examinations

Among the young women involved in this research, one of the most commonly cited reasons for not seeking sexual health care, and even health care more generally, is a fear of or a negative experience with Pap smears and pelvic exams. In Faith's words, "I don't like gynaecologists cuz they're like 90 and male and I feel uncomfortable with anyone over 25 near me who's male. So, I don't want to go to a gynaecologist who's like this old guy who's gonna poke me in the crotch. I'm just like, 'Yeah, um, no.'" Other research with homeless women has found that survivors of sexual abuse often report trauma-like responses after undergoing vaginal examinations (Wenzel et al., 2001). Building trust between physicians and young women is critical if these women are expected to undergo screening for HPV and STIs (Gelberg et al., 2004). Furthermore, women feel more comfortable receiving care from other women, who they feel can relate to them and who they are more likely to trust not to exploit them. Raven stated that, "If I could find a female one I'd probably go." The young women also expressed concern with doctors' approaches to pelvic exams, cringing at memories of the insensitivity demonstrated by the care providers who administered their first exams. Radha's first Pap experience involved, "waiting forever. I was super, super nervous. [The doctor] came in and did it in five minutes and ran away. I cried a lot." In Jean's case, she was pressured into having a Pap smear: "I've had a Pap smear because they didn't believe that I wasn't sexually active. They were doing an exam and they said something about my hymen being broken. So they did a Pap smear anyway. They didn't believe me. I don't know. It hurt a lot." While no woman expects a Pap smear or vaginal exam to be a pleasant experience, the degree of care exercised in the process clearly varies a great deal from provider to provider. If first experiences of pelvic exams are recalled as traumatic, painful, and humiliating, the chances that young women will continue with screening throughout their lives are slim. Particularly in light of some of these women's sexual practices, the decision to discontinue vaginal examinations has serious implications for their health and well-being across the life course.

Danika's first and only Pap smear experience is worth quoting at length as it evinces so many of the problems and barriers that homeless young women confront in dealing with their sexual health:

Because there was actually one time I went to Evergreen [a community and health centre for street-involved youth] and they were giving, um, Paps. They paid you $15 to get a Pap test done. It was just like, get this test done and they'll pay you for it. So I was like, oh sure. That was a really, really, really horrible experience. So it was in March I got this Pap test. And it hurt like hell. It was really, really painful. The lady, you know, she had this clamp and there was blood everywhere. It was just really bad. And I didn't even get paid for it because she couldn't get the sample that she needed. It was awful.

I had never been sexually active, but no one asked. And maybe everyone just assumed that everyone knows and that they're experienced. I don't know. I don't know. And it was another example of the lack of professionalism. Cuz you know anyone can go there and have it done. But they didn't really explain what I was going to have to endure. She just said, "oh yeah, read this form and sign it." You know there was no verbal explanation of what it was for, or what it was used for, or like why, you know. It was just there. Homeless youth. Homeless female youth. Get this test done. Get paid $15. And you know I was like well, I'm a student living in a shelter. I could sure use 15 bucks.

Then this other lady comes in and says, "Yes, it'll be painless. If it hurts just tell me." So when I said it hurts she reminded me that I had signed the form. I don't remember what the forms said. I've always wanted to go back and inquire about it, but it was just a really bad experience and I was so powerless. I just don't want to go back there. Seriously, I was like screaming, like "Ow!" and the lady told me that it couldn't be that bad. She was so rude. And there were guys in the room too for some reason. Well, right outside the curtain anyway. They could hear me if I said where it hurts and why. I don't know. The whole facility was just so ghetto. It was such a terrible experience. They were like, "Sorry. We can't pay you because you didn't complete the study." It was really, really brutal. I don't even want to bring it up again. I just want to forget about it.

To most people this story would be shocking, but when I shared it with other homeless young women, very few were surprised and several felt that the story validated their opinions of clinics for homeless youth. In analysing Danika's story for content, there are many significant damaging, and damning, points that require discussion in the attempt to understand why homeless female youth are not accessing sexual health services. As a researcher, I feel compelled to begin with the total disregard for the protection of vulnerable research participants. When I visited that particular health centre and inquired about these Pap tests for payment, the employee I spoke to had no recollection of any such program and thought it was possible that it was just a "one week thing." The rationale for providing incentives to encourage young homeless women to be screened for HPV and STIs is clear: rates of infection are high among homeless populations that are often difficult to reach, and, from a public health perspective, being able to treat STIs before they spread to others or create further complications for those infected, and the early detection of possible cervical cancers, have unquestionable benefit. However, offering cash incentives to vulnerable young women living in poverty requires extra vigilance and care on the part of the researchers and clinicians who are on the privileged end of the power spectrum. In Danika's experience, the vital protection of informed consent appears to have been revoked – signing a form does not mean that one is properly and fully informed about the conditions of her involvement. Moreover, to subject a research participant to such an experience and then fail to compensate, counsel, or care for her is sheer negligence.

Other salient issues at play in Danika's story have already been discussed in other contexts, but are brought into stark relief here: a young person with a critical lack of information about what a Pap test entails; a clinician who assumes that any homeless woman coming in for a Pap test is, or has been, sexually active; and total insensitivity on the part of those with significantly more social, economic, and political power. As she says above, the three most powerful feelings Danika experienced in this ordeal were pain, embarrassment, and powerlessness. The presence of men just outside the curtain reveals a total lack of foresight or attention to the context of young homeless women's lives or potential histories of violence. As is starkly demonstrated in Danika's narrative – that of a young woman who deals daily with stigma and a critical lack of basic resources while also attending university and working at a coffee shop – these inequities in health services delivery only serve to perpetuate the problems they are created to help ameliorate.

Conclusion

The focus of this chapter has been to examine the mental and physical health conditions that young homeless women are likely to be confronting. The empirical data relied upon here has demonstrated that mental and sexual health are not as straightforward as they are often characterized to be in policy and program decisions. In seeking care many of the young women who inform this research have had to weigh their health against affronts to their character and to their dignity. The mental health services required by many of the participants are difficult to navigate for fear of labelling processes which indicate that a diagnosis is a negative reflection on their character, rather than a negative reflection on a social safety net that has not protected them. For those who have experienced or continue to experience violence, the challenge of trust alone becomes a barrier to accessing services. In the realm of sexual and reproductive health, young women are seeking information that reflects their everyday lives and their heterogeneity. Women who are not sexually active want to be believed and to be able to ask the questions they need to ask in order to create healthy sexual relationships when they feel they are ready. Those who are sexually active want to feel safe to visit a provider who will not judge their behaviour and who will provide advice not just on how to protect themselves from STIs and pregnancy, but on how to negotiate sex in such a way that the experience is pleasurable and empowering. For young women on the street, connecting to health services is exceptionally difficult, both for reasons of trust and reasons of access. Dealing with menstruation alone can require significant amounts of time trying to acquire tampons and finding safe and private places to carry out basic hygienic activities. The next chapter engages with the ways in which young women are, or are not, seeking help with these health issues. All of the issues raised here must be understood within the context of these young women's everyday lives. Meeting the daily necessities of life, like shelter and food, must necessarily take priority; tending to health issues is often not a concern until pain or inability to function forces the issue, which often leads to an increase in emergency or crisis visits. Looking at barriers to health from a policy lens, as well as the lenses of gender, race, culture, and sexuality, paints a clearer picture of the ways in which young women struggle to negotiate with dignity their search for health services and resources.

7 Begging for Change: Barriers, Facilitators, and Implications for Policy and Practice

Introduction

Having examined the health issues that are most relevant to young women living in exceptional circumstances, I will now explore the barriers and facilitators young women encounter in accessing health services and discuss their implications for the delivery and implementation of policy and practice. Understanding the equity implications of these programs and policies requires a holistic conception of access that makes high-quality services available. Quality of care as defined by young people themselves is of fundamental importance in developing services that youth feel comfortable and confident accessing. Furthermore, the care must be accessible; providing services in clinical environments that are inhospitable, out of geographic reach, or that lack cultural competency will not improve youth's utilization or attachment to services.

I divide the barriers to accessing health services into three categories that reflect the gaps in services identified by the young women involved in this project: structural characteristics, clinical characteristics, and characteristics of space and place. In addition, cuts in funding, fragmentation, and downloading of services, as well as constraints faced by physicians seeking to care for marginalized populations, combine to prevent the most vulnerable from accessing quality care. This section also reflects on the considerable challenges of meeting the needs of diverse groups of individuals within the youth homeless population. Racialized and sexually diverse youth require targeted services that suit their particular needs and that reflect an understanding of their unique historical and social locations.

Young women were also eager to talk about those aspects of health and social services provision that enabled and empowered them in seeking solutions and creating options in their own lives. In this section I extend resiliency theory to acknowledge that relations of power must be unveiled to reveal who gets to define, and who is defined by, diagnostic labels. Resilient youth are the products of supportive structures rather than inherent personal characteristics. Agency and subjectivity combine with compassionate people and environments to create confidence and a sense of purpose for those who have often been alone and without reason to trust or confide in others. Social inclusion and relationship building are fundamental to the development of healthy young women with healthy futures.

Barriers to Accessing Health Services

In 2005, Street Health Toronto reported that 50 per cent of 360 homeless individuals surveyed described serious medical conditions for which they were not being treated as a result of an inability to follow the advice of their health care provider due to issues such as unsanitary living conditions, lack of housing, or poor nutrition. Because they have little choice but to prioritize the search for food, shelter, and work, many homeless youth place health care at the bottom of their list of needs. Many American studies of homeless young people suggest that they have inadequate access to primary care and that they often seek treatment in emergency departments when their conditions become too severe to ignore or self-treat (De Rosa et al., 1999; Ensign & Bell, 2004; Geber, 1997). In the United States, primary barriers to care include lack of insurance, anxiety over confidentiality, confusion over the rules of health care consent, and low tolerance for administrative tasks such as filling out paperwork or waiting for extended periods (Klein et al., 2000). Barriers such as a lack of insurance coverage are less relevant under a universal model of health care; however, it can become an issue for those living in Ontario if they lack an Ontario Health Insurance Plan (OHIP) card. For homeless youth who are new immigrants lacking official status, or for those who have lost their health cards or had them stolen, accessing health care is exceptionally difficult and potentially expensive. As Erin says, "That's the other thing, no health card, no birth certificate, no nothing. They don't like that over at the hospital, that's for sure. And then, of course, you have to go through the whole long-ass story of where you come from and where you're going and why you don't have a mommy and daddy. Everyone just assumes, right? But at one point I had some ID stuff, but shit gets stolen all the time." Frankford's (1997) research also notes that not having a health insurance card or using an incorrect health number means that physicians and lab technicians are not paid. For this reason, homeless people without an OHIP card are sometimes refused care. Furthermore, several young women in this research were under the impression that, despite Canada's universal health care coverage, they would have to pay to see certain types of doctors. The perception is that general medicine is covered, but specialist visits require payment. Otherwise, Canadian research on homeless youths' access to health services closely mirrors the data coming out the United States and Britain.

The structural characteristics that act as obstacles to accessing health care include constraints produced by the ways in which health care is financed, delivered, and organized (Daly et al., 2008). Structural barriers in place at hospitals and clinics, for example, include identification requirements, waits associated with processing intake forms, clinic hours, and clinic locations. Arielle, new to Canada, was frustrated by a clinic structure that was not explained to her in advance, likely due to a language barrier between herself and the administrative staff: "I first had to register. She put my name on the list but I didn't know about that and I was a bit angry with her. [She said,] 'No, [Arielle], listen, I must write your name on the list. You must be registered. It is one thing I must do.' 'But I am so sick.'" Structural barriers discussed in the research literature also include costs of prescription medication, lack of transportation, and, here in Canada, inability to obtain identification or social assistance because of homeless individuals' lack of a fixed address (Crowe & Hardill, 1993). To address this barrier, the SHOUT clinic, a Toronto-based health clinic specifically for homeless youth, offers free ID clinics for youth to procure identification on a regular basis, a practice that should be pointed out and commended. Young women frequently mentioned that mobility was an issue if they were unable to secure public transportation fare from shelter staff or sufficient funds when panhandling. Shelter staff provide residents with one token – good for a one-way journey on public transportation – per day, unless they have an established appointment, which they have to prove and which often requires them to divulge information that they would rather keep confidential. Trading privacy for transportation is often not worth the emotional cost and fear of judgment or stigmatization.

Many homeless young women are also unable to adhere to the advice of their physicians because of the costs associated with doing so. Even if a young person is working, minimum wage is currently set at $10.25 per hour, or $9.60 if one is under the age of 18 and working less than 28 hours per week (Ontario Ministry of Labour, 2010). These wages do not necessarily allow young women to budget for prescriptions, medical supplies, and nutrient-rich foods and adhere to the advice of their physicians.

In terms of clinical characteristics that create barriers to care, young women voiced many concerns about the places that have been designated for their care. Ensign (2001) asserts that one of the most significant issues with clinics designed for homeless youth is that they are designed by adults using an adult model of care, focusing mainly on reproductive health and paying little attention to the specific needs (such as sex-positive counselling or informal doctor-patient relationships) of out-of-the-mainstream youth. When young women feel they have been treated poorly in a particular clinic or by a particular provider, they sometimes reject the system altogether, assuming that all clinics and providers will make them feel the same way. Danika's experience at the health care clinic that botched her Pap smear affected her view of other health services: "I don't know why I don't use the health services. Either because I don't think my health is a big deal or because I don't think the services are really trustworthy. I feel like if I paid money for a service it would be better, but these free ones for youth aren't really trustworthy." Danika did not know that as long as she has her health card, she can visit health clinics throughout Ontario free of charge. Still, payment is the lesser issue when compared against her perception of the trustworthiness of youth clinics. Gender-mixed environments, frosty receptionists, and physical characteristics of the building itself – which can include anything from lack of building maintenance to glass dividers between patients and staff – are all viewed as reasons not to engage with services for fear of feeling unwanted or stigmatized (Crisis UK, 2007). As Danika continued, summarizing a range of reasons that homeless young women are not accessing care, "To offer services by category isn't really fair. Canada has free health care and everyone's supposed to be treated equal thing, but for homeless youth the building is crumbling, the staff aren't really, you know, it's not that they aren't trained, it's that they're not professional or they treat people like they're less deserving. These people are already down; they don't need to be pulled down further."

Negative experiences with and distrust in health care providers was the primary talking point when young women were asked about barriers to care. In other studies, too, women have reported hostile behaviour from practitioners that range from subtle innuendo to outright antagonism (Ensign & Panke, 2002). Hoffman and Coffey (2008) have labelled the two most common forms of treatment that homeless people face in their encounters with physicians: objectification and infantilization, whereby patients are treated either as numbers or as children. Radha voiced her frustration at experiencing both of these forms of treatment simultaneously, essentially being made to feel like a robotic child. First, she protested that her knowledge of her own body is devalued because of her age: "I don't really understand. [The doctor] just thought ... she didn't respect my ... I don't know, my idea. She thought I was too young to know my own body." Then, referring to the same doctor, Radha described feeling like a paycheque and not a person, "She does everything really, really fast, which is, I can't help but get the feeling that she knows she's paid by patient volume and once I'm in the office it's easiest to get me the fuck out as quickly as she can." Many doctors in Ontario are paid based on a fee-for-service model, and only allow patients to discuss one problem or concern per visit. Given the complex health needs of young homeless women who often suffer co-morbidities, this fee-for-service model of patient care fails to account for the context of people's lives; some would argue that the model is not benefiting anyone, homeless or housed.

Most of the young women also observed that accessing health services becomes an inevitable exchange of dignity for improved health. Jacobson (2009) refers to dignity work as the "activities individuals and collectives do in order to create, maintain, defend, or reclaim their own dignity or that of others." In this regard, homeless young women engage in dignity work not just with health care providers, but also with social services employees, social workers, and other members of the general population. As Savannah said, in the lives of homeless youth, this work is constant and exhausting: "It's actually pretty hard trying to convince people you aren't insane or a criminal just because you're homeless." All the young women noted that small changes to health services encounters would go a long way to making them feel more comfortable. Three of the eight women suggested that in all clinics, not just those for homeless people, intake should occur in a private room out of hearing range of other patients. Having their health concerns announced, followed by the inevitable check to confirm their no-fixed address status, means that they are subject not only to the scrutiny of the receptionist, but also that of other patients. In the case of street homelessness, maintaining confidentiality is even more crucial as the other patients in the clinic might be people they see on a regular basis or people with whom they trade sex.

In the discussion of barriers and facilitators to care, it is important to note that street youth face challenges that are both similar and different to those faced by youth living in shelters. Being visibly homeless creates a unique set of hurdles in maintaining, treating, and caring for health: street youth are more likely to be involved in drug use, report more serious health problems, and rely more heavily on emergency departments than do shelter youth (Ensign & Bell, 2004; Ensign & Santelli, 1997; Klein et al., 2000). Erin was quick to list the factors that affect her health and are attributable to street homeless, but she did not see these issues as anything to be concerned about: "I don't know, my health is fine, I guess. Maybe I get a lot of colds or whatever cuz I don't sleep very much or am outside too much or don't eat sometimes, but that's what happens, right? Not such a big deal. Definitely not going to a doctor about something like that." When street youth do visit clinics or emergency rooms and require labs or other tests, communicating results to those with no phone number or address is difficult (Eberle Planning and Research, 2001). Following treatment advice is equally difficult, especially when it requires rest, medication, or following a structured routine (ibid.). Erin explained the challenges she had after visiting a clinic: "So I went to this SHOUT clinic thing that is for street kids or something. And they give me pills or whatever to take, but I lost them, or maybe someone stole them off me, I dunno. But I didn't have them. So then a few days later I went to an emergency room cuz it got even worse and they hooked a needle into my arms and did some stuff that way, but then I still had pills so I had to hide them." If young homeless people get prescription medicine – whether they pay for them or are given drug samples by their physician – the prospect of selling those drugs on the street is tempting when it could mean a reprieve from sex work or several warm meals. Despite these differences between street and shelter youth, Erin shared the same primary desire of the other young women: that health care practitioners treat her with respect and respect the situation in which she lives without judgment or condescension. Furious about a former emergency room doctor's hostility at her "non-compliance" to physician's orders, Erin felt justified in her opinion that doctors are not for her:

Like at the emergency room they're all like, "Why didn't you take your pills?" and I was all like, "Um, I dunno, asshole, maybe because my mommy and daddy don't keep them at home and give them to me before they tuck me in." Like, they're such assholes and they make millions of dollars and just expect that you're like their kids at home in Richville and that you're going to walk out the hospital into your BMW. No fucking clue what it's like for us. And they look down on you and talk down to you and they know everything and you don't know nothing.

When a patient lacks social and family support and money, health care practitioners must account for context and attempt to find creative and non-traditional approaches to caring for homeless youth.

There is general consensus in the research literature that homeless youth tend to seek care only when their conditions become intolerable or interfere with their daily lives (De Rosa et al., 1999; Gelberg et al., 2004; Reid et al., 2005). The participants in this research tended to agree; as Danika said, "Me, myself, I'm like, meh, I'm OK, I'm not dying. I think when something goes really seriously wrong I'll start to think about my health." Homeless youth preferred self-care options to clinic options, which seems to signal that one possible intervention strategy might be to offer street and shelter-based self-care education seminars that would also teach young people about those aspects of their health with which they are unfamiliar, and provide advice on how to protect themselves (Ensign & Bell, 2004; Lifson & Halcón, 2001). Ideally, young homeless women would visit clinics but, as has been demonstrated, the lives of these young people are less than ideal. An ounce of prevention in this case is, indeed, better than a pound of cure. This is not to say that funding should be withdrawn or that new investments should not be made in clinics that specialize in health care for homeless youth, but rather to suggest alternative and innovative approaches that would empower individuals through knowledge and show respect for their circumstances. When homeless youth muster the energy that is required to seek health care and ask for help, and they are met with a one-size-fits-all solution that often does not work for them, they are quickly disillusioned by the inability of the health care system to meet their needs.

Race and Sexuality

Unique barriers also exist for those people who face racial, cultural, and sexual discrimination. Reducing health disparities and promoting equity require careful consideration of the ways in which cultural differences shape social realities and influence our understandings of, and access to, health services. There are several groups that are over-represented in the youth homeless populations: refugee and immigrant youth, sexually diverse youth, youth from black communities, and Aboriginal youth (Novac et al., 2002; Zerger et al., 2008). For refugee and immigrant youth, adapting to new cultural expectations while attempting to retain those of their parents often leads to family conflict and increased demands on young people (DeSantis et al., 1999). Ensign (2001) suggests that sexually diverse youth, too, find themselves living in two separate worlds, one of sexual diversity and the other of homophobia and heteronormativity. Research has shown that the primary users and benefactors of health services still tend to be white, English-speaking, educated, and middle-class (Carlson et al., 1990; Daly et al., 2008; Harris et al., 2001). When researchers and health care providers attempt to understand the sweeping consequences of racism and discrimination, they can better grasp the ways in which these critical social positions can both create and perpetuate homelessness and ill health, and, more importantly, what can be done to ally with racialized communities to deliver truly equitable health care.

Sexually Diverse Youth

Data shows that sexually diverse young women and trans people are over-represented in Toronto's homeless population – approximately one-third of homeless youth are sexually diverse (Novac et al., 2002; Whitzman, 2006). As Faith attested, many of these youth are pushed out of their homes because their parents or peers were unable to accept and embrace their sexuality: "And so, [Raven and I] started dating and things at home started to seem worse and worse, and my mom just hated the fact I was gay. I had come out to my mother, but at the same time she said, 'Oh, I accept it.' But, it was one of those, 'Oh, I accept it, just don't do it.'" Compared to heterosexual homeless youth, sexually diverse homeless youth are at even greater risk for violence and poor health outcomes (Walls et al., 2007). Youth who are considered sexual minorities, homeless and housed alike, are far more likely to experience physical and verbal abuse. Peers at school and on the street often make anti-gay comments and slurs, including using terms such as "gay" to refer to something that they do not like or disagree with (ibid.). When they lived in an all-women's shelter, Faith and Raven overheard more than one conversation between other residents "talking about how lesbians are gross and everything else like that. And how, why are they in like an all-girls' shelter when they're probably just here to check out all the girls." Lenz-Rashid's (2006) findings indicate that sexually diverse youth living on their own require additional help in coming to terms with being "different" in a heteronormative society, but that sexually diverse youth in care are not considered by policy-makers to be in need of any unique supports. In fact, group homes have often been found to be neither safe nor welcoming for sexually diverse youth (ibid.). Some youth, both heterosexual and sexually diverse, even suggested that Toronto's largest youth shelter is hostile towards sexual minorities due to its strongly religious affiliations.

As a trans-identified youth, Raven has complex health needs and faces intense discrimination in all facets of her life. The confusion over the difference between sex and gender created a particularly precarious situation when she and Faith, feeling safer at a women's-only shelter, were told to keep quiet about Raven's masculinized gender identity:

RAVEN: And then, when we came to Toronto, if I kept saying I was transgendered in the shelter I was in, because I was technically male, they would have shipped me off to a different shelter, cuz it was an all-female shelter, even though I looked female on the outside. And I wasn't going through any therapy.

FAITH: You can look male on the outside and be identifying as female there, but not the other way around.

Other shelter residents that I spoke to expressed their discomfort with having to shower in communal washrooms with trans residents who retained their male anatomy, but said that they would feel less discomfort with trans residents who looked female. My assertion here is not that the shelter policy is backwards, but that both male-to-female and female-to-male transgendered people should be given a choice to reside where they feel most comfortable and most safe. Raven feels like she has more masculine inclinations than feminine ones, but she still prefers the female pronoun and, as yet, inhabits a female body. Trans issues are undoubtedly complicated; however, it is for this very reason that they must be given due consideration. For trans people undergoing surgical body modification and hormone therapy, sensitive and non-judgmental medical care is essential; however, because homeless people are prohibited from undergoing these procedures due to the cost, that particular issue is less commonly discussed in the homelessness context. Homeless trans people are able to modify their bodies through their aesthetic choices, however. For Raven this means binding her breasts to obtain a more boyish figure, a choice that has implications for her health: "It hurts. That's why I only do it so often. I used to wrap my chest every second day. I'd go one day flat chest, one day boobs, one day flat chest, one day boobs. But eventually it started to hurt my ribcage and it started to shrink my ribcage." Because she has very little faith in doctors' abilities to be non-judgmental, Raven has not seen a health care provider about her health, her gender identity, or her ribcage.

Immigrant and Refugee Youth

Immigrant and refugee youth constitute other groups whose representation in shelters is greater than their representation in the overall population (Novac et al., 2002). On the surface, immigrant populations (who, of course, do not constitute a homogenous population) are not considered vulnerable in the realm of health. In fact, upon arrival they are generally in better health and have lower mortality rates than those born in Canada (Beiser, 2005). Through screening processes, Canada tends to select immigrants who are healthy, skilled, well educated, or young. Once immigrants enter the country, however, responsibility for their health status devolves from the federal department of Citizenship and Immigration Canada to the provincial Ministry of Health and Long-Term Care, whose policies offer little in the way of guidance for immigrant populations (ibid.). Refugees, conversely, generally enter the country in poorer health, and many, like Arielle, suffer from the effects of the persecution that catalysed their refugee claim. In addition, immigrant children, although they may initially be in good health, are three times more likely than children born in Canada to live in poverty (Beiser & Hou, 2002). Between 10 and 24 months after their arrival, immigrants and refugees, particularly those who lack social supports, become at high risk for developing a depressive disorder (Beiser, 1988; Beiser, 2005). Not coincidentally, this residency timeline mirrors the timeline around which many immigrant and refugee youth enter the shelter system. Resettlement experiences, then, have high potential to push immigrants and refugees into the category of people who are vulnerable to poorer health outcomes (Canadian Task Force on Mental Health Issues Affecting Immigrants and Refugees, 1988). Disturbingly, although researchers have known these statistics for more than 20 years, little has been done to ameliorate these disparities.

Aboriginal Youth

The legacy of racism and colonization inherited by Aboriginal youth is arguably Canada's most disgraceful injustice. The combination of the reservation system, forced relocation, residential schools, the existence of reserves without potable drinking water, and the continually paternalistic attitude of the federal government towards First Nations, Inuit, and Métis communities forms the foundation of the health and welfare crisis Aboriginal people face today (Adelson, 2005). The continuing familial dysfunction and mental ill health confronted by many Aboriginal peoples is engendered by this history of cultural erasure and by the assimilationist tactics still popular with the federal government today (Wesley-Esquimaux, 2007). Wesley-Esquimaux (2007), citing government suppression of Aboriginal cultural values, argues that the loss of storytelling traditions has quashed a vital source of education, which acted to instil values and to speak against harmful practices such as violence.

Canada's Aboriginal population encompasses 50 distinct nations living on 600 reserves and in cities across the country – this, too, is a diverse group (Hollands, 2001). Aboriginal women are by far the group most affected by violence in Canada: they are three times more likely than their non-Aboriginal counterparts to have been survivors of abuse, and two times more likely to experience violence than Aboriginal men (Besserer, 2001). Many members of the younger generation of Aboriginal women have grown up experiencing the consequences – such as sexual abuse and substance misuse – of residential schools on their parents and grandparents. Adelson (2005) reports the disturbing statistic that "up to 75 per cent of the victims of sex crimes in Aboriginal communities are women and girls under the age of 18. 50 per cent of those are under age 14 and almost 25 per cent are under the age of 7" (p. S55). Both Savannah and Jean fall into the latter 25 per cent, as both experienced multiple incidents of sexual abuse by the age of 10, and still more by the age of 18. Given all of these factors, it is not surprising that Canada has the highest youth suicide rate among Aboriginal youth in the world (Ungar, 2007). The intergenerational nature of this violence has been called "historic trauma": a phenomenon that is common to Aboriginal peoples and which has "covertly shaped individuals' lives and futures, and has had devastating consequences for entire communities, regions, and countries" (Wesley-Esquimaux, 2007, p. 66). Clearly

Canada – at its federal, provincial, and municipal branches of government – needs to focus on genuine partnerships with Aboriginal people to create serious and sustained policy change in order to begin to resolve the social, cultural, and economic crises being faced by so many Aboriginal people. The self-determination of Aboriginal communities is crucial to health and well-being. Although Aboriginal youth often qualify for tax exemptions and free university tuition, many cannot make use of these benefits until they escape the poverty and abuse that makes higher education seem, as Jean said, like "a far-off dream." The ways in which younger generations remember and understand their past also contribute to what Wesley-Esquimaux (2007) calls "dis-ease": the new epidemics, like substance misuse and violence, that relate to the mental health issues faced by individuals and communities, and which stem from negative or disrupted forms of cultural identification. On some reservations, lack of access to resources, such as culturally appropriate health care or even safe drinking water, that other Canadians take for granted, leaves Aboriginal peoples "with a sense that they are on the inside looking out, with little recourse but to join the rest of the world" (ibid., p. 63). This sense of powerlessness experienced by many individuals living on reserves has initiated a wave of Aboriginal migration into Canada's urban centres; Savannah is one of many who have come to Toronto searching for self-improvement opportunities or escaping violence: "I couldn't live on the res anymore. With [my ex-boyfriend] beating on me and just the way things are over there. Back at home I wouldn't do nothing, cuz I didn't want to meet anybody, and if I did go out, it was always drinking with the boys. We'll see what Toronto does for me." Toronto has one Aboriginal health centre, Anishnawbe Health Toronto, which is based on the Aboriginal wellness model. Both Jean and Savannah have been there and give it good reviews; however, this is just one clinic that treats patients as unique individuals whose physical, emotional, and spiritual health are all considered part of health care and it is the exception rather than the norm.

Homeless Aboriginal youth spent a great deal of time recounting stories of the blatant racism and discrimination they face in the shelter system, in group homes, and even on public transportation. As Jean said, "I've heard people's thoughts before me, 'Hey, you drunk Indian. Are you dreaming of beer or welfare?'" Further compounding the effects of stigmatization and discrimination, many young people internalize feelings of helplessness and belittlement in the face of these racist comments. Moreover, young women often feel like they have little re-course in dealing with those who insult and disparage them, and often turn to cutting or violence as an outlet for their anger, as Savannah experienced:

> They were just making racial comments cuz I was the only Native Ameri-can living there at the time. They would just say like little racial comments in the end. I would try to ignore it and next day, it would keep going on and on until I finally just had enough of it and I just snapped on these girls. I just, I couldn't take it any more like, that's when I started to isolate my-self. I would like stay in my room, listen to music, try to cool off in the day, but then I would get in trouble because the staff said I'm not socializing. I said, "How am I supposed to socialize when people are making rude ra-cial comments to me?" The staff won't do nothing.

Savannah's comments illuminate the chain of events that leads to her violent outbursts: the bigoted attitudes of others, which are not con-demned by those who should protect her; isolationist coping strategies; and feelings of powerlessness in her own place of shelter. Following these incidents Savannah almost invariably finds herself in courtrooms and in police custody – a poor substitution for the healing of trauma. Ineffective responses to these hurtful historic and present-day struc-tural issues are a significant contributor to the dis-ease faced by young, displaced Aboriginal peoples.

Although Canada's Aboriginal peoples face a number of daunting challenges, they are, of course, much more multi-dimensional and agentic than discourses of victimization might suggest. While it is true that Aboriginal women confront higher rates of violence than any other group in the country, they are also often the innovators and supporters of initiatives and movements targeted at improving the health of indi-viduals within their communities (Wesley-Esquimaux, 2007; Yee, 2011). Furthermore, many youth, who currently constitute 56 per cent of the Aboriginal population, are also becoming integrally involved in the bet-terment of their communities (ibid.). Aboriginal researchers, activists, and healers are beginning to create and explore health care models that integrate the best of traditional practices with the best of Western medi-cal practices in order to create hybrid clinics and practices, which have been well-received by Aboriginal and non-Aboriginal patients alike (ibid.). Many non-Aboriginal health care providers are embracing the practice of treating people holistically and as members of communities and societies to which they have varying degrees of access and in which they hold varying degrees of power. Youth, too, are taking a leading role in teaching their peers and communities about HIV and decolonization through arts-based workshops and seminars (Flicker, 2009). Aboriginal peoples are taking steps forward to healing not just individual ailments, but long and traumatic histories of injustice and loss. As Wesley-Esquimaux (2007) asserts, "Only by deconstructing historic trauma and (re)membering the past, will Indigenous peoples see each other from the oppositional realms they occupy in existing dominant and resistant cultural structures" (p. 68). Aboriginal youth are mobilizing communities to reclaim their ancestral rights to self-determine decisions over their own bodies and spaces (Yee, 2011). These efforts deserve sustained support from governments and funding agencies, and from critical and committed non-Aboriginal allies. Most of all, they require the recognition that Aboriginal youth can and do empower each other and make vital differences in their own communities.

Policy Barriers

In its current form, Canada's health care system is not working for homeless people (Deber, 2003). This is not because health care is publicly provided – public health care is necessary and advantageous in a number of ways – but rather because of how health care is currently delivered, financed, and organized. Cuts in funding, fragmentation, and downloading of services, along with constraints faced by physicians seeking to care for vulnerable populations, combine to build fences rather than bridges for homeless young people and, indeed, all those experiencing poverty and social exclusion. Hospitals, for example, tend to focus on cases that are acute and episodic, downloading chronic and comorbid conditions – those most commonly faced by homeless populations – to community agencies whose resources are already stretched to maximum capacity (Daly et al., 2008). The type of integrated services that are required by most people in exceptional circumstances are not offered, for the most part, outside of targeted clinics for marginalized individuals, such as clinics for homeless youth or Community Health Centres. There are a number of health and social policies that limit access for vulnerable people, and homeless youth feel those limits acutely; fixing the system that creates these barriers is advantageous not just to those in need, but to society at large. A visit to the emergency room costs the government at least $400 and a bed in an in-patient ward costs more than $1,000 a day, which means that if each person in the shelter system was able to use the emergency room even one time less than current rates of usage, there could be health care system savings of up to $2 million dollars per year (Street Health, 2005).

Beyond accessing health services, one of the largest policy challenges that homeless youth face is the lack of social assistance. Of course, this is a reality faced by low-income boys and adults, men and women alike, but the situation is made even more difficult for those who suffer the double marginalization of youth and poverty. Ontario Works (OW) provides a single person $535 per month, the Ontario Disability Support Plan (ODSP) allows $950 per month. Working full-time at adult minimum wage provides $1,520 per month, while young workers can earn up to $924 per month working the maximum 28 hours specified under the so-called student wage – noting the assumptions inherent in the label (ibid.). In Toronto, paying rent and other bills and buying food and other necessities are not feasible on these amounts, let alone if one is supporting dependents. Transportation costs to get to and from appointments can also prove unmanageable. Several of the young women participating in this research, including Radha, mentioned that friends or family members irked them by suggesting that the system was giving them a free ride: "My dad, first of all, thinks it's a much more idyllic situation than it is. He's like great, free rent and food. I'm like, you're stupid. It's not like that at all." Nobody who lives in a shelter thinks that their situation is a good deal. Having to ask for the smallest of things and being dependent on the kindness of strangers just to get from point A to point B, does not inspire self-confidence.

Insufficiencies in OW and ODSP often mean that social assistance recipients use the personal needs portion of their cheques to supplement their basic shelter allowance to cover their rent. Key research involving 130 low-income Canadians showed that 40 per cent of those who had been prescribed medication in the previous 12 months had not filled an average of three prescriptions (Williamson & Fast, 1998). One hundred percent of the people who were from working poor families cited their inability to pay for drugs as the primary reason not to fill prescriptions and indicated that one of the largest disincentives to seeing a physician is that they fear their doctor will prescribe medications that they cannot afford (ibid.). Social support recipients are provided with drug cards to cover the cost of prescription drugs as well as dental and vision care for children; however, the OW recipients in this research indicated that they had been prescribed medications that were not covered by OW and that, because they were receiving OW as independents, they were unable to claim vision and dental expenses despite being under the age of 18. This is another prime example of the ways in which social policy seems to see youth as adults and children simultaneously, depending on which better suits the political agenda. Those who are homeless and do collect social assistance also talked about the so-called "special diet" supplement that is available to individuals whose doctors indicate that they have a health condition, such as diabetes or celiac disease, that requires special dietary components. A nutritional deficit such as that experienced by homeless and other impoverished individuals, however, does not count as a health condition. As Erin says, "I eat from garbage cans some nights. That's my special diet. I probably need some extra nutrition."

Similarly, pregnant women receive a monthly allowance from OW in order to meet the developmental needs of the fetus. However, this additional support is not available after the child is born. Protecting the health of the fetus for nine months treats the fetus as though it were not a part of the woman, and fails to recognize that, in order for a woman to care for a child beyond its birth, her nutrition as well as that of the child remains critical. Policies like this perpetuate the position of those who see women only as vessels for children.

The ways in which health care is delivered to homeless youth is critical in their decisions to visit a clinic or provider. Caring for this population requires a shift away from traditional models of service delivery and towards creative thinking that understands homeless youth culture and that takes health care out of buildings and hospitals and onto streets and into shelters, exchanging white coats for jeans and T-shirts (Barry et al., 2002). For homeless youth, assessments and discussions of their health and medical history are bound to take longer than normal, especially for individuals attempting to share difficult histories with a complete stranger. In this case, coordination between service providers and agencies is necessary to ensure that the health of youth is being treated holistically through social services, housing, and health workers who understand that caring for homeless youth requires "flexibility and forgiveness" (Novac, 2006, p. 25).

When speaking about the delivery of health care, discussing the roles of physicians is both unavoidable and obligatory, especially in light of the fact that all the young people in this study reported that their relationship with their physician was a, if not *the*, critical factor in seeking or avoiding care. In so doing, however, I am not questioning the intentions or hard work of health care providers, but rather recognizing that physicians, nurses, and volunteers are also subject to constraints within the health care system, albeit from differing positions of power (Hoffman & Coffey, 2008). In every profession there are those who are excellent at their jobs, and those who are not – health care is no exception.

Both service providers and their clients have complained that the current system emphasizes individual problems and deficits rather than skill building and the expansion of personal resources (Sistering Toronto, 2002). When community or clinical programs are funded on the basis of necessity and individual diagnoses, running programs that build capacity is difficult if not impossible. Of course, among traditional physician-based organizations these programs are even more difficult to find, not necessarily due to a lack of funding, but due to a lack of experience with and understanding of the needs of vulnerable populations. The unique challenges faced by homeless young women, and homeless people generally, should be included in medical school curricula and rotations (Hunter et al., 1991). Creating a medical school rotation during which students are required to practice in clinics for vulnerable populations and on outreach buses which travel to different neighbourhoods to deliver care would sensitize young physicians to the needs of marginalized individuals (ibid.). Incorporating this sort of training into the professional development of more senior physicians would be equally valuable. Erin articulated the need for more doctors to understand her situation:

> I am the one in charge of my life and my body. Then, too, take the way I have to live into your brain when you tell me things. Like, "make four more appointments to check up later." Or, "Take these pills every day at exactly the same time." Shit. These assholes want me to wear a watch. Seriously? I wear a watch, I get jumped. Back to the doctors cuz I'm bleeding all over the street. Then where am I supposed to keep that little card thingy they give you so you remember your appointment. I dunno what day of the week it is, what time it is. I wish doctors would come out here and see this. Like, so I could just say, um, hey I got this homeless thing.

The number one request of the young homeless women I interviewed is that the physician actually stop and listen to what they are saying, rather than overwhelming them with clinical expertise. When the physician truly listens, the young person can explain their presenting issue as well as other issues that could be contributing or exacerbating that condition; by providing explanations that lack jargon, physicians can help young women to feel more in control of their bodies and their health (Ensign & Panke, 2002). Acquiring skills to work with vulnerable populations would logically also enhance physicians' practice with mainstream patients.

O'Connell (2004) suggests that effective care for homeless people begins with bringing clinicians into streets and shelters, or what he calls "home" visits, highlighting the critical need for physicians to develop relationships with their patients. Health care practitioners who use this mobile approach have found that the quality and continuity of care they can provide to homeless individuals is exceptional; however, this option is more time consuming, minimally funded, and little valued by those outside the homeless community (ibid.; Hwang et al., 2000). Under the current fee-for-service system, alternative service delivery is difficult, especially because so many homeless individuals lack health cards. If a patient does not have a health card, they have to pay out-of-pocket for health services; if they cannot do so, doctors end up providing the services for free. As such, this model actually provides financial disincentives for physicians (Hwang et al., 2000). Given these facts it comes as little surprise that physicians are disinclined to work outside of the traditional structures of health delivery. Those doctors who are willing to work with vulnerable people in alternative service models are often unable to do so for extended periods of time as they become overworked, underpaid, and emotionally exhausted. Clearly, the creation of, and support for, alternative remuneration for street health practitioners would greatly assist in lowering barriers to care for homeless young people.

The organization of health care delivery also requires attention if access is to be improved for homeless young women. Service providers who work with homeless and marginally housed women have emphasized the lack of coordination, as well as the physical distance, between services throughout Toronto that require women to travel from one end of the city to the other in order to meet their diverse needs (Sistering Toronto, 2002). Navigating the system, both physically and intellectually, is a daunting task, particularly for newcomers to the city. When dealing with intimate partner violence, for example, women must interact with several parts of the service system at once: justice, health, housing, and social services must be accessed individually and in various locations (Harris et al., 2001). Already dealing with the consequences of trauma, survivors of violence must then travel through a line of services that often comes to look like a game of broken telephone: the person at the first agency refers the woman to another agency that refers her to another and so on until she finds herself back at the beginning.

The lack of discharge planning is another matter of great concern to homeless young women and shelter staff alike. Traditional health care institutions, including most hospitals in Toronto, do not coordinate or communicate with the shelters into which still-ailing women are released. Even though shelter workers become the "family" these young people go "home" to, the workers are not informed about follow-up appointments, medications, or treatment plans (Sistering Toronto, 2002). Furthermore, many patients are now forced to leave the hospital before they are ready, due to a lack of funding, space, or resources at the hospital. Downloading care onto families and into the home is problematic enough for mainstream families who often lack the knowledge and time required to care for a sick family member, but for shelter staff it is nearly impossible as they, too, lack medical training and are working to their maximum capacity without taking on the responsibilities for a sick young person. As with the mainstream population, it is generally other women who shoulder the duties of care giving. As Erin and others explained, in their friendship circles the young women were the ones who gave up a day of panhandling or other work to care for a sick friend: "Oh god! Can you imagine a guy sitting there and making sure someone doesn't puke to death? Yeah, right. That's a girl job. Girls just care more about what happens to people so they wait around and do what they can, right?" Neither the street nor shelters are appropriate spaces for people who require care or for those who need rest, quiet, or reduced stress.

The way health care services are funded can act as both a barrier and a facilitator in homeless young women's access to care. Funding is lacking for programs that specifically target difficult-to-reach populations. Instead, hospitals – which, with only a handful of exceptions, are not attuned to the needs of diversely situated patients – receive the bulk of health care dollars (Daly et al., 2008). Again, the case of women dealing with domestic violence is a primary example worth repeating given how many women become homeless as the result of family or intimate partner abuse. Community-based shelters for abused women receive funding for counselling services (Sistering Toronto, 2002). This type of funding, however, is not made available to emergency hostels despite the fact that significant numbers of women fleeing violence find refuge in these locales. In addition, even if they have long and complex histories of abuse, women who are homeless but not recently abused are not able to access counselling and support services at these shelters (ibid.). Finding a place to stay at all requires a great deal of effort on the part of homeless young women. If they are not in the right place of refuge, the services available to them are limited. Moreover, the longer one is homeless and left without support, the more likely one is to experience re-victimization or develop more intense depressive feelings. Homeless people often view community health centres (CHCs) as the best places to seek care because services are co-located, focus tends to be on harm reduction, and OHIP cards are not required. In Toronto, however, several CHCs have reached their capacity and are unable to accept new admissions, in large part because they expend their budgets on caring for non-insured clients (Sistering Toronto, 2002). In 2002, the Ontario Ministry of Health and Long-Term Care (MoHLTC) had not funded any new CHCs in 10 years and 80 per cent of CHCs were not accepting new files (ibid.). In 2005, the MoHLTC created 22 new CHCs and 17 satellite CHCs to respond to the clear need for services of this kind (MoHLTC, 2008). As of 2011, a total of 73 CHCs serve approximately 357,000 people in 110 communities throughout Ontario (Glazier et al., 2012). While the situation of CHCs has improved there remains a great need to fund models of care outside of the traditional realm. Health buses – which travel around the city to provide health care to homeless and under-housed individuals in their own neighbourhoods – and other alternative models of care on the streets and in shelters, which young women indicate that they prefer, require increased funding and support.

As Dunn (2000) asserts, in terms of social policy, the value of ameliorating social inequalities exists in the fact that they persist both temporally and geographically. These inequalities are evinced in most causes of death, despite changes in the leading causes of mortality; they continue even in the face of universal medical coverage; and they are not linked just to those in the poor minority, but instead appear across all groups and classes. Hierarchy and access to power, no matter where one is positioned on the ladder, correspond with health status (Coburn, 2004; Wilkinson, 1996). For society's most vulnerable, health outcomes are poorest and access is the most fraught. Creating health and social policies that address these inequities requires solutions that are innovative, trans-disciplinary, culturally competent, well supported, and well staffed.

Facilitators

Depending on her social location, the priority care needs of a young woman may differ from those of other homeless youth – a new immigrant often requires different services than one born in Toronto, a heterosexual young woman has different health concerns than one who is LGB2TQ. The Toronto Teen Survey Report (Flicker, 2009) found that Aboriginal youth and youth living in shelters both report that drop-in services are a key priority; transgender youth value clinics that provide comprehensive services; immigrant youth wish to choose the gender of their providers; and newcomer youth need health care providers who speak their language. When an individual is a member of two or more of these groups, which is the case for many of the young women in this research, her needs compound and become more complex. In sharing their life stories and their opinions, the young women often engaged in what Hoffman and Coffey (2008) refer to as "talking back": a form of resistance in the process of subject formation that, although necessarily embedded in power relations, allows some room for personal agency. In most cases their reason for avoiding health services had little to do with clinic regulations, but rather with the desire to avoid the judgment and stigma that they viewed as a violation of their dignity (ibid.; Jacobson, 2009). In this case, the act of abstaining from, or opting out of, health care constituted the dignity work in which they were involved. Facilitators for young women, then, are those interactions that preserve and promote dignity by allowing agency and providing support. As Wesley-Esquimaux (2007) contends, "we want to protect against making people fit the symptom or disease from any other perspective than their own" (p. 63).

Youth in this study and others have said that the most useful and dignity-promoting health care services are those that account for the context of their lives (Ensign, 2004). In other words, cultural competency is a necessary component of accessing health care. Ensign and Panke (2002) define cultural competency as "a set of congruent behaviours, attitudes, and policies that come together in a system, agency, or among professionals to enable them to work effectively in cross-cultural situations" (p. 167). Culturally competent care, then, occurs when providers see their relationships with clients as dynamic – as an exchange rather than a monologue, in which the life story and experiences of the patient are valued and relied on to make informed diagnoses and provide appropriate treatment options. Importantly, culture does not solely refer to racial, linguistic, and cultural diversity, but also to the unique culture of homeless young people, who experience life differently than do housed youth or adults in general, as Erin pointed out: "[Doctors] don't have a clue. Like how many thousands of dollars does it cost to go to school to be a doctor. Lots of thousands, I bet. I'm living off ten dollars a day. Sometimes not even that much. And don't treat me like I'm stupid because I'm young. Age is just a number. And I bet I'm smarter than a lot of people with doctor school too." Culturally competent care requires health care providers to recognize youths' strengths and perseverance in the face of adversity and acknowledge the positive attributes of youth, rather than just those that are more negative or risky.

Working with homeless youth requires a lot of care: caring about the individual, caring about their ideas, and caring about the strength they exhibit just in being able to access services in the first place. Non-verbal cues, such as lowered eyes, crossed arms, or shaking hands, can sometimes provide as much information as asking questions and can also help to prevent misinterpretation on the part of the provider (Wesley-Esquimaux, 2007). Gathering the history of a patient should be seen as analogous to the hearing of a story, much the same as I have described the storytelling process and its effect in this research. Any patient discussing their life with a provider is telling a story situated in a particular time and a particular place. Culturally competent care requires that practitioners accept the story that a patient presents as the interpretation of his or her life as he or she sees it, not as a fiction to be interpreted by one who knows better, as Danika suggested: "They can definitely take more time to get some background on the person. You know, are you working? Where do you live? Who was your last health person? Rather than saying, 'OK, name, birthday, OK we'll see you.' Just get a better idea of who you are as a person and know first what you think about yourself before deciding who you are for you." As Wesley-Esquimaux (2007) asserts, this tendency to interpret and therefore create one's own representation of the patient is especially problematic when a health care practitioner is working with patients who come from a different cultural context. In various communities, such as Arielle's Congo or Savannah's reservation, illnesses may be understood as the result of different factors or treated with different approaches than in urban Canada. Wesley-Esquimaux avers that in delivering competent care, "we have to step through our own cultural orientation and be in theirs as much as possible" (p. 63). Providers must understand that in the case of homeless youth, a young person has risked damaging their self-esteem to seek that person's care. That a vulnerable young person has placed any trust in an adult authority figure should be viewed as an honour not to be taken lightly – helping youth to re-establish trust in adults is as important as treating physical ailments.

As Erin articulated, young women, not doctors, are the experts on their own lives and histories. Too often, physicians, both because of their training and socialization, believe their role is to tell patients what is wrong and how to fix it – the exchange of information is seen to flow unidirectionally (Ensign, 2001). Physicians must bear in mind that any interaction between a provider and her or his patient is a relationship. As such, listening to and validating patient experience, much as one would do in their personal relationships, is an integral part of that professional connection (ibid.). One of the young women's most commonly stated desires was to have continuity of care and be seen by the same doctor at the same clinic, as Danika said: "You know, it's nice to see the same person. They can follow your progress and they know you and you don't see someone new every time. Like, have a relationship, not just an appointment." Having a home base for health where young homeless women are treated with respect, feel safe, and can build trust in a provider is crucial to ensuring that homeless youth are treated holistically rather than as one ill body part at a time. The idea of having someone to talk with had great appeal for young people who felt that visiting a doctor involved being seen and not heard, spoken to but not spoken with. Radha explained her frustrations with one physician she visited: "He just didn't listen to me at all. He told me what I should be feeling instead of asking me how I was feeling. I just want to talk about general things that were happening to me." For health care providers, nurturing their relationships with their homeless clients is key to building the trust that will allow young women to feel safe in divulging information that they see as secret or shameful – the sort of information that can provide context for their mental and physical health problems.

In many locales youth-friendly programs based on integrated services and cultural competency have proved to be successful in better addressing the needs of youth and out-of-the-mainstream youth. Nonetheless, Barry and colleagues (2002) advocate upgrading youth-friendly services to the level of youth-centricity: creating services around the wishes of youth themselves, rather than adjusting typical or adult services to meet youth halfway. Understanding the ways in which adult policies, such as social assistance, disenfranchise young people is critical to crafting integrated services that will meet their health needs on a social as well as a physical level. Clearly, homeless youth require assistance as they transition from dependence to independence. Being thrown into adulthood with no signposts or support only exacerbates pre-existing health and social problems. Guides that offer clinicians tips to provide better care for homeless youth include recommendations such as not insisting that one know the young person's birth name, structuring clinic hours to suit the needs of youth, and providing youth with clear information on their rights as patients and their rights in regard to their patient files (Ammerman et al., 2004). For instance, all young women under 16 who go to an emergency room are required to provide their parents' or guardians' address and phone number in order for staff to contact an adult on the young person's behalf, as Raven found out: "It was really embarrassing. My mom doesn't know anything about me. The only thing is they had to call my mother, cuz I was 15." Certainly there are cases in which parents should be contacted; however, the lives of homeless youth often require particular consideration. Erin, for instance, refuses to visit a clinic for fear that when she indicates she is without parents, clinic staff will call child services; of all the worries she carries, being reported to the Children's Aid Society is by far the greatest. Ammerman and colleagues (2004) also note that there is often a mismatch between the biological age of homeless youth and their maturity levels. In this case, life course stage, again, becomes a more effective measure for how young homeless women should be treated. Young women know a great deal about how to treat themselves when they have a cold or flu or minor cuts and burns – most of the young women in this research indicated that self-care was preferable to being seen by a physician in cases where they could be treated without antibiotics or clinical interventions. Physicians, then, must take their patients' knowledge into account when diagnosing and planning treatment for young people as paternalism only further distances youth from the health care system. Facing the stereotypes of both homelessness and adolescence, the women I interviewed are seeking providers that see them as more than just young and homeless.

Homeless women across the spectrum of age, race, culture, sexuality, and ability report that traditional health services are not addressing their needs (Sistering Toronto, 2002). Most homeless young women first seek health advice from social services providers, like social workers or shelter staff, not from those trained in health care. In the case of street youth, health information is garnered from the Internet or from older, although still young, women. In some cases, street youth like Erin access services from providers such as Street Health, which offers mobile outreach workers who visit communities on a regular basis to provide medical care. Such services are non-judgmental and require no identification or proof of age. These outreach workers are present in the community on a regular basis and are familiar with the context of homeless people's lives. In other words, young women are seeking information from sources with which they have relationships of trust. Moreover, these sources can also provide confidentiality and information about other types of social services that homeless people can tap into.

Given complicated histories with psychiatric hospitals, prisons, and residential schools, another frequently suggested approach to service delivery was to locate health services outside of institutional settings. Health buses were seen as a good method of accessing care by those living in shelters and on the street; not requiring an appointment or having to leave places that were seen as safe were key to service access. As Erin suggested, women-only services are also an important factor in the organization and delivery of services, especially for those with histories of abuse or those who are employed in sex work: "It would be good if there was a bus just for women. Like a women-only place even could be good. I dunno. I don't want to stand around talking about my vag with all the perverts standing around me and listening." The young women often reminded me that even if streets seem dangerous, women often see them as safer than hospitals. Changing attitudes and physical locations are certainly key to creating more accessible health environments for young women; however, education is absolutely central to keep young people from repeating mistakes they may not even be aware they are making, to empower young people to make informed decisions, and to help them and their partners help each other (Gelberg et al., 2004). Education, social services, and health care that are co-located in the same non-institutional setting could go a long way to encouraging young women to be proactive about their health and welfare.

Resilience

The vast majority of the research literature written about homeless youth focuses on deficits and risk; however, there also exists a mounting body of literature demonstrating the great resilience and fortitude of young people living in exceptional circumstances. Mostly the domain of children's mental health researchers and clinicians, resilience approaches are shifting the focus away from psychopathology (Ungar, 2007). According to Gilgun (1999), resilience manifests itself in a young person's ability to cope with extreme or prolonged stress and is seen as an indicator of well-being and the ways in which it is successfully achieved. Possessing this ability to cope positively, resilient youth report lower levels of hopelessness and exhibit fewer suicidal tendencies (Kidd & Carroll, 2007; Rew et al., 2001). Many researchers have delimited sets of qualitative measures to determine young people's resiliency levels: future orientation, spirituality, adaptability, self-confidence, and hope (Kidd, 2003; Lindsey et al., 2000; Rew & Horner, 2003). Because of the nature of homeless young people's lives, they are more likely to rely on their own skills and tactics to survive or thrive in their situation, rather than depend on assistance from others. Kidd and Shahar (2008) refer to these skills as self-resources: intelligence, efficacy, and personal fortitude. Self-esteem, however, was found to relate to resiliency and to soften the blows of loneliness more than any other variable (ibid.). As Danika expressed, taking bad experiences and learning from them is crucial for positive development: "Oh yeah, I think those bad things that have happened have made me who I was. I just became like a really mature person. I went through some real hardships and that's kind of made me a person who wants successes and I am moving toward that."

Community-based research also indicates that spirituality is often a critical resource tapped by homeless women in times of hardship, although a notable disconnect exists between secular health and social services and the strength that many women muster as a result of their faith (Sistering Toronto, 2002). Arielle's faith in God is the foundation on which she builds her survival strategy: "I am the child of God. I pray a lot. I love praying. It's better to spend time praying than hanging around in the market. I love praying and I like people who pray." Arielle firmly believes that God delivered her from the war and willed her passage to Canada so that she could make a better life for herself. As a result, she is staunchly committed to overcoming her hardships and moving forward with her life. The same can be said of Danika, whose faith and belief in the power of prayer get her through difficult days and weeks. Both of these young women are committed to their faith and to school and have a solid future orientation. This personal strength is often unrecognized by secular providers who underestimate the power of belief to carry these young people forward.

Despite pages of clinical records reporting their ill health and poor mental state, all of the young women involved in this research expressed hope for the future and proposed solutions to the gaps in their service needs. Future plans were always stated with dedication and excitement. For Savannah, "My plan is to like finish school and get my license. Then go to university. Get a degree in hospitality. Or go to George Brown and do a course in like culinary arts. Eventually have a family." Notably, three of the eight young women aspired to become architects – professional women who build homes with solid foundations. These strengths and aspirations must be nurtured and developed as they provide positivity in lives that are often full of negative attitudes and discriminatory barriers.

Throughout the psychology-informed literature on resilience, there is a strong emphasis on individuals and on individual strengths and behaviours. As Martineau (1999) attests, "The resiliency discourse imposes prescribed norms of school success and social success upon underprivileged children identified as at-risk. The effect is that non-conforming individuals may be pathologized as non-resilient. Emphasis remains wholly on the individual and this, individualism is a dominant ideology embedded in the mainstream resiliency discourse" (p. 11). Pathologized on a regular basis, the last thing homeless young women need is another negative label that fails to account for their social circumstances. For this reason I use Ungar's (2007) definition of resilience in this work: "resilience is the outcome from negotiations between individuals and their environments, to maintain a self-definition as healthy" (p. 87). This way of thinking about resiliency recognizes that homeless youth do not exist in a bubble and that context matters. Where one is and has been is much more telling than individual personal traits that are apparently innate rather than structural. To this end, I have seen through the course of this research that all of these young women possess forms of resilience, and that those who are the most resilient, including Danika, Faith, and Raven, are also the ones who have the most social support. Resiliency is nurtured and created in supportive communities. Once again relations of power must be unveiled to show who gets to define and who is defined. For instance, Jean would probably be the least likely to be labelled resilient due to her struggles with concurrent mental illnesses; however, her displays of courage are perhaps all the more impressive because of, not in spite of, her situation: "Do you ever get that feeling in the subway? I get that all the time. It's annoying, but you just think, if I make it home I'll be OK. Yeah, I feel that all the time, but I always get to where I'm going without killing myself. It takes a lot of guts to do that." Although Jean is not the poster child for resilient behaviour, this, too, is an example of a remarkable form of resilience that requires coping with a multitude of factors to preserve one's health and safety.

Without genuinely listening to, and actually hearing, these young women's stories, we are neglecting their strengths and their everyday assets. Hearing stories provides researchers and clinicians a window to locate what Ungar (2007) has called "narratives of resilience": positive self-constructions that are concealed beneath survival behaviours and chaotic environments (p. 90). Young women are more than capable of defining their own strengths and weaknesses, and of attributing those characteristics to their social locations and life histories. Self-definition provides these women with the opportunity to create themselves and to recognize their capabilities rather than their shortcomings (Stephen, 2000). Situated in the midst of discourses imposed upon them from without, definitions from within provide forms of resistance against those that would seek to tell them who they are and what they are capable of. Despite feeling constantly measured against typical teenagers, the young women interviewed here realized that, as a result of living in exceptional circumstances, they possessed skills and perspectives uncommon to those their age. Erin said, "But I think we see through the bullshit a whole lot more. You have to when the real world is always kicking your ass." Recognizing the ways in which adversity has created positive skills in the midst of a challenging environment dovetails with Stephen's (2000) assertion that "notions of homelessness as a 'hopeless' state require modification to accommodate a conception amongst young women as being that of an alternative stage of transition for those whose previous circumstances, they believed, offered few prospects, security and hopes for the future" (p. 458). Unique skills and genuine hope for a better future – qualities that each of these young women possess – deserve more sustained attention. Their preference for the term "young women in exceptional circumstances" – as developed in the shelter and adopted by young women themselves – reveals the ways in which they desire to be seen and understood in the same ways they understand themselves: as normal women walking less traditional paths towards success.

Relationships

Resilience and positive health outcomes are integrally linked to young women's positive relationships, whether they are social, familial, or environmental supports. Detachment from school and family limits the social supports available to young people living independently, and research has shown that low parental socio-economic status is a key factor in the appearance of health disparities (Benoit et al., 2007). According to Dunn (2000), there are two ways in which social support influences health: social support may reduce perceived feelings of stress by calming the neuroendocrine system and making individuals less reactive, or the benefits of social support accrue because individuals are aware that others will be there to assist them in times of need, thereby elevating self-esteem and sense of control. The latter, more social form creates predictability and control because routine social interaction and positive role modelling create mirroring behaviours and teaches appropriate social roles (ibid.). Moreover, Kidd and Shahar (2008) found that secure models of attachment are correlated to higher levels of resilience because they enhance youths' abilities to gain further support through those pre-existing relationships and reinforce to young people that they are capable of forming secure attachments to trusted individuals.

Young homeless women's relationships with their parents and guardians are not straightforward; although the young women often speak of abuse and ill treatment in their homes, they also describe positive interactions with their parents (Benoit et al., 2007). For example, Raven explains that even after her mother kicked her out of the house, she still provided support by purchasing basic necessities: "Eventually she started helping me out every now and again, like near Christmas time I asked her, 'Well Mom, I'm cash short on groceries, can I get a few things?' 'Oh yeah, well what do you need?' 'Well I need butter, ketchup, toilet paper, preferably.' Little stuff like that. Staples and like condiments and stuff like that. Mostly stuff that's pretty good. She came through and she bought like a huge bag." Although Raven's relationship with her mother is strained, she knows that her mom can help her when she is in a serious bind or going without basic necessities. That said, there have also been times when Raven was street homeless and her mother failed to provide for her. Nonetheless, this example provides a more complex picture than those that are usually painted of the parents of homeless teens.

For the most part the young women in this study who were clearly in the process of creating stability or moving forward had an important, supportive woman in their life, whether she was a social worker or extended relative. Family characteristics, such as emotional ties to family or parental mental health, as well as environmental characteristics, such as ties to an adult or regular attendance at a particular program, have been shown to increase resiliency in young homeless people (Drapeau et al., 2000). In the case of the young women involved in this research, grandmothers were an important source of support for five of the eight participants, including Savannah: "[M]y grandma, around wintertime, my grandma took me to live with her for about a couple weeks, just to get away from [here]. And then, I was doing good. I was staying away from doing all that stuff. With my grandma, that's my home." In other instances, grandmothers were supportive of the young women's diverse sexual identities and had a hand in raising the girls at various points in their lives. In several cases tensions between mothers and grandmothers meant that the young women were forced to sever their connections to their grandmothers, but were able to re-form these bonds once they had left their parental home.

For those who are entirely removed from their families, non-family supports are critical to creating the bonds of trust necessary for accessing health and social services, and for forming stable attachments to mainstream society. Notably, for many young women enrolled in school, these attachments took the form of teachers. As Radha says, in terms of her health care, "my teachers have been my best support of anyone." Teachers take on significant responsibilities for their growing numbers of students, and Arielle, Faith, Raven, and Radha have depended on teachers for support outside of school curricula, in finding social workers and shelters, and even in dealing with unscrupulous landlords. Erin, who is unattached to both school and family, locates her social support in the form of trusted friends who helped her learn the ropes of living on the street: "Like, they showed me food banks and places around here that you could stay where you weren't like totally out in the public. And they were my friends, I guess. It's a lot like that Peter Pan movie in a way, these kids that don't have families and they just have each other." Connecting to particular peers and disengaging with others was seen to be critical to surviving on the street; those who were trying to move forward in positive ways or who had particular knowledge were seen as people to "hang on to." Choosing not to isolate herself and to associate with positive people displays strength of character, which may explain why Erin was the only street-involved youth who was able to attend all of the scheduled interviews to participate in this research. In examining the relationships that homeless young women value and create, it is evident that social role modelling and program integration have far-reaching consequences for how youth will fare over time and across the life course.

Conclusion

This chapter has relied on the empirical evidence provided by eight young women to draw a more comprehensive picture of the landscapes in which homeless young people attempt to navigate health and social services. These landscapes are fraught with steep hills and locked doors, but there are also key points of entry into spaces of care that need to be nurtured and improved upon. The complex health needs of young homeless women suffering from a spectrum of mental health issues and physical health concerns demonstrates the ways in which the fee-for-service model of patient care fails to account for the context of people's lives, privileging particular parts over the complete individual. In the case of homeless youth, creating coordinated, youth-centric services means developing innovative service delivery and funding models that pay attention to youth's own concerns and desires, while collaborating with health care providers to ensure that remuneration is commensurate with the amount of emotional and physical labour they are required to contribute. Caring for this population requires a shift away from traditional models of service delivery and towards creative thinking that takes health care out of clinical spaces and into streets and shelters.

In 1971, Julian Tudor Hart proposed what he called the "inverse care law," which stated that, "the availability of good medical care tends to vary inversely with the need of the population served. This inverse care law operates more completely where medical care is most exposed to market forces, and less so where such exposure is reduced" (p. 405). More than 40 years later, his hypothesis still stands. Moreover, as privatization encroaches on publicly provided care, we see that the gap between haves and have-nots is growing. Hart discusses the importance of providing medical care, but specifies that this care must be quality care – care that is equitable, not just accessible. Achieving this goal requires the creation of health and social policies that address inequality and encourage innovation and collaboration across ministries, sectors, and providers. These policies must also be supported by strong communities, which nurture resiliency. Breaking down barriers requires multi-level solutions that reflect the complexity of youth homelessness landscapes. By listening to their voices, we take one step further in emphasizing the equalizing potential of privileging caring in health care.

8 Living in a Material World: Challenges and Change

One critical part of the future is our children. The way we bring them up is an indication of how we feel about the future; and of course our attitudes to the young and ideas on how they should be educated reveal much about the present [...] Without a strong sense of how we want the future to be, the government tends to revert to a default position, thinking mainly about how children will fit into the economy.

(Davison, 2005)

Introduction

The final chapter of this story attempts to weave together the threads of the previous chapters in order to create a tapestry rather than a linear series of stitches. The issues faced by homeless young women are complex and heterogeneous; meeting their needs requires innovation in programming and commitment to equity-focused policies, while policy development itself requires the genuine input of the communities that programs are designed to serve. The goal of health equities-planning is to reduce differences in health status that "are avoidable, unfair and systematically related to social inequality and disadvantage" (Gardner, 2009, p. 18). Policy, then, requires a sustained focus on health outcomes, not health outputs. In other words, the effectiveness of a given policy or program should be evaluated by the quality of its results, not quantity. The role of neoliberalism in these measurements cannot be ignored and in this analysis I strive to illustrate the ways in which neoliberal ideology is undermining health equity and creating further disparities. I examine the areas of policy that were most frequently raised as barriers throughout young women's lives. Many of the policy recommendations discussed here are drawn from an interview question that asked the participants what they would tell government officials given a 10-minute audience. Others are the result of my analysis of their day-to-day struggles.

From this discussion, I will evaluate particular policies that have been influenced by neoliberalism and its tenets. While the preceding chapter covers policy barriers in health services, this chapter focuses on other social policy areas that are outside the umbrella of the Ministry of Health and Long-Term Care, in an attempt to make connections between social services and health and to advocate inter-ministerial collaboration in working on this complex issue. Systemic change does not come easily but, as this chapter argues, it begins with the process of democratic renewal that engages citizens in active roles in consultation. Although executing this task in an equitable way will require time, patience, and genuine engagement, integrating young service users into the decision-making process will result in more inclusive, equitable policies for all.

Given Toronto's recent election of Rob Ford, a right-wing, populist mayor, one doubts that the situation of homeless young people and, indeed, many others in need of social support and services, will see positive change in the next several years. Ford's budget intends to dramatically reduce spending on shelter beds for the homeless, proposing to cut 40,000 shelter beds throughout the city (City of Toronto, 2011). These cuts are unsurprising from a man who was recorded in a meeting of Council saying that he would prefer a "public lynching" to a public discussion of the construction of a homeless shelter in his ward (Mahoney, 2010).

In Canada, trends towards privatization of health care have already had disastrous effects on women's health. Wilkinson (1996), among others, postulates the income inequality hypothesis, which asserts that the degree of income inequality, rather than the wealth of a nation, is the most significant determinant of differences in health status. Degrees of hierarchy and social cohesion also determine the health of a society's population. Coburn (2004) has complicated this hypothesis by adding neoliberalism as a determinant in this equation: nation states that are social democratic in nature will perform better in health status than those that espouse neoliberal forms of government. Under the suppositions of the income inequality hypothesis, marginalized and poor people are likely to bear the brunt of neoliberal policies. When governments cut social spending and indulge private interests they assume that households and communities will internalize solutions: caregivers, community agencies, volunteers, and the poor are most likely to feel the negative impacts of these types of policies (Armstrong et al., 2001). As the previous chapters have illustrated, social policy in the multiple policy arenas that serve the needs of homeless youth often perpetuate the plight of young people by failing to recognize the roots of their complex situations. Our society tends to criminalize rather than care for youth, and poverty, housing insecurity, and histories of violence are neglected in favour of an out-of-sight, out-of-mind approach that blames the individual without regard to the larger social structure. Accountability and outcomes measurement are built into government-funded projects and institutions, but the accountability in question is to the funder rather than to the client. Quantitative measures of numbers served and how quickly cannot capture the qualitative nature of change and growth in young people's lives. We must adjust our conception of what counts as evidence of program success. Policies that inadvertently lead to social exclusion must be replaced by policies that create and nurture genuine democratic citizenship. Meeting this objective by creating public spaces for participation and meaningful dialogue among all members of society – young and old, rich and poor – is vital to vibrant civic activity. As the chapter will demonstrate, youth are carving out new spaces for citizenship even in the face of the neoliberal social policies that ostracize and exclude them.

Neoliberalism

As global capitalism becomes further entrenched, Western economies, including Canada's, are becoming more and more reliant on the service sector to provide jobs for citizens. These jobs are increasingly part-time and casual, and do not provide benefits and job security for those who have little choice but to accept what is on offer in an ever more competitive job market. This neoliberalized economic structure is increasing the gap between rich and poor as inequalities become starker and people struggle to pay higher rents and costs of living. In Canada, social entitlements, once thought to be the hallmark of Canadian identity and citizenship, have been destabilized and hollowed out by neoliberal values that promote self-sufficiency and economic competition, turning a blind eye to the need for a strong welfare state (Morrow et al., 2004). Cuts to public services and income supports have allowed the rich to grow richer as state policies cater to the interests of capital at the expense of secure union jobs, and programs and services that allow those in need to find the assistance necessary to achieve their potential. In short, equity has all but disappeared from the political agenda in the last 30 years. Varney and van Vliet (2008) have noted a strong correlation between increasing state privatization and decentralization and the growing reliance of individuals on community agencies and informal supports. Cuts in funding, fragmented services, policies that allow once-public jobs to be auctioned off to the highest private bidder, and reductions in costs have been termed "new poverty management" or "accumulation by dispossession" (DeVerteuil, 2003, p. 361; Harvey, 2005, p. 7). The privatization and commodification of public assets, alongside the hollowing out of the welfare state and an inequitable taxation structure, have resulted in a government that is overly influenced by corporate will and largely inattentive to the needs of the less fortunate.

The expectation of independent responsibility even in the face of illness and misfortune and an assumption of nuclear family membership, alongside a lack of attention to the social structures that create inequalities, combine to create a state in which citizenship is defined by wealth – the more one earns, the more one belongs. Perhaps more startling, however, is the rationale for this agenda, which is obscured behind rhetoric that is both appealing to, and socially inscribed in, people's day-to-day lives; the rhetoric of freedom, independence, and choice has allowed the more nefarious aspects of neoliberalism to go unchecked and unnoticed by many, even those who suffer its consequences on a daily basis (Curry-Stevens, 2006). People are now more dependent on themselves, on their families, and on services they can purchase through the market rather than their government. In the case of homeless young people who have neither family nor the means to attain privately rendered services, a clawed-back welfare state leaves them not only struggling, but believing their struggle is their own and exists as a result of their personal failings. Savannah demonstrates this thinking: "I dunno. Maybe if I tried harder at school or something things would be better. I always think of all the stuff I shoulda done different and maybe I wouldn't be in this place." As Baker (2005) asserts, "claims on the welfare state are made by individuals which further reinforces the idea that individuals are increasingly responsible for their lives under increasingly consumerist principles of citizenship" (p. 231). Those who promote consumerist values falsely inform citizens that success is readily available to all, providing one purchases the right products, maintains a certain lifestyle, and works hard. Moreover, these claims to equality based on personal merit exist across social positions, such as gender – a fact that is readily exemplified in the rampant commercial success of slogans like "girl power." Under this logic, oppression is not socially produced and reproduced but is attributable to one's own failure to seize opportunity. Danika articulates this logic well when she remarks, "Um, I don't see any barriers because I almost like force my own opportunities to happen. Like if I want something I have to go and get it." Principles of democracy quickly, and intentionally, become elided with individualism and market rule.

Regardless of claims that meritocracy erases social positions, the outcomes and effects of neoliberal agendas are highly gendered. Principles of economic individualism have encouraged women to enter the workforce while still expecting them to espouse conservative family values such as raising children and tending to family. With little to no subsidization for child care or caregiving, women are taking on double burdens in order to make ends meet, and they are doing so in a policy climate that takes little notice of their integral role in social reproduction. This is especially the case for lone parents and those who are precariously employed or who have partners who are precariously employed (Armstrong & Laxer, 2006). The unencumbered equality promised by neoliberal discourse successfully borrows its rhetoric from the liberal feminist movement, which sought to create workplace opportunities for women who had previously been excluded from certain segments of the labour market. In so doing, the focus shifted from collective interest to individual entitlement, whereby women are supposedly unfettered contenders in an unfettered market (Baker, 2005). As Bryson (2001) maintains, however, the co-option of liberal feminist discourse only serves to illustrate its limitations as the structure of gender relations, especially as manifested in social reproduction, are still not remedied today.

The most striking language borrowed from the feminist movement and implemented in favour of the neoliberal agenda is that of choice – another slippery concept that is viewed unproblematically by, and is indeed the supposed panacea of, neoliberalism. The notion of unfettered choice is attractive to those who believe that constraints are surmountable for those who are self-motivated enough to "choose" to overcome them. Of course, a concept like choice is also difficult to critique given that its opposite, choicelessness, so readily conjures images of restricted freedoms and lack of agency; however, the creation of false dichotomies such as these only assist the neoliberal agenda and provide ready weapons in fear-mongering campaigns. Moreover, after decades of fighting for women's right to choose their own paths in reproduction and employment, one does not wish to underemphasize the importance of choice. The problem, then, is not choice itself, but rather its context-free implementation, which fails to account for the many ways in which options are limited to particular groups of people and extended to others. This research has demonstrated the ways in which many of the conditions and circumstances of young people's lives are not created by their choosing, but by any number of outside constraints that limit and circumscribe choice. Choices are not made by individuals in isolation, but are integrally affected by the situations in which they find themselves: poverty, relationships, and social position all bear directly on one's ability to grow and prosper. Certainly these young women are more than capable of making decisions and are agentic in many facets of their lives; however, insofar as inequalities and marginalization are justified by the emphasis on the power of individuals to choose, the rhetoric of choice often obscures the larger processes that are at play in social exclusion. As Danika says, "I also think a lot of people have the idea that youth come here by choice. Not very many of us would choose this living situation if we had another option. When you have no money, choice looks a lot different." McRobbie (2004) refers to this internalized process as the "re-regulation" of women through choice, arguing that we must remain attentive to the ways in which our decisions are constrained, compelled, and complicated.

Lack of government spending on welfare and social programming, combined with high unemployment, an economic recession, and the privatization of jobs and services has created particularly precarious terrain for young people. The rhetoric of individualism encourages young people to achieve, especially through higher education and higher incomes. While many young people today remain financially reliant on their parents well into their twenties and live at home longer than previous generations, those who are pushed out or leave parental homes at an early age are placed at an enormous disadvantage, especially in a knowledge-based economy (Jeffrey & McDowell, 2004). Further, the public policy-making process of the post-war years has been replaced by an emphasis on corporate interest, creating a re-engineered system in which citizens' voices and concerns are eschewed in favour of economic competition, leaving young people with the decaying remains of a once stronger and more compassionate welfare state.

Notably, however, the young women involved in this research were quick to espouse individualism and condemn dependency – Jean, for instance, often referred to her and her peers as "leeches" or "burdens" – without realizing that the same neoliberal rhetoric that cut the services and funding they require to move forward legitimizes these internalizations. Attributing personal responsibility to social problems that are deeply rooted in systemic inequalities effectively privatizes the experiences of those young people who struggle and who find themselves on the homelessness spectrum.

Regardless of their socio-economic status, young women in exceptional circumstances are exposed to the rhetoric of choice and personal attainment through private means. As Baker (2005) asserts, "young women's experiences as neoliberal subjects expose the difficulties and tensions that are obscured by the seductive concepts of individual choice and personal responsibility and the promise of achievement and improved life" (p. 226). The seeming guarantee that independent initiative, hard work, and self-improvement will result in upward social mobility is central to the future-oriented narratives of those young women who are, for example, more likely to believe in the benefits of gaining part-time, temporary employment than they are to value the benefits of mental health services. In the same vein, most of the participants believed that the objectives of feminism had been met and that women had achieved equality. In most cases, youth was seen as the primary barrier to accessing housing, social assistance, and general personal advancement, but gender was seen as relatively unimportant. Faith said that being female was at the bottom of her list of concerns about equality, "cuz people don't discriminate against women as much as like way back. Now they've got other things to discriminate against, like being young." Each participant was able to identify ways in which gender created significant disadvantages and unique circumstances; however, these were attributed to individual behaviours rather than structural constraints, as demonstrated by Savannah's description of an interaction with her landlord: "He thought I was going to sleep with him for the rent. So next time I made sure that I wasn't wearing anything low cut or nothing." Savannah's impression was that gender was a disadvantage in certain one-on-one encounters, but was not a larger social or structural issue. As was the case in Baker's (2005) research, the young women involved in this project were keen to divorce themselves from claims of disadvantage due to race, class, or gender, preferring instead to rely on discourses of meritocracy that downplay the role of inherent inequalities and legitimize the actions of the privileged and powerful.

The mass adherence to the politics of personal responsibility also creates conditions under which empathy towards the poor and disenfranchised is diminished or altogether absent. The resultant social exclusion stemming from this type of apathy obscures relations of ruling, creating further constraints for those who lack freedom of choice. Under neoliberalism, many mainstream citizens often feel, at best, as though those who are on social assistance are well-treated by the state and, at worst, that social assistance recipients are abusing the system as they are too lazy to use their independent initiative to seek gainful employment (Baker, 2005). Welfare state concepts like shared vulnerability and collective responsibility are all but forgotten in neoliberal discourse that privileges the economic advancement of the individual over the betterment of society as a whole. As Green (2006) highlights, neoliberal policy discourse tends to talk about people who "fall into poverty" and the ways in which poverty is an object to be attacked or warred upon in and of itself, rather than the consequence of unjust social relations, further eclipsing the role of structural inequality while positioning poverty as a threat to the mainstream rather than to the health and well-being of those who experience it daily. The state has a role to play in ensuring the health and income status of those who are homeless; however, in recent years under neoliberal agendas, welfare reform measures have been some of the most harmful as governments have continued to cut all but the "most deserving" from the eligibility list (Gilmour & Martin, 2003). Under the Harper government the "most deserving," who receive extended benefits, are long-tenured workers with minimal past use of the system (Service Canada, 2009a). Redistributive factors are meant to have an equalizing effect by raising the incomes of those on the bottom through transfers and lowering the incomes of those at the top through taxation, but these measures are not applied inclusively. Moreover, the move towards workfare policy has attached deservingness of social assistance to labour market participation, which often means finding work in menial and poorly paying jobs. Those who do qualify for social assistance are subject to surveillance, and their homes, intimate partnerships, and spending habits are scrutinized (Green, 2006). Cutbacks to social services create double jeopardy for those who are without homes as the hollowing out of the welfare state also affects the capability of providers to do their jobs to the best of their abilities. Caseworkers who provide Ontario Works or Ontario

Disability Support Program dollars learn to be suspicious of client behaviour and follow protocol to the letter, allowing little, if any, room
for context specificity or individualized solutions (Hoffman & Coffey,
2008). Discourses of recipients' culpability for their own socio-economic
situations produce hostility and scepticism in the eyes of those who are
unable to see the ways in which people living in poverty become dependent on a system that provides only the bare minimum and which
often fails to provide essential services like mental health counselling, thus creating a cycle of reliance upon a flawed system. Moreover,
young people in exceptional circumstances are attuned to this hostility,
and, consequently, come to internalize these perceptions of homeless
people. In so doing, young people further individualize themselves in
order to separate their experience from those of others who are "abusing the system" or are "welfare bums." As McNaughton (2006) argues,
unequal access to scarce social resources and the individuals' desire to
dissociate themselves from a stigmatized group may serve to individualize their collective social issues and to legitimate the stereotypes perpetuated by neoliberal values. Having a marginalized insider verify the
prejudices of the mainstream only strengthens the neoliberal hold over
a weakened welfare state. Finding a delicate balance between critiquing
state policy and recognizing the power of those same policies to bring
about positive change becomes crucial to the project of strengthening,
improving, and rebuilding a welfare state that nurtures the potential
and broadens the possibilities of each of its citizens.

Social Policy

As has been demonstrated throughout this research, creating solutions
to youth homelessness must necessarily cover a broad spectrum of policy areas in order to be fully realized – health, community and social
services, housing, aboriginal affairs, child and youth services, education,
and correctional services must all play an integrated and integral role to
successfully create interventions to assist young people through prevention, protection, and transitions to stability. Researchers, policy-makers,
and practitioners alike must remember that progressive social policy has
the potential to create real and meaningful change, especially in the lives
of marginalized individuals who depend so heavily on those policies for
survival. That said, there is a strong impetus to tie social policy to economic incentive and work force participation. Take, for example, Martin
and Pearson (2005) on the benefits of "active social policies": "[W]e must

not forget that in doing so, active social policies not only help the poorest and the most disadvantaged in society. More and more productive workers mean healthier economies, and everyone gains from that" (p. 8). As Jenson (2008) notes, these ideas of the role of social policy assume that policy's primary function is less about ensuring the well-being of the disadvantaged and more about economic incentive. This is an argument to which mainstream tax-paying citizens can attach themselves: helping others helps yourself. However, these notions also reflect and bolster a strongly neoliberal agenda which fails to address the social relations that create poverty to begin with and perpetuates the conditions under which some grow rich while others remain poor.

The 1990s brought significant changes to the social policy context and the 1995 tabling of the *Budget Implementation Act* created some of the most pressing transformations of all when the federal government rescinded the Canada Assistance Plan (CAP) and introduced the Canada Health and Social Transfer (CHST). The CHST eliminated national standards for social assistance and replaced them with a combined block transfer for social assistance, health, and post-secondary education (Morrow et al., 2004). The far-reaching effects of the CHST have been detrimental for social services such as shelters, which became more vulnerable, less stable, and further reliant on per-diem funding (ibid.). The offloading of services onto provincial and municipal governments meant that those services that were once guaranteed began to disappear or downsize, creating gaps for homeless individuals as well as for women fleeing violence. Already underfunded community programs and volunteers were left to manage on shoestring budgets, attempting to provide the most with the least. Nonetheless the federal government defended its actions as integral to reducing the deficit and becoming more competitive in emerging global markets (ibid.). While provincial and municipal governments deal with cuts in funding, First Nations governments have even fewer resources. In 2006–07 the federal government provided a total of $6 billion to all First Nations and Aboriginal people to fund all services (Canadian Centre for Policy Alternatives, 2009). This figure includes services that non-Aboriginal people receive from all three levels of government: primary and secondary education, roads and infrastructure, and all other services provided by the federal government (ibid.). In that same fiscal year, Ottawa transferred $20.1 billion – or 8.5 cents of every tax dollar – to the provinces and territories for health care, while a remarkable 7 cents per dollar was funneled into the Department of National Defence (ibid.). Combined, these statistics expose the inequities that are created and actively maintained by policy that emphasizes the health of the military-industrial complex over the health of its citizens, especially those who depend on social welfare for their survival and reintegration into mainstream society. Given these budget decisions, in the context of years of racist social policy, it comes as no surprise that the Aboriginal community is over-represented in the homeless population or that the homeless population suffers from poor access to the health and social services that should be in place to protect them.

Youth

I'm saying the prime minister should have changes so that kids who are teenagers can be OK on their own. Kids my age have kids. Lots of them do. So how can you say they're not grown-ups when they're raising kids too. If you're old enough to have a baby, you're old enough to live on your own. We need help with that.

(Erin)

The politicization of childhood influences the social policy that affects the lives of young women in exceptional circumstances. This is especially true in what Leira and Saraceno (2008) identify as the "changing patterns of defamilialization and refamilialization of social care and their implications for patterns for social solidarity" (p. 357). Defamilialization connotes several factors at once, including young people leaving, being removed from, or pushed out of their family homes and the extension of childhood from a private family matter to the realm of public concern, particularly in light of child poverty within the family unit. Refamilialization, on the other hand, is occurring in social policies where so-called "family values" place the onus on families, and particularly mothers, to privately provide for themselves. Children and young people are discussed within policy discourse as future contributors to the economy rather than as active beings in their own right. Britain's statement in 2004 on social policy in regard to children provides a salient example of this "almost, but not quite" citizenship status: "Investment in children to ensure that they have opportunities and capabilities to contribute in positive ways throughout their lives is money well spent and it will reduce the cost of social failure" (as quoted in Jenson, 2008, p. 2). The problem here is not that this statement is untrue or that investment in children does not build a brighter future, but rather that children are viewed as an investment in the economy – as a means to an end, not as individuals in need of immediate support or, more importantly, as people who already represent the failure of the social safety net.

Student welfare – the assistance given to those between the ages of 16 to 18 – for example, is meant to ensure that young people are able to complete their schooling despite their disaffiliation with their families of origin; the funds, however, cannot be paid out until youth assign a trustee who can ensure that their money is being spent wisely (Mann et al., 2007). The clear message sent to young people by these policy restrictions is that even though they are living independently, they are as yet incapable of making decisions – although they will be capable of doing so in the coming year or two. Moreover, if a student welfare recipient fails to attend school on a regular basis, her support is revoked and she is ineligible to reapply to the Ontario Works program until she is 18 (Nichols, 2008). The failure to examine context specificity in these cases gives youth living independently one chance to get it right while navigating the largely unsigned path to accessing housing, social services, health care, and other basic necessities. The rigidity of policy allows no room for real-life obstacles, and, although people and circumstances change, the ways in which policy can be administered do not (ibid.). Likewise, at the federal level, supports for youth fall under the jurisdiction of the Youth Employment Strategy which, again, emphasizes young people's labour force participation. This is not to say that young people should not work, but rather to suggest that for many homeless young women, direct entry into the workforce is a flawed solution when maintaining employment depends so heavily on being healthy, housed, stable, and supported. Redirecting funds, or better yet, creating new long-term, stable funding for community initiatives that treat youth holistically rather than simply as future employees would go farther to actually beginning to eradicate inequities. As Klodawsky and colleagues (2006) assert, caring is an essential ingredient that must be added to policy-making in order to create continuity in supports that are integrative and sensitive to the heterogeneity of the population.

Housing

I went to 13 different foster homes and group homes and stuff. Then I moved into shelters. I think that's how I was supposed to do it. No one told me to do nothing else.

(Jean)

Homelessness by its very definition demands attention to housing and shelter policies, which are essential factors in facilitating life transitions out of precarious living situations and into lives of stability and independence. However, without due attention to other sectors and a more integrated service system, youth will be only marginally better off. For example, staff at youth shelters are constrained by policy that limits their access to information and their professional capabilities: probation and police officers, as well as Children's Aid Society (CAS) workers, have the right to demand information from shelter workers, but the same right is not extended reciprocally due to apparent privacy infringements (Nichols, 2008). When those who are working with youth on a daily basis and in an intimate setting are not extended the same privileges as those in law enforcement, problems emerge in terms of what constitutes care and support in the lives of young people who require, above all, social support from trusted individuals. Likewise, in order to lower the number of young people who find themselves living in shelters and on the streets, policies could be reworked to allow young people to remain in care beyond the age of 18 or to increase the levels of support, both financial and social, granted to youth as they make the transition from being in care to independence (Raising the Roof, 2009).

Criminalization

I know it's not right, but what else can I do to stay alive?

(Erin)

Law enforcement and criminal justice policies, too, act as significant barriers for homeless young people. The need to garner income to cover basic necessities often places youth in precarious forms of work, such as prostitution, drug trafficking, panhandling, or squeegeeing. Law enforcement officials hand out tickets to homeless youth for a range of petty crimes from loitering, to panning, to fare jumping on public transit – activities that, when more carefully examined, may be youths' only means of accessing the public spaces, basic income, and transportation services that the mainstream urban population takes for granted. Kulynych (2001) argues that when seen in this light youth are "treated as problems to be addressed, not persons to address" (p. 262). Discourses of risk cast homeless youth as objects rather than subjects, creating the sense that the public requires protection from their actions, rather than that youth require protection from the public. By this syllogism, streets are made unsafe by street youth, not for street youth, when, indeed, policies that criminalize the survival activities of young people effectively push them to the margins and underground where they are even less safe and even more vulnerable.

Harm reduction strategies that provide safe spaces and link hard-to-reach populations to supportive relationships and programs are often quashed by NIMBYism and public perceptions which refuse to accept that addiction counselling and safe sexual practices actually help to reduce criminal activity in communities. Harm reduction accepts young people as they are, realizing that even at a young age people carry a lot of baggage, and works on establishing ties with the services they need to begin creating trusting relationships and getting back on their feet (Raising the Roof, 2009).

Violence

> And because, they're ... most of us women, we're like, I'd say about 60 per cent of us women are in abusive relationships and we're scared. We can't just say, "I'm gonna leave you, stop." It's not easy. Some people think ... some people think it's just like a switch you can just switch off and on. It's not. There's like so many things you gotta do.
>
> (Savannah)

The feminist agendas of the past several decades have pushed intimate partner violence to the forefront of the social policy landscape. Once considered a private matter between families, domestic and intimate partner violence is now understood to fall within the purview of government and legal action. Those who experience sexual, physical, and emotional abuse have come to rely on services and supports provided through state funding as they attempt to rebuild their lives and move forward independently from those who have abused them. However, cuts in funding to social services and the downloading of services to underfunded community agencies as a result of the introduction of the CHST in 1995 has meant that many survivors of violence cannot access the supports they need. In 1996, research conducted with survivors of violence found that women reported social assistance cuts as the number one reason for remaining in or returning to an abusive household (Du Mont & Miller, 2000). Under fiscal policies that provide only the bare minimum, shelters become temporary reprieves rather than havens that allow women, and often their children, to rebuild.

Research has inarguably demonstrated that funding social programs for abused women is far more cost-effective than the legal expenses of persecuting perpetrators – including incarcerating them – or the health care expenses of those who are taken to emergency rooms or hospitalized from the injuries sustained at the hands of their abusers (Morrow et al., 2004). While it is unfortunate that the emphasis on cost-saving measures garners the most support for these programs, it appears to be the necessary angle to provide these young women with the supports they require. On a human level, however, our greatest concern should be the more than 500 Aboriginal women that have disappeared or been found murdered in Canada in the last 15 years – an atrocity that has prompted the United Nations to require that Canada report back on what is being done to address such a gross violation of human rights (Canadian Centre for Policy Alternatives, 2009). Eliminating violence against women requires a trans-disciplinary, multi-sectoral approach that recognizes the structural inequalities that perpetuate violence while also examining the ways in which categories of gender, race, class, sexuality, age, and ability intersect with poverty, colonialism, and social exclusion to create the conditions under which violence against women continues to be such a pressing issue (Cope & Darke, 2002; Morrow et al., 2004). This approach requires not just consultation, but meaningful discussion and contribution from women themselves and from members of the communities that are the most affected by, and least mentioned in, the policy discourse around violence: racialized women, lesbian women, trans people, women working in the sex industry, and women living with disabilities.

Accountability and Outcomes

> It would be nice if the government thought that it owed us something and not the other way around.
>
> (Radha)

There is an increasing emphasis within the policy realm on program accountability and outcomes measurement, especially for government-funded programs. While accountability and evaluation certainly have their place, questions about what is being measured and how, alongside understandings of to whom these programs are accountable, need to be examined. In the majority of cases these measures stem from business management models that are ultimately concerned with numbers and generalizations rather than focusing on the clients (Hoffman & Coffey, 2008). In measuring homelessness in this way, regardless of the objective of the agencies, those who are homeless become objects to be quantified rather than subjects to be engaged with (ibid.). Moreover, when programs must be evaluated in particular ways and according to particular metrics, there is little room for dynamic change within organizations – staff must adhere to the practices that are under measurement and are limited in their ability to respond in individualized ways. This is particularly complicated in complex systems that are affected by policy directives from multiple ministries and multiple levels of government; caregivers must often adapt on the spot to respond appropriately to the shifting needs of clients, but are frequently unable to do so because of program limitations that require accountability to funders rather than clients. Evidence and evaluation within social services organizations must be reconsidered. Considering multi-method approaches that combine local qualitative knowledge with quantitative objectives would at least allow for the voices of workers and clients to be incorporated into reviews and outcomes measurement.

If policy-makers' understandings of homelessness do not concur with the ways in which young people are experiencing homelessness, social policy will not be able to address the needs of this heterogeneous population (McNaughton, 2006). One-size-fits-all solutions based on accounting and supposedly objective, value-free measurements will not resolve the multitude of issues faced by young people in exceptional circumstances. Evaluation is a valuable and necessary practice and interventions that are well-researched, community-informed and policy-relevant require strong evidence that is based on the study of aspects of programs and services that actually make a difference, or fail to make a difference, in the lives of those they are in place to support. For example, monitoring the outcomes of the welfare of youth leaving care by merging data from the Children's Aid Society and youth shelters demonstrates the capabilities of this type of objective. Having this cross-sectoral data would allow for the improvement of existing programs because, if implemented and designed sensitively, it would tell the story of what happens to youth after they leave the child welfare system and what they need to make that transition smoother. Similarly, cross-ministerial government poverty reduction plans carry the potential to ensure that decision-makers at all levels develop equitable and sustainable objectives that are achievable by governments within the term of their mandate (Canadian Centre for Policy Alternatives, 2009). Accountability in social services should be to clients who benefit from continuity of care and from the continuity of the programs that work best for them. Outcomes measurement and evaluation should be used to improve access and to provide solid, context-specific evidence that informs policy decisions. The measures that work for business do not always work for dynamic and complex human relationships.

As much as governments justify cuts in funding as necessary to reduce deficits and rein in spending, these reductions are often driven by a neoliberal impulse to generate surpluses for big business. For example, in 2009, when banks and auto manufacturers revealed that their poor business practices had jeopardized the stability of the economy, it was those receiving large bonuses and private incentives, rather than homeowners foreclosing on properties, who were bailed out (Ritholtz, 2009). Increasingly, there are calls from Canada and from countries around the world to incorporate an ethics of care into the policy structure, demanding that more funds be earmarked for social programming and that those funds be directed in context-specific ways that reflect diverse youths' own wishes and needs rather that simply focusing on labour force training and participation (Klodawsky et al., 2006; Sevenhuijsen, 1998). Although state power is diminished by the goals of privatization, there must be a concerted effort to stop and reverse the hollowing out of the welfare state to make it more representative of genuine democratic practices that support and reflect the opinions of citizens. In 1999, Jim Flaherty, who was then Ontario's Attorney General, voiced his and his government's commitment to public safety when he introduced the bill that became *The Safe Streets Act*: "Our government believes that all people in Ontario have the right to drive on the roads, walk down the street, or go to public places without being or feeling intimidated. They must be able to carry out their daily activities without fear. When they are not able to do so, it is time for government to act." If all people in Ontario have the right to safety and security, homeless young people are once again being let down by those who have promised to protect them. Indeed, we see here another example of an ostensibly universal commitment being made only to high-income taxpayers at the expense of those struggling to get by.

Citizenship

Homelessness and Social Exclusion

The question of who constitutes "all people" in the above quotation becomes significant in light of the realities of a weakened welfare state and neoliberal understandings of citizenship's constitution by labour market participation. Increased surveillance and regulation of public places and spaces has meant that individuals who live outside the boundaries of these economic expectations, living on the peripheries and at no fixed address, face discrimination and are made the object of criminal discourse, effectively invalidating their rights as citizens (Desforges et al., 2005). These interactions between apparatuses of the state and individuals lead to exclusion or inclusion in political forums, insider or outsider status, and overall power to change or control the conditions under which one lives. Without the social and cultural capital necessary to participate in the political process – be it through voting, memberships on boards and advisory committees, or simply seeing oneself reflected in the makeup of legislative bodies – one may be a nominal citizen, but lack a true sense of belonging or group membership. Citizenship scholars, including Walker (2006), emphasize the value of understanding citizenship as a practice that is dynamic and evolving, rather than as a particular group of rights or responsibilities. In so doing, citizenship is understood as a project of engagement rather than as a status that is assumed by simplistic labels or even the ability to vote. Being and feeling like a citizen of a particular nation or community is about more than casting ballots, where one was born, or where one lives; it is about finding a voice that speaks to one's needs, that reflects one's values, and that creates a sense of belonging regardless of age, income, or situation.

For people who are homeless, social exclusion becomes a major barrier to accessing services, creating community, and developing the social ties necessary to feel connected to society. Social inclusion adherents focus not on individual-level behaviours, but rather on "those processes that lead to the marginalization and exclusion of individuals and social groups, including the influence of public, economic and social policies, programmes, institutions and actors," giving emphasis to social justice, seeking to reduce disparities and building a more equitable society (Labonte, 2004, p. 258; Reutter et al., 2005). Too many reports and papers speak to poverty solely in economic terms, failing to consider that poverty is not only about a lack of resources, but also about powerlessness and the barriers that accrue to those who are excluded from meaningful participation in the decisions that most affect their lives. Policy documents often neglect the impact of marginalization on citizenship and political participation – the absence of home, then, is felt not just locally but also globally in the lives of homeless individuals. Importantly, however, this disenfranchisement does not mean that those who are without homes are without agency or opinion. On the contrary, they intimately understand and negotiate their situations within those very power structures that render them social outsiders. Their active participation is crucial to create policy and social change that will support those living in non-mainstream environments, understanding that these environments are inhabited in specific ways by specific individuals and recognizing that these spaces and places, as well as experiences, are far-removed from the lives of most policymakers and decision-makers. Sistering Toronto (2002) strongly recommends that the health care system, and I would argue all ministries and social services organizations, increase the number of homeless women on boards, committees, and in public education initiatives, thereby increasing the likelihood that the voices of the marginalized are heard.

The creation of public spaces that reflect an inclusive and democratic understanding of "public" is also crucial to the task of social inclusion, especially for homeless youth. The monitoring of spaces by closed-circuit television systems, private security guards, and sprinkler systems effectively warns homeless people that they are not included, wanted, or welcome to participate in civic life; this surveillance forces homeless people into liminal spaces that further jeopardize their health and safety (Hodgetts et al., 2008). This very physical form of exclusion prohibits a sense of belonging to a city or community, creating further mistrust and alienation among those who should, by right, be able to participate in civil society (Mitchell, 2003). Spatial separation and social exclusion demonstrate the ways in which opportunities become even further limited for homeless young people. As Walker and Walker (1997) assert, social exclusion is "[t]he process of being shut-out, fully or partially, from any of the social, economic, political or cultural systems which determine the social integration of a person in society. [It] may, therefore, be seen as the denial (or non-realization) of the civil, political and social rights of citizenship" (p. 8). Homeless youth, despite being at the centre of much debate about public safety, are barred from the conversations and community forums that decide their fate, their ability to live safely, and the ways in which they are publicly perceived (Gaetz, 2004). Policies that understand homeless individuals as part of the community of local, provincial, and national citizens have a greater chance of actually impacting outcomes for housed and homeless people alike (ibid.). Creating communities that are inclusive and responsive to all requires intentionally engineering opportunities for the meaningful participation of those who face barriers to access.

Citizenship for (Homeless) Youth

While mainstream upper- and middle-class youth are leaving home later, being educated for longer periods of time, and depending on parents well into their twenties, marginalized youth have no such benefits, further polarizing them both in terms of income and opportunity (Klodawsky et al., 2006). While they are subject to these restrictions and funneled into low-paying, low-control jobs or experiencing a complete lack of employment, they are also further removed from the conduits for political participation – lack of leisure time, lack of education, and a surplus of other worries create poor conditions to seek out civic membership. Moreover, several studies have shown that young people in general are indifferent or cynical about mainstream politics and are, therefore, less likely to attach themselves to political parties (Wyness, 2006). Despite assumptions to the contrary, youth are not lazy or incompetent when it comes to political participation, but tend rather to affiliate themselves with single issues or campaigns that focus on one-time political action, such as protests or marches (ibid.). This is true of homeless youth as well. As Faith said, "In my opinion, I would vote if something they were saying caught my attention. If there was nothing that caught my attention, and there was nothing going to help me, then what's the point in voting?" Notably, however, Faith and Raven had participated in an Ontario Coalition Against Poverty rally because they understood the organization as one which could actually impact their current situation and which had reached out to invite their participation, taking the time to explain why the issues mattered. Bessant (2004) has argued that the problem with youth participation is not that young people are apathetic, but rather that they have few options for participation that they see as meaningful and effective. Faith pointed to a critical issue when she said that political campaigns do not speak to issues that catch her attention, signalling that young homeless people's issues are unaccounted for and that young people themselves are rarely listened to. Erin articulated this point when she suggested, "Maybe get those government people to talk to teenagers about this stuff, right? Like, wanna know what we want? Come outta the big office and ask me. Trust me, I'll tell you."

Edwards' (2007) study on youth political participation is particularly enlightening insofar as she explains that low electoral enrolment cannot be resolved simply by educating young people in civics courses. She certainly does not discount the importance of education; however, she suggests that education alone is not sufficient, especially for youth that face structural and social barriers. These same individuals are less likely to be enrolled in formal education to begin with, not to mention that those without fixed addresses have a difficult time with voter registration and enrolment. The resultant disenfranchisement of marginalized youth further demonstrates how state apparatuses perpetuate rather than ameliorate social exclusion among out-of-the-mainstream youth. Danika also spoke to the ways in which the very discourses that are meant to catalyse political discussion are constructed around an "us-versus-them" mentality that casts particular populations as homogenous groups that are seen as either undeserving or deserving of pity, which further entrenches stereotypes and objectification:

> And we feel marginalized. These impressions that [homeless youth] don't want to work, they just want to be on social assistance while the rest of the population has to support them. Or, you know, "These refugees, we have to help them assimilate. They're from a war-torn country, so we have to help them." Those refugees. These people who are on drugs. They squander resources. You know they're just categorizing people without knowing anything about them.

Given these stereotypes and generalizations, youth often felt more empowered by not participating in a system that views them in such a derogatory light. The general consensus of the young women who participated in this study was that parties on the right of the political spectrum vilified them while parties on the left of the spectrum presented them as undifferentiated, unagentic objects of pity. Some women felt that they would side with the left-leaning parties for fear of having no social support at all, but none felt at all empowered by this decision.

For those under the age of 18, citizenship becomes even more slippery and channels for participation are further limited. As has been detailed in this research, governments assume for the most part that in childhood the majority of the costs of dependence are managed privately by families and that children are to be socialized by their parents in order to become contributing members of society (Hearst, 2004). Children, then, figure into political discourse as future citizens, rather than as citizens in their own right. As Qvortup (2005) states the problem, "It is children's fate to be waiting – patiently waiting to become adults, to have their contributions recognized, to have a say in societal matters, to be part of the citizenry" (p. 5). What, then, would citizenship look like for those under the age of majority? In Neal's (2004) estimation, citizenship for children is defined as "an entitlement to recognition, respect and participation [...] These basic needs are as crucial to children's well-being as their needs for care and protection" (p. 1). Taken together, it becomes clear that children must be recognized as more than adults in chrysalis form – children, particularly those without familial supports, must be recognized as people with specialized interests, requiring particularized forms of representation. Erin's situation demonstrates the importance of recognizing young people as individuals in their own right: "Well in January I'll actually be 16, which is the greatest thing ever. Because then I can get welfare and live in a shelter if I want to. Which I don't. But it … means I'll be a quote-unquote 'actual adult' in the eyes of the law. It's so screwed up because I don't think I can be more adult than I am now, but I'm not 16, so I'm left to rot in the street." Notably, at 16, Erin's application for student welfare will still be subject to great scrutiny and she will be told to find an adult trustee to monitor her spending. Given Erin's mistrust of adults, this requirement may be enough to send her underground until her eighteenth birthday, by which time she will have been living on the streets for four years.

Ruxton (2005) makes the point that, under the assumptions of neoliberalism, some children are a more risky investment than others, which translates to increased spending on those with labour market potential and decreased spending on those who are more likely to require a greater amount of support in order to attain "productive" status as defined by work force participation. Funding training and schooling endeavours is a means to this end; however, funding mental health programs or harm reduction strategies is several steps removed from this objective and is, by this measure, less valuable. Homeless young people, despite facing multiple barriers that are usually no fault of their own, are thus less able to achieve their potential and the problem of how to increase the political participation of such young people in order to create a more equitable society remains. Children cannot be invested with the same citizenship rights as adults, nor can they be brushed off as people in the making (Lister, 2008). In fact their need to be recognized as citizens results from their being equal to, but different from, adults (Neal, 2004). As is clear from the narratives of the young women in this research, age does not necessarily reflect the maturity or competence of particular individuals. Despite being considered children under the law, they are already engaging in the affairs of adults: working, living independently, having sex, surviving alone, interacting with health and social services, and being profoundly affected by a political system in which they are unrepresented and little considered.

Children's right to self-determination is a much-debated topic in the discipline of childhood studies, but it is one that requires serious consideration in light of the ways in which children are currently represented under legal and social policy. Wyness (2006) differentiates between two types of children's rights: welfare rights and rights to self-determination. His distinction is interesting in several ways, not least his point that children themselves never actually possess welfare rights insofar as actions are always taken on a child's behalf – adults determine what is in the best interest of the child. Under this formulation, children's own thoughts on the matter are rarely if ever taken under consideration. Because she is under 16, Erin can be apprehended under the Child Welfare Act regardless of whether or not she wants to be, or will be pushed further and further away from mainstream supports. Self-determination rights do allow that children have the right to make certain decisions on their own behalf, even if they are contrary to what adults have defined as being in their best interest (ibid.). This is not to say that young children with limited ability to reason should be able to undermine their parents' decisions, but rather that those who are advancing through the life course at a faster than normal rate should have meaningful input and the ability to participate in the decisions that are affecting their present and future well-being. Wyness (2006) attempts to further explicate the argument for children's rights to moderate self-determination in asserting that rights of this kind "[open] up possibilities for hearing children, consulting and working with children and creating new spaces for children's contributions, even if this means children appealing to the 'natural' authority of adults" (p. 236). The central idea is to open up spaces in which children's voices can be heard so that young people can be empowered to choose the paths that are best for them, often with the support and guidance of adults who are not just hearing but listening.

Advocating for the increased participation of young people in the political process is advocating for the achievement of a truly democratic society in which the voices of the oppressed are as important as the voices of the powerful. Without the right to vote – which is a limited form of political engagement – young people require channels that allow them to become citizens in their own right. Lowering the voting age will do little to rectify the lack of representation of the young, and the young and impoverished in particular, in the decision-making process. The fact that young people continue to require the protection of the state or their families does not mean that they should not also be able to participate if they choose to and are given viable options to do so (Lister, 2008). Social inclusion requires more than "marginal insider" status (Jenson, 2008). Posting an advertisement requesting youth to participate on boards or even in research is not a sufficient means of including young marginalized people. True social inclusion of homeless young people involves community-based participatory practices and sensitivity to their unique needs and constraints. Homeless young people want to be respected and reflected in the policies that shape their lives. As Erin says, "I think the people who make [policy] are definitely not teenagers. Like, no self-respecting teenager would make these things up." Those adults who do create policy need to be attuned to the ways in which their decisions impact the lives of those for whom they are deciding. Remembering what it was like to be a child or a teenager is not sufficient, advisable, or possible. Asking young people about their lives and experiences is the only way to truly understand what is needed, wanted, and achievable.

A Web of Inclusion: The Potential of the Internet

Adolescents' interactions with and through the Internet have become a popular topic of discussion among adults and youth alike. With the rise of social networking sites such as Facebook, alongside email, instant messaging, blogs, webcams, and new cell phone technology, youth are plugged in and turned on. Although the dangers of these new technologies receive the most attention from the media and parents, the electronic environment creates new venues for identity creation, peer-group formation, play, and self-expression for this generation of youth (Ito et al., 2008). Focusing on the empowering elements of these new technologies allows for the consideration of the Internet as a potentially equalizing force in the lives of young people; however, if this equalizing potential is to be realized we must first acknowledge that those youth who are marginalized and have limited access to these technologies may also be severely disadvantaged and further marginalized by the unequal distribution of these resources. The inability to access computers or the Internet can indeed lead to an acute form of social exclusion, which has been termed "information poverty" or the "digital divide": the segregation of marginalized individuals from information that connects them to employment, services, and social networking opportunities (Facer & Furlong, 2001; Katz & Aspden, 1997; Koss, 2001). It is, therefore, a mistake to think of all young people as the beneficiaries of the digital revolution as those who are unable to take advantage of its benefits may feel unskilled or anxious about its applications or the expectation that they intuitively understand software and program components.

Katz (1996) has called today's youth the "digital generation of cyberkids," arguing that "children are at the epicenter of the information revolution, ground zero of the digital world" (p. 1). This notion of the cyberkid has captured the imagination of adults, disrupting the traditional power structure between adults and children, and unsettling the binary in ways not dissimilar to notions of the street kid. Online, young people are seemingly outside the control of adults, inhabiting spaces in private, public, and unfamiliar ways which pose a threat to the established order. Constructions of childhood are shaken by stories of young people hacking the databases of banks and private corporations, creating viruses, or, on a smaller scale, texting naked photos or becoming addicted to gaming instead of playing outside (Facer & Furlong, 2001). In these tensions, then, we locate the paradox and the potential of technologies that are at once threatening and groundbreaking. For young homeless individuals, however, the concern is more about access and less about hacking or software engineering. Closing the digital gap would allow marginalized individuals access to those resources that provide information about job searches and shelter addresses, as well as those that create opportunities for social inclusion. Policy-makers, researchers, and those who work on the frontlines with marginalized youth must recognize the need to develop programs and policies that equalize access and empower marginalized youth to connect with the broader, even globalized, publics created by the Internet (Mehra et al., 2004). As Arielle explained, "I like to go to the library. I like to use the computer, to type, and try to find things. I can do this in French, which is easier for me and I can find things in French or practice my English.

I can find things out about the war at home." Despite being thousands of miles away from everything familiar, the Internet provides Arielle with a sense of connection to her own language and to the country she grew up in. Her isolation and alienation are lessened by her sense of belonging to a larger, globalized community. In terms of social capital, the Internet needs to be viewed more as an opportunity-builder for youth. The knowledge community of Internet users provides users with a certain amount of expertise, which can be shared or employed to create new skills and environments in which to participate. Moreover, the anonymity provided by the Internet, while often considered a threat to young women in particular, also removes visible markers of socio-economic status and allows young homeless people to be whoever they wish to be without fear of stigmatization or exclusion. For young women in exceptional circumstances who often live in crowded spaces and under great surveillance, the Internet also provides a space in which they have autonomy and privacy, a chance to create online spaces that are theirs alone. While we cannot entirely dismiss claims of the dangers posed by the Internet and we must educate Internet users on safe practices, we must also not allow a desire to control youth spoil the potential that exists for online communities and resources to enhance the lives of those for whom the benefits of the Internet far outweigh the costs.

danah boyd (2008) researches the implications of new technologies, particularly social networking sites, for young people. Her work suggests that teenagers push for access to online communities or publics because it is in these spaces that they are able to create social lives and nurture new identities. As my research has shown, adults and authority figures who seek to create tangible separations between the worlds of adults and children often limit young people's access to physical public spaces. This form of isolation reminds young people of their marginalized position in society and provides an even starker reminder of the double marginality experienced by homeless youth who attempt to use these spaces to interact and to survive (ibid.). The Internet, however, presents new opportunities for youth to delimit their own public spaces and to create publics in the privacy of their own rooms, in libraries, at drop-in centres, or in shelters. In this vein, Mehra and colleagues (2004) advocate the adoption of a situated approach to technologies that is less concerned with the direct effects of technologies and more with the mutually constitutive relationships formed between people and technology: technology affects the way people perform activities and people affect the way that technology is employed. At different times and in different places, under the control of different users, the applications of technology will change – the ways in which young homeless women access the Internet, for example, is much different than the ways in which a university professor would do so. As a microcosm of the overall social order, the Internet can either reflect the current, exclusionary social order or become a more inclusive space where participation is different, but democratic.

The ways in which youth use the Internet vary greatly within the heterogeneous group. Youth who are interested in particular topics or games can find an online community of other people who are equally enthusiastic about that particular subject matter, decreasing the sense of social isolation that is often felt by those young people who are "different" (Ito et al., 2008). Here too the barriers between youth and adult are at least partially torn away as everyone's expertise is valued and the need to discuss age and authority does not exist in a faceless forum. As boyd (2008) asserts, schools are the usual publics that most young people use to form connections and to interact with peers. For homeless youth who have loose or no ties to school or who are marginalized in that environment, the online publics of the Internet offer new alternatives for building relationships and for interacting with those like them, thus validating their experiences and creating social support networks. Erin explained how her ability to access the Internet at public libraries – although it is important to note its conditional nature – allows her to keep in touch with other friends who are street involved and provides her with a productive use for her limited leisure time: "Some days though I'll go to a drop-in or to a library. You can sometimes, as long as you look not dirty or drunk or whatever, spend a lot of time in the library and they even have Internet and stuff there for free. So I can go online and check my emails and surf and go on MSN [instant messaging]." The primary focus for policy-makers, then, should be to ensure that marginalized individuals have access to these forms of support – which are enacted and initiated locally by young people themselves – through the creation of computer stations in the places most visited by marginalized youth: shelters, drop-in centres, health clinics, and libraries, or through free-usage Internet cafes. In fact, having access to computers and the Internet in such places might even encourage youth to interact with service providers in other ways.

The meaning of social capital is contentious and employed differently in different disciplines; however, most agree that although social capital is good for individuals, it should benefit society as whole. When one invests in a particular group, she is not the sole benefactor of that capital investment, but rather the benefits accrue to the group in which she has invested (Coleman, 1988). Putnam (1995), who is one of the most widely read theorists on social capital, believes that the Internet is a detrimental element in the destruction of social capital because online social contacts are virtual rather than tangible. In my research, however, it seems fairly clear that access to the Internet does, in fact, have the potential to increase social capital and social inclusion. Each of the young women involved in this research indicated that a favourite activity was surfing the Web for any number of reasons, from education, to seeking health information, to chatting on instant messaging platforms. Young women maintained social contacts online; as Danika explained, whether these were friends they met online or in person, keeping in contact through the Internet was listed as a crucial coping mechanism: "Yeah. Some of my friends have left the shelter and got into their own housing. It's cool that I can keep in touch with them because it reminds me that that is a possibility for me too. It keeps me in touch with the people who know what it's like, to be like, to do this." Young people who feel isolated or alone are more likely to have weaker ties in their everyday lives and the online communities to which they belong help compensate for that lack of connection (Subrahmanyam & Lin, 2007). The Internet is a space that is entirely public, open to all who have access, and does not belong to any person or group; people from all classes and categories are invited to share their opinions, write blogs, or give advice. In this sense the Internet breaks down the boundaries that homeless young women experience in their everyday lives, opening up a space for identity development and self-empowerment.

Three of the eight young women in this study spoke about their involvement with online games that served multiple functions in bettering their day-to-day lives. Although this particular example does not reflect the larger youth homeless population, it demonstrates one of the ways in which technology is creating connections and inclusivity for homeless young women. Using their shelter Personal Needs Allowance – which speaks to the value young women place on these forums – these young women found Internet cafes where they could log into multi-player online games. Williams (2006) is astute in arguing that the social study of online games is critical at this juncture because networked gaming forms entirely new ways of interacting, new forms of community, and new social phenomena that are becoming normative and evolving more quickly than they can be analysed or examined.

Games, he goes on to say, "do not exist in a social vacuum, and the reason to study them has as much to do with what's happening outside of games as it does with what's happening in them" (p. 14). This is true on a number of levels for the young homeless women that involve themselves in these sorts of games. Outside of the game, Faith and Raven experience social exclusion in a multitude of forms, from being ostracized at school to being stigmatized in shopping malls. However, within their online community of choice – the game of World of Warcraft, affectionately known to them as WoW – all players are equal, players pursue a common goal, and exchanges happen on the basis of reciprocity. As I participated in their day-to-day lives, I learned that WoW fulfilled a number of needs in their lives. Faith and Raven, as well as Jean, focused particularly on the guild aspect of the game – the aspect that created interdependency between players. In guilds, characters complete tasks in spaces in which they are not only connected to other players, but are also responsible for the maintenance of group welfare, performing what can undoubtedly be referred to as virtual caring responsibilities (Williams et al., 2006). The higher the level of in-group caring the more likely a guild is to gain prestige and advance through the ranks of the game, although remarkably this social element is not engineered into the game, but is rather an unintended consequence of meeting its objectives (ibid.). Williams and colleagues (ibid.) found that in their interviews with WoW players, many participants agreed that their game friends were "as real as any real-life friendship and described situations that could only be described as strong, bonding-type social support, such as having someone to listen to personal problems" (p. 352).

These new technologies have interesting applications in building self-esteem and social capital, especially among their more marginalized players. These games, for example, last months and years at a time, put players in constant contact with new people with whom they work collaboratively, and allow for chatting with friends outside the world of the game. As Raven says, "[Guild] members become friends because you're always trying to get ahead, but you can't do that unless the other people get ahead too. So you're always meeting people. Oh yeah, a whole jubilee of friends." Having left school and lacking any public space to hang out in without being lectured or accused of loitering, Raven and Faith find social ties, community, and human connection online.

Williams (2006) theorizes that, "the demand for human connection has been static but stymied by the real, it has moved into the virtual. As a result, social ties have moved online as part of a virtual community trend" (p. 15). Faith verified these social ties and reflected upon her citizenship in the WoW community:

> I've met some really great people on WoW and they don't care that I'm a lesbian. They don't care that I'm homeless. They say that in WoW everyone is cool and everyone has something special that only they can add. At guild when we make decisions everyone gets to say what they think is best. Then we talk about it and pick the best thing. It's a lot of choices. We don't get a lot of those, you know?

Given this powerful description of the ways in which she feels like she belongs to a community of equals, it is not much wonder that Faith and Raven spend all of their extra money on WoW. While many people would consider using taxpayer dollars to play computer games imprudent, we must consider what it is that young people are finding in video games that they are unable to find in real world society. If we are unable to provide homeless youth with meaningful connections and a sense of community in their offline lives, perhaps it is our failure to build an inclusive society and not video games that requires criticizing.

Contributions from Non-Marginalized Citizens

> If public space is not to be experienced as a private affair, but as a vibrant sphere in which people experience and learn how to participate in and shape public life, it must be shaped through an education that provides the decisive traits of courage, responsibility, and respect, all of which connect the fate of each individual to the fate of others, the planet, and global democracy.
>
> (Giroux, 2008, p. 612)

Most members of the general population have more access to opportunities, resources, and services than do those who are homeless, especially if those people are young and on their own. As Gaetz (2004) highlights, secure housing is perhaps the foremost consideration; however, social, political, and material status also bear heavily on one's likelihood to feel included and attain social capital. Likewise, most mainstream Canadians see themselves reflected in the constitution of government and boards, although that reflection is much more blurred for members of racialized communities and people of diverse sexualities. Mainstream Canadians are also more likely to be politically informed and to know who to go to in order to lobby for a particular issue or cause, which allows them to feel at least partially represented in the larger system. A meaningful interpretation of the concept of social solidarity should be rooted in the notion that "individuals have obligations to their fellow human beings which go beyond the negative freedom of respecting their liberty and extend into mutual assistance and support" (Baker, 2005). In other words, those who are fortunate enough to be securely housed, well-fed, healthy, and gainfully employed have an obligation to assist those who are less fortunate. Understanding homelessness not as an individual failure, but as a result of greater social barriers is perhaps the first step in getting the mainstream population involved in bettering the situation of homeless communities. Helping Canadians to debunk myths about homeless youth and the threat they represent, as well as to create an appreciation of the contexts from which these young people come and the ways in which they have been let down by social failures, requires public education and nuanced, balanced reporting from the mainstream media (Raising the Roof, 2009). Encouraging the media to engage with homeless individuals and to tell the personal stories of real people, rather than simply relying on facts and figures, would facilitate the re-imagining of the homelessness narrative as that of subjects rather than that of objects. In fact, a 2005 study by Reutter and colleagues demonstrated that people who understand poverty as the result of social circumstances are more likely to be in favour of social spending and social protection than are those who view poverty as the result of individual choices. Public policies are shaped around the will of the majority and their values, beliefs, and interests are key in the creation of programs and the funding of initiatives (ibid.). Using our collective agency to create change and deliver social justice allows us to fulfil our obligations to others and to nurture citizenship for the many as well as for the few.

9 A Journey of a Thousand Miles: One Conclusion

Recognizing diversity and meaningful participation in research requires much more than constructing "the homeless" as objects. Lacking the subjectivity that allows for understanding the heterogeneity of the population and the genuine inclusion of those living in poverty, research and policy only contribute to the misconceptions that further disenfranchise marginalized populations. The role of narrative-based research, then, is to make visible the interactions between the self-defined subject and the social structures that have come together in creating the complex situations which young homeless people navigate under a particular set of constraints. Focusing on individuals' perceptions of events over the life course, whether that spans 15 years or 80, allows for new ways of knowing outside of the quantifiable and the positivist. Stepping away from approaches that attribute the causality for homelessness to individual behaviours highlights the very real systematic and structural inequalities that create and sustain poverty, ill health, and social isolation. Narrative, then, brings faces to numbers, illuminating personal identities while creating a forum for local solutions as imagined by those who navigate the system every day and who know better than anyone what they need to overcome what often seem like insurmountable obstacles. The stories embedded in this research do not represent some sort of ultimate truth, but rather reveal that understandings of what constitutes evidence and expertise need to change in order to reflect the opinions of those who have traditionally been forced to remain silent. Homeless young people exist within a web of power relations in which they hold multiple subject positions and are influenced greatly by constructions of age, gender, race, ability, and sexuality, to name but a few (Hoffman & Coffey, 2008). The ability to overlay dominant narratives with counter-stories provides a conduit for the presentation of a richer, more complex account of the worlds of marginalized people (Roe, 1994). The contradictions that exist within and between the narratives of young women in exceptional circumstances provide critical insight into the complicated and dynamic worlds of young people, confirming that one-size-fits-all solutions are not really solutions at all. The power of narrative is to provide space for young people to explain themselves and to demonstrate agency and resistance – however limited – in the face of stigma and stereotypes that exclude them from the conversations of their lives.

Toronto serves as a point of congregation for many homeless young women who leave, whether by choice or by force, the rural or suburban places of their childhood in search of better lives, more services, and a new start. Each bridge, shelter, drop-in centre, and sidewalk serves as a point of reference on a large and sprawling map that must be navigated by young travellers who have rarely been treated well and who have a deep-seated mistrust of those who are meant to protect them. This journey, then, is fraught with challenges, has no restart button, and lacks a defined end point which marks a clear place to return to safety. The geography of youth homelessness is not a simple one and no two individuals experience the landscape in quite the same way; however, poverty, as we know, is now thought to be one of, if not the, major determinant of ill-health (Raphael, 2004a; Reutter et al., 2005). Poverty is not an item carried in some people's baggage and not in others, but a series of social relations in which each of us is involved. The backdrop of neoliberalism has created caverns and craters in the social fabric, cordoning off public spaces and criminalizing the people who rely on those spaces for sustenance and safety. Thus, it is up to those in the mainstream population, policy-makers, and health and social services providers to collaborate with young people and, indeed, all homeless people, to create worlds in which they can become empowered and better equipped – in which they can attain not just the feeling but also the reality of belonging. These worlds are public, inclusive, digital, and concrete. They are online and offline. They are equitable, just, and empowering. But most of all they are worlds in which each citizen is entitled to health, happiness, and the opportunity to realize their potential.

Describing the situations faced by homeless young women, however, is not enough. Shedding light on the issue is critical, but creating workable solutions is the only way to ameliorate what can only be described as injustice in a country that prides itself on the principles of social justice. Interventions research that keeps an eye on the problem, while focusing on the solution can help young homeless people recover to a good life characterized by happiness and fulfilment, achieving more than just the clinical conception of health as the absence of disease. Affordable housing strategies are one large piece of this solution: providing people with a door, a key, and a private space to perform the most basic of human functions is, obviously, a priority. Project teams in Toronto, Vancouver, and across Canada are beginning to implement an innovative housing first strategy, known as At Home/Chez Soi, for those who have mental health issues and sleep on the streets, whereby individuals are moved directly from streets to apartments with no provisos or paternalistic rules and regulations around drug use, service attachment, or behavioural modification (Mental Health Commission of Canada, 2009). While this intervention caters solely to a particular segment of the homeless community, it is a forward-thinking project that places the needs of homeless individuals first. Preliminary data out of the Vancouver site show that there has been a decrease in the number of people who are homeless, and At Home/Chez Soi is cited as one of the reasons for that decrease (Mental Health Commission of Canada, 2012). Rather than adhering to a model that starts at service attachment and leads on an upward continuum towards housing, this program recognizes that by the end of the upward continuum most people have fallen off the track. Of course, adequate incomes are also a necessary step in solving homelessness for all people, regardless of age or mental health status. Progressive taxation policies, sufficient social assistance, and a liveable minimum wage are all basic requirements in the search for solutions to homelessness. In terms of health, I have attempted here to demonstrate that positive health outcomes are not just about equal access to health care, but also about the creation of equal opportunities to access health care and supports in the first place. Even if homeless populations were as healthy as housed populations, homelessness would still be a critical social issue. Creating equitable access to the social determinants of health means eradicating poverty as much as it means visiting a general practitioner on a regular basis.

For young people, these interventions must be youth-centric, taking into account their unique situations and their unequal position in the legal and social structures that infantilize them at the expense of their health and well-being. Youth require a distinct plan of action that is tailored to their needs and that recognizes the ways in which the needs of young people differ from the needs of adults. For instance, policies must accept that some young people will not fare well in the traditional school system; creating programs that uniquely serve their needs, that consider their context, that are participatory in nature, and that are not necessarily attached to labour force participation, would go a long way to helping young people stay attached to the social assistance they desperately require. Treating youth with respect and dignity and as equals in social and health services provision is necessary to build supportive and trusting relationships with adults. While this objective may seem outside the job description of health care providers, anyone who is interested in doing their job well and in serving the community will recognize the long-term benefits of practicing social inclusion as much as they practice medicine or process applications. Realizing these goals can only happen through collaboration with youth, service providers, policy-makers and researchers. This type of community-based participatory research is slowly gaining a foothold in the research community and, hopefully, funding agencies and decision-makers will start to see that although partnering requires more resources and is more time-consuming than traditional work, it has the potential to create real, workable, and inclusive solutions. These policy changes are critical for youth, but they also signal the necessity of improving policies that affect all low-income people in the province: adequate income and shelter supports, socially inclusive health services, and meaningful participation in the policy that affects them most of all.

As Dana Brunanski argues, "programs and services are only part of the solution. We need societal change and community-level healing, in order to create a world where more of our youth can choose a good path" (as quoted in Saewyc et al., 2008). Her comments are directed specifically at the needs of Aboriginal youth, and it is important to note again that Aboriginal youth are especially vulnerable and in need of supports in this greater community of homeless youth. Positive societal change, however, would benefit all homeless young people if realized equitably and would benefit us all. Youth in particular must be assured that they can make mistakes without feeling like the rest of their adult lives are at stake. Living independently with few resources and social supports while attending school, eating nutritiously, dealing with poor mental health, paying bills, and developing friendships is a challenge and requires room to make mistakes. If, for example, a young woman living in a shelter is unable to attend school on regular basis while coping with all of her other competing needs, she should not be punished with the withdrawal of her social assistance payments. Regardless of social status, youth is a time in which we are learning, experimenting, and discovering who we are as individuals, and making and learning from our mistakes is a crucial element of that life course stage. Social change, then, involves recognizing that it is worth caring for the whole individual, not just the pieces that might create a productive worker. Catering to "diversity, complexity and particularity" is fundamental in caring for young people in exceptional circumstances (Klodawsky et al., 2006, p. 431).

T.S. Eliot (1943) once wrote, "We shall not cease from exploration/ And the end of all our exploring/ Will be to arrive where we started/ And know the place for the first time" (p. 46). What is research, if not exploration? My objective in this book has been to weave a story that is at once popular, academic, and theoretical, a story that can be understood by the many as well as by the few, a story that is at once mine and not mine. Ultimately, this is the story of eight young women, but it speaks to the stories of thousands of others like them. My hope is that having read this work, the reader can return to its opening paragraphs having learned something new or having garnered a different perspective on the needs of homeless young women and a desire to explore solutions. The truths about the stories imparted within this research could not have been told without those eight young women who told me that their stories needed to be heard. Hopefully through the course of this research you will, as I have, come to hear them and to better understand their truths, their fictions, and their lives.

Youth Resources List

Youth Without Shelter

Address: 6 Warrendale Court, Toronto, Ontario, M9V 1P9
Intersection: Kipling Ave. and Albion Rd.
Office phone: (416) 748-0110
Email: communications@yws.on.ca
Web address: www.yws.on.ca

Shout Clinic

No Ontario Health Insurance card is necessary.
Address: 168 Bathurst St., Toronto, Ontario, M5V 2R4
Intersection: Bathurst St. and Queen St.
Office phone: (416) 703-8482
Web address: www.ctchc.com

Eva's Initiatives

Address: 215 Spadina Ave., Suite 370, Toronto, Ontario, M5T 2C7
Intersection: Spadina Ave. and Dundas St. W
Office phone: (416) 977-4497
Email: info@evas.ca
Web address: www.evasinitiatives.com

Frontier College – Beat the Street

Address: 425 Adelaide St. W, Ste. 701, Toronto, Ontario, M5V 3C1
Intersection: Spadina Ave. and King St. W

Office phone: (416) 979-3361
Email: bts@bts.frontiercollege.ca
Web address: www.frontiercollege.ca/english/learn/programs_beat_
    the_street.html

Justice for Children and Youth

Address: 415 Yonge St., Suite 1203, Toronto, Ontario, M5B 2E7
Intersection: Yonge St. and Gerrard St. E
Office phone: (416) 920-1633
Email: info@jfcy.org
Web address: www.jfcy.org

Native Child and Family Services of Toronto

Address: 30 College St., Toronto, Ontario, M5G 1K2
Intersection: Yonge St. and College St.
Office phone: (416) 969-8510
Email: info@nativechild.org
Web address: www.nativechild.org

Oolagen Community Services

Address: 65 Wellesley St. E, Suite 500, Toronto, Ontario, M4Y 1G7
Intersection: Church St. and Wellesley St. E
Office phone: (416) 395-0660
Email: ocs@oolagen.org
Web address: www.oolagen.org

Sketch–Working Arts for Street-Involved and Homeless Youth

Address: 180 Sudbury St., Toronto, Ontario, M6J 3H2
Intersection: Queen St. W. and Dufferin St.
Office phone: (416) 516-1559
Email: info@sketch.ca
Web address: www.sketch.ca

Street Kids International

Address: 38 Camden St., Ste. 201, Toronto, Ontario, M5V 1V1

Intersection: Spadina Ave. and King St. W
Office phone: (416) 504-8994
Email: info@streetkids.org
Web address: www.streetkids.org

Turning Point Youth Services

Address: 95 Wellesley St. E, Toronto, Ontario, M4Y 2X9
Intersection: Jarvis St. and Wellesley St. E
Office phone: (416) 925-9250
Email: turningpoint@turningpoint.ca
Web address: www.turningpoint.ca

Evergreen Centre for Street Youth/Evergreen Health Centre

Address: 381 Yonge St., Toronto, Ontario, M5B 1S1
Intersection: Yonge St. and Gerrard St. E
Office phone: (416) 977-7259
Email: healthcentre@ysm.ca
Web address: www.ysm.ca

Youth Link

Address: 747 Warden Ave., Toronto, Ontario, M1L 4A8
Intersection: Eglinton Ave. E. and St. Clair Ave.
Office phone: (416) 967-1773
E-mail: info@youthlink.ca
Web Address: www.youthlink.ca

Rainbow Health Ontario

Address: Sherbourne Health Centre, 333 Sherbourne St., Toronto, Ontario, M5A 2S5
Intersection: Yonge St. and Gerrard St. E
Office phone: (416) 324-4168
Web address: www.rainbowhealthontario.ca

References

Acosta, O., & Toro, P.A. (2000, Jun). Let's ask the homeless people themselves: A needs assessment based on a probability sample of adults.
American Journal of Community Psychology, 28(3), 343–366. http://dx.doi.
org/10.1023/A:1005105421548 Medline:10945121

Adams, B.N., & Sydie, R.A. (2001). *Sociological Theory.* Thousand Oaks, CA:
Pine Forge Press.

Adelson, N. (2005). *The Embodiment of Inequity: Health Disparities in Aboriginal
Canada.*

Aldridge, R. (1996). *Youth Homelessness: National Report.* Brussels: UK
FEANTSA.

Ammerman, S.D., Ensign, J., Kirzner, R., Meininger, E.T., Tornabene, M., &
Warf, C.W. (2004). *Homeless Young AdultsAages 18–24: Examining Service
Delivery Adaptations.* Nashville: National Health Care for the Homeless
Council.

Andrews, M., Squire, C., & Tamboukou, M. (2008). Introduction. In M. Andrews, C. Squire, & M. Tamboukou (Eds.), *Doing Narrative Research* (pp. 1–
22). London: Sage.

Archard, D. (1993). *Children: Rights and Childhood.* London: Routledge.

Arendt, H. (1958). *The Human Condition.* Chicago: The University of Chicago
Press.

Arendt, H. (1965). *Eichmann in Jerusalem: A Report on the Banality of Evil.* New
York: Viking Press.

Arendt, H. (1994). In J. Kohn (Ed.), *Essays in Understanding 1930–1954.* New
York: Harcourt Brace.

Armstrong, P., Armstrong, H., & Coburn, D. (Eds.). (2001). *Unhealthy Times.*
Toronto: Oxford University Press.

Armstrong, P., & Laxer, K. (2006). Precarious Work, Privatization, and the Health Care Industry: The Case of Ancillary Workers. In L. Vosko (Ed.), *Precarious Employment: Understanding Labour Market Insecurity in Canada (pp. 115–40)*. Montreal: McGill Queen's Press.

Arnett, J. (2005). The developmental context of substance abuse in emerging adulthood. *Journal of Drug Issues, 35*(2), 235–254. http://dx.doi.org/10.1177/002204260503500202

Astbury, J. (1999). *Gender and Mental Health*. Working Paper Series No. 99, 8. Cambridge, MA: Harvard Center for Population and Development Studies.

Baker, J.L. (2005). *The Politics of Choice: Difficult Freedoms for Young Women in Late Modernity*. PhD dissertation, James Cook University, Queensland, Australia.

Bannerji, H. (2000). *The Dark Side of the Nation: Essays on Multiculturalism, Nationalism and Gender*. Toronto: Canadian Scholars' Press.

Barham, P., & Hayward, R. (1991). *From the Mental Patient to the Person*. New York: Routledge. http://dx.doi.org/10.4324/9780203207079

Barry, P.J., Ensign, J., & Lippek, S.H. (2002, Apr). Embracing street culture: Fitting health care into the lives of street youth. *Journal of Transcultural Nursing, 13*(2), 145–52. http://dx.doi.org/10.1177/104365960201300208 Medline:11951718

Beiser, M. (1988, Jan). Influences of time, ethnicity, and attachment on depression in Southeast Asian refugees. *American Journal of Psychiatry, 145*(1), 46–51. Medline:3337292

Beiser, M. (2005, Mar–Apr). The health of immigrants and refugees in Canada. *Canadian Journal of Public Health, 96*(Suppl 2), S30–S44. Medline:16078554

Beiser, M., Hou, F., Hyman, I., & Tousignant, M. (2002). Poverty and Mental Health Among Immigrant and Non-Immigrant Children. *American Journal of Public Health, 92*(2), 220–7. http://dx.doi.org/10.2105/AJPH.92.2.220 Medline:11818295

Benoit, C., Jansson, M., & Anderson, M. (2007). Understanding health disparities among female street youth. In B.J. Ross-Leadbeater & N. Way (Eds.), *Urban Girls Revisited: Building Strengths (pp. 321-37)*. New York: New York University Press.

Benoit, C., Jansson, M., Hallgrimsdotter, H., & Roth, E. (2008). Street youth's life-course transitions. In A. Leira & C. Saraceno (Eds.), *Childhood: Changing Contexts (pp. 325-56)*. Bingley: Emerald Group Publishing. http://dx.doi.org/10.1016/S0195-6310(07)00011-7

Bessant, J. (2004). Mixed messages: Youth participation and democratic practice. *Australian Journal of Political Science, 39*(2), 387–404. http://dx.doi.org/10.1080/1036114042000238573

Bessant, J. (2005). Principles for developing youth policy. *Policy Studies, 26*(1), 103–16. http://dx.doi.org/10.1080/01442870500042031

Besserer, S. (Ed.). (2001). *A Profile of Criminal Victimization: Results of the 1999 General Social Survey*. Ottawa: Statistics Canada.

Bezanson, K. & Luxton, M. (Eds.). (2006). *Social Reproduction: Feminist Political Economy Challenges Neo-Liberalism*. Montreal, Kingston: McGill-Queen's University Press.

Bhabha, H. (1994). *The Location of Culture*. London: Routledge.

Boenisch-Brednich, B. (2002). Migration and narration. *Folklore, 20–2*, 64–67.

Bondi, L., & Rose, D. (2003). Constructing gender, constructing the urban: A review of Anglo-American feminist urban geography. *Gender, Place and Culture, 10*(3), 229–45. http://dx.doi.org/10.1080/0966369032000114000

Bondi, L., & Burman, E. (2001). Women and mental health: A feminist review. *Feminist Review, 68*, 6–33. http://dx.doi.org/10.1080/01417780122133

Booth, R.E., & Zhang, Y.M. (1997, Nov 25). Conduct disorder and HIV risk behaviors among runaway and homeless adolescents. *Drug and Alcohol Dependence, 48*(2), 69–76. http://dx.doi.org/10.1016/S0376-8716(97)00113-0 Medline:9363405

boyd, d.m. (2008). *Taken Out of Context: American Teen Sociality in Networked Publics*. Berkeley, University of California, Berkeley.

Braveman, P. (2006). Health disparities and health equity: Concepts and measurement. *Annual Review of Public Health, 27*(1), 167–94. http://dx.doi.org/10.1146/annurev.publhealth.27.021405.102103 Medline:16533114

Brickman, B.J. (2004). 'Delicate' cutters: Gendered self-mutilation and attractive flesh in medical discourse. *Body & Society, 10*(4), 87–111. http://dx.doi.org/10.1177/1357034X04047857

Briere, J., & Gil, E. (1998, Oct). Self-mutilation in clinical and general population samples: Prevalence, correlates, and functions. *American Journal of Orthopsychiatry, 68*(4), 609–20. http://dx.doi.org/10.1037/h0080369 Medline:9809120

Brooks, A. (1997). *Postfeminisms: Feminism, Cultural Theory, and Cultural Forms*. New York: Routledge.

Bryant, T. (2004). Housing and health. In D. Raphael, (Ed.), *Social Determinants of Health: Canadian Perspectives* (pp. 217–32). Toronto: Canadian Scholars' Press.

Bryson, L. (2001). Motherhood and gender relations: Where to in the twenty-first century. *Just Policy, 24*, 12–23.

Budget Implementation Act, 1995, S.C. 1995, c. 17.

Burstow, B. (2005). Feminist antipsychiatry praxis – women and the movement(s): A Canadian perspective. In W. Chan, D. Chunn, & R.

Menzies (Eds.), *Women, Madness and the Law: A Feminist Reader* (pp. 245-58). London: Glasshouse.

Callaghan, M., Farha, L., & Porter, B. (2002). *Women and Housing in Canada: Barriers to Equality*. Toronto: Centre for Equality Rights in Accommodation.

Canada Health Act 1984 (U.K.), 1984, c.11.

Canadian Centre for Policy Alternatives. (2009). *Alternative Federal Budget 2009: Beyond the Crisis. A Budget for a Strong and Sustainable Future*. Ottawa: CCPA.

Canadian Charter of Rights and Freedoms, Part I of the Constitution Act, 1982 being Schedule B to the Canada Act 1982 (U.K.), 1982, c. 11.

Canadian Institutes of Health Research, Natural Sciences and Engineering Research Council of Canada, Social Sciences and Humanities Research Council of Canada (1998). *Tri-Council Policy Statement: Ethical Conduct for Research Involving Humans (with 2000, 2002 and 2005 amendments)*. Ottawa.

Canadian Task Force on Mental Health Issues Affecting Immigrants and Refugees. (1988). *Once the Door Has Been Opened: Mental Health Issues Affecting Immigrants and Refugees in Canada*. Ottawa: Ministry of Supply and Services Canada.

Caplan, P. (1987). *The Myth of Women's Masochism*. Toronto: New American Library of Canada.

Caplan, P. & Cosgrove, L. (Eds.). (2004). *Bias in Psychiatric Diagnosis*. New York: The Rowman & Littlefield Publishing Group.

Carlson, D., Martinez, A., Curtis, S., Coles, J., & Valenzuela, N. (1990). *Adrift in a Sea of Change: California's Public Libraries Struggle to Meet the Information Needs of Multicultural Communities*. Sacramento: California State Library Foundation, Center for Policy Development.

Chamberlayne, P., Bornat, J., & Wengraf, T. (Eds.). (2000). *The Turn to Biographical Methods in Social Science*. New York: Routledge.

Chouinard, V. (2006). On the dialectics of differencing: Disabled women, the state and housing issues. *Gender, Place and Culture, 13*(4), 401–17. http://dx.doi.org/10.1080/09663690600808528

Christopoulou, N., & de Leeuw, S. (2005). Children making media: Constructions of home and belonging. In J. Knorr (Ed.), *Childhood and Migration: From Experience to Agency* (pp. 113–36). Bielefeld: Transcript Verlag.

Christopoulou, N., & de Leeuw, S. (2008). Changing childhoods: Migrant children and the confrontation of uncertainty. In A. Leira & C. Saraceno (Eds.), *Childhood: Changing Contexts* (pp. 239–64). Bingley: Emerald Group Publishing. http://dx.doi.org/10.1016/S0195-6310(07)00008-7

City of Toronto. (2007). *What Housing First Means For People*. Toronto: City of Toronto.

City of Toronto. (2011). *City of Toronto 2011 Budget*. Toronto: City of Toronto.

Coburn, D. (2001). Health, health care and neo-liberalism. In P. Armstrong, H. Armstrong and D. Coburn (Eds.), *Unhealthy Times* (pp. 45–65). Toronto: Oxford University Press.

Coburn, D. (2004, Jan). Beyond the income inequality hypothesis: Class, neo-liberalism, and health inequalities. *Social Science & Medicine, 58*(1), 41–56. http://dx.doi.org/10.1016/S0277-9536(03)00159-X Medline:14572920

Cole, A.L. & Knowles, J.G. (Eds.). (2001). *Lives in Context: The Art of Life History Research*. New York: AltaMira.

Coleman, J.S. (1988). Social capital in the creation of human capital. *American Journal of Sociology, 94*, S95–S120. http://dx.doi.org/10.1086/228943

Connell, R.W. (1991). Live fast and die young: The construction of masculinity among young working class men on the fringes of the labour market. *Australian and New Zealand Journal of Sociology, 27*(2), 141–71. http://dx.doi.org/10.1177/144078339102700201

Connell, R.W. (2002). *Gender*. Cambridge: Polity.

Connell, R.W. (2005). *Masculinities*. Berkley: University of California Press.

Conrad, P., & Schneider, J.W. (1980). *Deviance and Medicalization: From Badness to Sickness*. Philadelphia: Temple UP.

Cope, A., & Darke, J. (2002). *Trans Inclusion Manual for Women's Organizing: A Report for the Trans/Women Dialogue Planning Committee and the Trans Alliance Project*. Vancouver, BC: The Trans/Women Dialogue Planning Committee and the Trans Alliance Project.

Courtwright, A.M. (2009, Feb). Justice, stigma, and the new epidemiology of health disparities. *Bioethics, 23*(2), 90–6. http://dx.doi.org/10.1111/j.1467-8519.2008.00717.x Medline:19531162

Crawley, S.L., & Broad, K.L. (2004). "Be your(real lesbian)self: Mobilizing sexual formula stories through personal (and political) storytelling. *Journal of Contemporary Ethnography, 33*(1), 39–71. http://dx.doi.org/10.1177/0891241603259810

CRISIS UK. (2007). *Homeless Women: Homelessness Careers, Homelessness Landscapes*. London: Crisis.

Crowe, C., & Hardill, K. (1993, Jan). Nursing research and political change: The street health report. *Canadian Nurse, 89*(1), 21–4. Medline:8425165

Cummins, S., Curtis, S., Diez-Roux, A.V., & Macintyre, S. (2007, Nov). Understanding and representing 'place' in health research: A relational approach. *Social Science & Medicine, 65*(9), 1825–38. http://dx.doi.org/10.1016/j.socscimed.2007.05.036 Medline:17706331

Curry-Stevens, A. (2006). Rooting social policy advocacy in social movements. *Canadian Review of Social Policy, 56*, 113–30.

Daly, T., Armstrong, P., Amstrong, H., Braedley, S., & Oliver, V. (2008). *Contradictions: Health Equity and Women's Health Services in Toronto*. Commissioned Report. Toronto: The Wellesley Institute.

Davis, A. (1981). *Women, Race and Class*. New York: Random House.

Davis, M. (1992). Fortress Los Angeles: The militarization of urban space. In M. Sorkin (Ed.), *Variations on a Theme Park: The New American City and the End of Public Space* (pp. 154–80). New York: Hill and Wang.

Davison, S. (2005). Opportunity knocks. *Soundings, 31*, 7–9.

Deber, R.B. (2003, Jan). Health care reform: Lessons from Canada. *American Journal of Public Health, 93*(1), 20–4. http://dx.doi.org/10.2105/AJPH.93.1.20 Medline:12511378

de Lauretis, T. (1984). *Alice Doesn't: Feminism, Semiotics and Cinema*. Bloomington: Indiana University Press.

Department of Finance Canada. (2009). Budget 2009: Canada's Economic Action Plan. Ottawa: Department of Finance Canada.

De Rosa, C.J., Montgomery, S.B., Kipke, M.D., Iverson, E., Ma, J.L., & Unger, J.B. (1999, Jun). Service utilization among homeless and runaway youth in Los Angeles, California: Rates and reasons. *Journal of Adolescent Health, 24*(6), 449–58. http://dx.doi.org/10.1016/S1054-139X(99)00040-3 Medline:10401975

DeSalvo, L.A. (1990). *Virginia Woolf: The Impact of Childhood Sexual Abuse on Her Life and Work*. New York: Ballantine Books.

DeSantis, L., Thomas, J.T., & Sinnett, K. (1999, Apr). Intergenerational concepts of adolescent sexuality: Implications for community-based reproductive health care with Haitian immigrants. *Public Health Nursing (Boston, Mass.), 16*(2), 102–13. http://dx.doi.org/10.1046/j.1525-1446.1999.00102.x Medline:10319660

Desforges, L., Jones, R., & Woods, M. (2005). New geographies of citizenship. *Citizenship Studies, 9*(5), 439–51. http://dx.doi.org/10.1080/13621020500301213

Despres, C. (1991). The meaning of home: Literature review and directions for future research and theoretical development. *Journal of Architectural and Planning Research, 8*(2), 96–115.

DeVerteuil, G. (2003). Homeless mobility, institutional settings, and the new poverty management. *Environment and Planning, 35*(2), 361–79. http://dx.doi.org/10.1068/a35205

Douglas, M. (1991). The idea of a home: A kind of space. *Social Research, 58*(1), 287–307.

Doyal, L. (2000, Sep). Gender equity in health: Debates and dilemmas. *Social Science & Medicine, 51*(6), 931–939. http://dx.doi.org/10.1016/S0277-9536(00)00072-1 Medline:10972436

Drapeau, S., Beaudoin, S., & Marcotte, R. (2000). The resilience of youth in care: Implications for intervention. *Intervention (Amstelveen, Netherlands)*, *112*, 37–43.

Dua, E., & Robertson, A. (1999). *Scratching the Surface: Canadian Anti-Racist Feminist Thought*. Toronto: Women's Press.

Du Mont, J., & Miller, K.L. (2000). Countless abused women: Homeless and inadequately housed. *Canadian Women's Studies*, *20*(3), 115–29.

Dunn, J. (2000). Housing and health inequalities: Review and prospects for research. *Housing Studies*, *15*(3), 341–66. http://dx.doi.org/10.1080/02673030050009221

Dunn, J.R., Schaub, P., & Ross, N.A. (2007). Unpacking income inequality and population health in North American Cities: The peculiar absence of geography. *Canadian Journal of Public Health*, *98*(S1), S10–S17.

Eberle Planning and Research. (2001). *Homelessness — Causes & Effects: The Relationship between Homelessness and the Health, Social Services and Criminal Justice Systems*. Vancouver: British Columbia Ministry of Social Development and Economic Security.

Edwards, K. (2007). From deficit to disenfranchisement: Reframing youth electoral participation. *Journal of Youth Studies*, *10*(5), 539–55. http://dx.doi.org/10.1080/13676260701600070

Ehrenreich, B., & English, D. (1978). *For Her Own Good: 150 Years of Experts' Advice to Women*. New York: Anchor Press, Doubleday.

Eisner, E.W. (1981). On the differences between scientific and artistic approaches to qualitative research. *Educational Researcher*, *10*(4), 5–9.

Eliot, T.S. (1943). *Four Quartets*. New York: Harcourt Brace Jovanovich Publishers.

Ellis, R.L. (2002). *A Feminist Qualitative Study of Self-Mutilation*. Masters Thesis, Virginia Polytechnic Institute and State University, VA.

Ensign, J. (2001, Apr–Jun). "Shut up and listen": Feminist health care with out-of-the-mainstream adolescent females. *Issues in Comprehensive Pediatric Nursing*, *24*(2), 71–84. http://dx.doi.org/10.1080/01460860119440 Medline:11817429

Ensign, J. (2004, Aug). Quality of health care: The views of homeless youth. *Health Services Research*, *39*(4 Pt 1), 695–708. http://dx.doi.org/10.1111/j.1475-6773.2004.00253.x Medline:15230923

Ensign, J., & Bell, M. (2004, Nov). Illness experiences of homeless youth. *Qualitative Health Research*, *14*(9), 1239–54. http://dx.doi.org/10.1177/1049732304268795 Medline:15448298

Ensign, J., & Panke, A. (2002, Jan). Barriers and bridges to care: Voices of homeless female adolescent youth in Seattle, Washington, USA. *Journal of Advanced Nursing, 37*(2), 166–72. http://dx.doi.org/10.1046/j.1365-2648.2002.02067.x Medline:11851784

Ensign, J., & Santelli, J. (1997, Aug). Shelter-based homeless youth: Health and access to care. *Archives of Pediatrics & Adolescent Medicine, 151*(8), 817–23. http://dx.doi.org/10.1001/archpedi.1997.02170450067011 Medline:9265885

Evans, R.G., Barer, M.L., & Marmor, T.R. (Eds.). (1994). *Why Are Some People Healthy and Others Not?* New York: Aldine DeGruyter.

Facer, K., & Furlong, R. (2001). Beyond the myth of the 'cyberkid': Young people at the margins of the information revolution. *Journal of Youth Studies, 4*(4), 451–69. http://dx.doi.org/10.1080/13676260120101905

Farmer, P. (2003). *Pathologies of Power.* Berkeley: University of California Press.

Favazza, A.R., & Conterio, K. (1989, Mar). Female habitual self-mutilators. *Acta Psychiatrica Scandinavica, 79*(3), 283–9. http://dx.doi.org/10.1111/j.1600-0447.1989.tb10259.x Medline:2711856

Featherstone, M. & Wernick, A. (Eds.). (1995). *Images of Aging: Cultural Representations of Later Life.* London: Routledge.

Finkelstein, M. (2005). *With No Direction Home.* Toronto: Thomson.

Finlay, L. (2000). Aching for Affection. *Chatelaine, 73,* 135–9.

Fitzpatrick, S. (2000). *Young Homeless People.* London: Macmillan. http://dx.doi.org/10.1057/9780230509931

Flicker, S. (2009). *Taking Action: Using Arts-Based Approaches to Developing Aboriginal Youth Leadership in HIV Prevention.* CIHR Grant.

Flicker, S., Flynn, S., Larkin, J., Travers, R., Guta, A., Pole, J., & Layne, C. (2009). *Sexpress: The Toronto Teen Survey Report.* Toronto: Planned Parenthood Toronto.

Fonow, M.M., & Cook, J.A. (1991). *Beyond Methodology: Feminist Scholarship as Lived Research.* Bloomington: Indiana University Press.

Foucault, M. (1973). *The Birth of the Clinic.* London: Routledge.

Foucault, M. (1975). *Discipline and Punish.* New York: Random House.

Foucault, M. (1978). *The History of Sexuality.* Trans. R. Hurley. New York: Penguin Books.

Foucault, M. (1980). *Power/Knowledge: Selected Interviews and Other Writings, 1972–1977.* Ed. C. Gordon. New York: Pantheon.

Fournier, L., & Mercier, C. (1996). *Sans Domicile Fixe.* Montréal: Méridien.

Frank, J.W. (1995). Why 'population health'? *Canadian Journal of Public Health, 86*(3), 162–4.

Frankford, B. (1997). Comment: Impact on health care adds to the social cost of homelessness, MDs say. *Canadian Medical Association Journal, 156*(4), 481–4. Medline:9054814

Gaetz, S. (2004). Safe streets for whom? Homeless youth, social exclusion, and criminal victimization. *Canadian Journal of Criminology and Criminal Justice, 46*(4), 423–56. http://dx.doi.org/10.3138/cjccj.46.4.423

Gaetz, S. (2009). *Backgrounder: Who Are Street Youth*. Toronto: The Homeless Hub. Retrieved from http://www.homelesshub.ca/Library/Who-are-Street-Youth-46117.aspx

Gaetz, S., O'Grady, B., & Vaillancourt, B. (1999). *Making Money: The Shout Clinic Report on Homeless Youth and Unemployment*. Toronto: Central Toronto Community Health Centres.

Galabuzi, G.E. (2004). Social Exclusion. In D. Raphael, (Ed.), *Social Determinants of Health: Canadian Perspectives* (pp. 235–52). Toronto: Canadian Scholars' Press.

Gardner, B. (2009). Social Determinants of Health Inequalities: Health Professions Appeal and Review, and Other Ontario Boards and Organizations [PowerPoint slides]. Retrieved from http://www.wellesleyinstitute.com/files/HealthEquityNow.pdf

Geber, G.M. (1997, Nov). Barriers to health care for street youth. *Journal of Adolescent Youth, 21*(5), 287–90. http://dx.doi.org/10.1016/S1054-139X(97)00111-0 Medline:9358291

Gelberg, L., Browner, C.H., Lejano, E., & Arangua, L. (2004). Access to women's health care: A qualitative study of barriers perceived by homeless women. *Women & Health, 40*(2), 87–100. http://dx.doi.org/10.1300/J013v40n02_06 Medline:15778140

George, R.M. (2005). Youth Leaving Care – How Do They Fare? Briefing Paper. Modernizing Income Security For Working Age Adults Project.

Giddens, A. (1991). *Modernity and Self-Identity: Self and Society in the Late Modern Age*. Cambridge: Polity Press.

Gilgun, J.F. (1999). Mapping resilience as process among adults with childhood adversities. In H.I. McCubbin, E.A. Thompson, A.I. Thompson & J.A. Futrell (Eds.), *The Dynamics of Resilient Families* (pp. 41–70). Thousand Oaks: Sage.

Gilmour, J., & Martin, D.L. (2003). *Head, Heart and Hand: Partnerships for Women's Health in Canadian Environments—Volumes I and II* (pp. 353–81). Ed. P. VanEsterik. Toronto: National Network for Environment and Women's Health.

Giroux, H.A. (2008). Beyond the biopolitics of disposability: Rethinking neoliberalism in the New Gilded Age. *Social Identities, 14*(5), 587–620. http://dx.doi.org/10.1080/13504630802343432

Glazier, R., Zagorski, B.M., & Rayner, J. (2012). Comparison of Primary Care Models in Ontario by Demographics, Case Mix and Emergency Department

Use, 2008/09 to 2009/10: ICES Investigative Report. Toronto: Institute of Clinical Evaluative Science.

Goering, P., Paduchak, D., & Durbin, J. (1990, Jul). Housing homeless women: A consumer preference study. *Hospital & Community Psychiatry, 41*(7), 790–4. Medline:2365314

Goldsack, L. (1999). A haven in a heartless home? Women and domestic violence. In T. Chapman & J. Hockey (Eds.), *Ideal Homes?: Social Change and Domestic Life* (pp. 121–32). London: Routledge.

Goodley, D., Lawthom, R., Clough, P., & Moore, M. (2004). *Researching Life Stories: Method, Theory and Analyses in a Biographical Age*. London: Routledge.

Graham, H. (2004). Social determinants and their unequal distribution: Clarifying policy understandings. *Milbank Quarterly, 82*(1), 101–24. http://dx.doi.org/10.1111/j.0887-378X.2004.00303.x Medline:15016245

Green, M. (2006). Representing poverty and attacking representations: Perspectives on poverty from social anthropology. *Journal of Development Studies, 42*(7), 1108–29. http://dx.doi.org/10.1080/00220380600884068

Greene, J.M., & Ringwalt, C.L. (1996). Youth and familial substance users' association with suicide attempts among runaway and homeless youth. *Journal of Substance Use and Misuse, 31*(8), 1041–58. http://dx.doi.org/10.3109/10826089609072286

Gubrium, J.F., & Holstein, J.A. (1998). Narrative practice and the coherence of personal stories. *Sociological Quarterly, 39*(1), 163–87. http://dx.doi.org/10.1111/j.1533-8525.1998.tb02354.x

Gubrium, J., & Holstein, J. (2009). *Analyzing Narrative Reality*. London: Sage.

Harding, S.G. (1991). *Whose Science? Whose Knowledge?: Thinking from Women's Lives*. New York: Cornell University Press.

Harris, R., Stickney, J., Grasley, C., Hutchinson, G., Greaves, L., & Boyd, T. (2001). Searching for help and information: Abused women speak out. *Library & Information Science Research, 23*(2), 123–41. http://dx.doi.org/10.1016/S0740-8188(01)00066-4

Harvey, D. (2005). *A Brief History of Neoliberalism*. New York: Oxford University Press.

Health Canada (2004). *Overview of the Canada Health Act*. Ottawa: Health Canada. Retrieved from: http://www.hc-sc.gc.ca/hcs-sss/medi-assur/cha-lcs/overview-apercu-eng.php.

Hearst, A. (2004). Recognizing the roots: Children's identity rights. In P.B. Pufall & R.P. Unsworth (Eds.), *Rethinking Childhood* (pp. 244–62). New Jersey: Rutgers.

Herman, J.L. (1997). *Trauma and Recovery: The Aftermath of Violence—From Domestic Violence to Political Terror*. New York, NY: Basic Books.

Hermer, J., & Mosher, J. (2002). Introduction. In J. Hermer & J. Mosher (Eds.), *Disorderly People: Law and the Politics of Exclusion in Ontario* (pp. 11–22). Halifax: Fernwood Publishing.

Hick, S. (2001). The political economy of war-affected children. *Annals of the American Academy of Political and Social Science, 575*(1), 106–21. http://dx.doi.org/10.1177/0002716201575001007

Hill-Collins, P. (1991). *Black Feminist Thought: Knowledge, Consciousness, and the Politics of Empowerment*. New York: Routledge.

Hill-Collins, P. (2000). *Black Feminist Thought: Knowledge, Consciousness, and the Politics of Empowerment* (Revised 10th Anniversary, 2nd Edition). New York: Routledge.

Hockey, J., & James, A. (2003). *Social Identities across the Life Course*. New York: Palgrave Macmillan.

Hodgetts, D., Stolte, O., Chamberlain, K., Radley, A., Nikora, L., Nabalarua, E., & Groot, S. (2008). A trip to the library: Homelessness and social inclusion. *Social & Cultural Geography, 9*(8), 933–53. http://dx.doi.org/10.1080/14649360802441432

Hoffman, L., & Coffey, B. (2008). Dignity and indignation: How people experiencing homelessness view services and providers. *Social Science Journal, 45*(2), 207–22. http://dx.doi.org/10.1016/j.soscij.2008.03.001

Hollands, R. (2001). (Re)presenting Canadian youth: Challenge or opportunity? In M. Gauthier & D. Pacom (Eds.), *Spotlight on Canadian Youth Research* (pp. 99–117). Quebec: University of Laval Press.

Horne, O., & Csipke, E. (2009, May). From feeling too little and too much, to feeling more and less? A nonparadoxical theory of the functions of self-harm. *Qualitative Health Research, 19*(5), 655–67. http://dx.doi.org/10.1177/1049732309334249 Medline:19380501

Homelessness Partnership Secretariat. (2012). *2011 Shelter Capacity Report*. Ottawa: Human Resources and Skills Development Canada.

hooks, b. (1984). *Feminist Theory from Margin to Center*. Cambridge: South End Press.

hooks, b. (2000). *Feminism is for Everybody: Passionate Politics*. Cambridge: South End Press.

Hou, F., Chen, J., & Statistics Canada -. (2003, Feb). Neighbourhood low income, income inequality and health in Toronto. *Health Reports, 14*(2), 21–34. Medline:12658862

Huey, L., & Berndt, E. (2008). 'You've gotta learn how to play the game': Homeless women's use of gender performance as a tool for preventing victimization. *Sociological Review, 56*(2), 177–94. http://dx.doi.org/10.1111/j.1467-954X.2008.00783.x

Hughes, J., & Dvorsky, G. (2008). Postgenderism: Beyond the gender binary. IEET White Paper 3. Hartford, CT: Institute for Ethics and Emerging Technologies. Retrieved December 20, 2010, from http://ieet.org/archive/IEET-03-PostGender.pdf

Hulchanski, D. (2007). *The Three Cities within Toronto: Income Polarization among Toronto's Neighbourhoods, 1970–2000*. Toronto: Centre for Urban and Community Studies.

Hunter, J., Getty, C., Kemsley, M., & Skelly, A. (1991). Barriers to providing health care to homeless persons: A survey of providers' perceptions. *Health Values and Achieving High Levels of Wellness, 15*(5), 3–11.

Hwang, S.W., Windrim, P.M., Svoboda, T.J., & Sullivan, W.F. (2000, Jul 25). Physician payment for the care of homeless people. *Canadian Medical Association Journal, 163*(2), 170–1. Medline:10934979

Ifekwunigwe, J.O. (1999). *Scattered Belongings: Cultural Paradoxes of "Race," Nation and Gender*. New York: Routledge.

Impett, E.A., & Tolman, D.L. (2006). Late adolescent girls' sexual experiences and sexual satisfaction. *Journal of Adolescent Research, 21*(6), 628–46. http://dx.doi.org/10.1177/0743558406293964

Ito, M., Horst, H., & Bittanti, M. boyd, d., Herr-Stephenson, B., Lange, P.G., Pascoe, C.J., & Robinson, L. (2008). *Living and Learning with New Media: Summary of Findings from the Digital Youth Project*. Berkeley: MacArthur.

Jackson, M. (Ed.). (1995). *At Home in the World*. Sydney: Harper Perennial.

Jackson, M. (2002). *Politics of Storytelling: Violence, Transgression and Intersubjectivity*. Copenhagen: Museum Tusculanum Press.

Jacobson, N. (2009). A taxonomy of dignity: a grounded theory study. *BMC International Health and Human Rights, 9*(1), 3. http://dx.doi.org/10.1186/1472-698X-9-3 Medline:19239684

James, A., & James, A. (2008). *Key Concepts in Childhood Studies*. London: Sage.

James, K. (2001). "I just gotta have my own space!": The bedroom as a leisure site for adolescent girls. *Journal of Leisure Research, 33*(1), 71–90.

Jeffrey, C., & McDowell, L. (2004). Youth in a comparative perspective: Global change, local lives. *Youth & Society, 36*(2), 131–42. http://dx.doi.org/10.1177/0044118X04268375

Jenks, C. (2005). *Childhood* (2nd ed.). New York: Routledge.

Jenson, J. (2008). Children, new social risks and policy change: A Lego future? In A. Leira & C. Saraceno (Eds.), *Childhood: Changing Contexts* (pp. 165–92). Bingley: Emerald Group Publishing. http://dx.doi.org/10.1016/S0195-6310(07)00012-9

Jones-Johnson, R., Rew, L., & Weylin-Sternglanz, R. (2006). The relationship between childhood sexual abuse and sexual health practices of homeless adolescents. *Adolescence, 49*(162), 222–34.

Justice For Children and Youth. (2006). Bill 52 – Learning to 18: Legislative Concerns and Qualified Praise. Toronto: Canadian Foundation for Children, Youth and the Law.

Katz, C. (1993). Growing girls/closing circles: Limits on the spaces of knowing in rural Sudan and U.S. Cities. In C. Katz & J. Monk (Eds.), *Full Circles: Geographies of Women Over the Life Course* (pp. 88–106). London: Routledge.

Katz, J. (1996). The rights of kids in the digital age. *Wired, 4*(120), 166-71.

Katz, J., & Aspden, P. (1997). Motivations for and barriers to Internet usage: Results of a national public opinion survey. *Internet Research, 7*(3), 170–88. http://dx.doi.org/10.1108/10662249710171814

Kearns, R.A., & Joseph, A.E. (1993, Sep). Space in its place: Developing the link in medical geography. *Social Science & Medicine, 37*(6), 711–17. http://dx.doi.org/10.1016/0277-9536(93)90364-A Medline:8211286

Kearns, R., & Smith, C.J. (1994). Housing, homelessness, and mental health: Mapping an agenda for geographical inquiry. *Professional Geographer, 46*(4), 418–24. http://dx.doi.org/10.1111/j.0033-0124.1994.00418.x

Kelly, K., & Caputo, T.C. (2001). Responding to youth at risk. In M. Gauthier & D. Pacom (Eds.), *Spotlight on Canadian Youth Research*. Quebec: University of Laval Press.

Kidd, S.A. (2003). Street youth: Coping and interventions. *Child & Adolescent Social Work Journal, 20*(4), 235–61. http://dx.doi.org/10.1023/A:1024552808179

Kidd, S.A. (2004). "The walls were closing in and we were trapped": A qualitative analysis of street youth suicide. *Youth & Society, 36*(1), 30–55. http://dx.doi.org/10.1177/0044118X03261435

Kidd, S.A. (2007). Youth homelessness and social stigma. *Journal of Youth and Adolescence, 36*(3), 291–9. http://dx.doi.org/10.1007/s10964-006-9100-3

Kidd, S.A., & Carroll, M.R. (2007, Apr). Coping and suicidality among homeless youth. *Journal of Adolescence, 30*(2), 283–96. http://dx.doi.org/10.1016/j.adolescence.2006.03.002 Medline:16631925

Kidd, S., & Shahar, G. (2008, Apr). Resilience in homeless youth: The key role of self-esteem. *American Journal of Orthopsychiatry, 78*(2), 163–72. http://dx.doi.org/10.1037/0002-9432.78.2.163 Medline:18954180

Kilbride, K.M., Anisef, P., Baichman-Anisef, E., & Khattar, R. (2000). *Between Two Worlds: The Experiences and Concerns of Immigrant Youth in Ontario*. Toronto: CERIS.

King, T. (2003). *The Truth About Stories*. Toronto: House of Anansi Press.

Klein, J.D., Woods, A.H., Wilson, K.M., Prospero, M., Greene, J., & Ringwalt, C. (2000, Nov). Homeless and runaway youths' access to health care. *Journal of Adolescent Health, 27*(5), 331–39. http://dx.doi.org/10.1016/S1054-139X(00)00146-4 Medline:11044705

Klodawsky, F. (2006). Landscapes on the margins: Gender and homelessness in Canada. *Gender, Place and Culture, 13*(4), 365–81. http://dx.doi.org/10.1080/09663690600808478

Klodawsky, F., Aubry, T., & Farrell, S. (2006). Care and the lives of homeless youth in neoliberal times in Canada. *Gender, Place and Culture, 13*(4), 419–36. http://dx.doi.org/10.1080/09663690600808577

Klonsky, E.D., Oltmanns, T.F., & Turkheimer, E. (2003, Aug). Deliberate self-harm in a nonclinical population: Prevalence and psychological correlates. *American Journal of Psychiatry, 160*(8), 1501–8. http://dx.doi.org/10.1176/appi.ajp.160.8.1501 Medline:12900314

Koskela, H. (1997). 'Bold walk and breakings': Women's spatial confidence versus fear of violence. *Gender, Place and Culture, 4*(3), 301–20. http://dx.doi.org/10.1080/09663699725369

Koss, F. (2001). Children falling Into the digital divide. *Journal of International Affairs, 55*(1), 75–90.

Kraus, D., Eberle, M., & Serge, L. (2001). *Environmental Scan on Youth Homelessness*. Ottawa: Canada Mortgage and Housing Corporation.

Kulynych, J. (2001). No playing in the public sphere: Democratic theory and the exclusion of children. *Social Theory and Practice, 27*(2), 231–64.

Labonte, R. (2004). Social inclusion/exclusion and health: Dancing the dialectic. In D. Raphael (Ed.), *Social Determinants of Health: Canadian Perspectives* (pp. 253–66). Toronto: Canadian Scholars' Press.

Langille, D. (2004). The Political determinants of health. In D. Raphael, (Ed.), *Social Determinants of Health: Canadian Perspectives* (pp. 283–96). Toronto: Canadian Scholars' Press.

Lansdown, G. (2006). International developments in children's participation: Lessons and challenges. In K. Tisdall, J. Davis, M. Hill, & A. Prout (Eds.), *Children, Young People and Social Inclusion*. Bristol: Policy Press.

Laye-Gindhu, A., & Schonert-Reichl, K.A. (2005). Nonsuicidal self-harm among community adolescents: Understanding the "whats" and "whys" of self-harm. *Journal of Youth and Adolescence, 34*(5), 447–57. http://dx.doi.org/10.1007/s10964-005-7262-z

Leadbeater, B.J., Blatt, S.J., & Quinlan, D.M. (1995). Gender-linked vulnerabilities to depressive symptoms, stress, and problem behaviours in adolescents. *Journal of Research on Adolescence, 5*(1), 1–29. http://dx.doi.org/10.1207/s15327795jra0501_1

Leavy, P.L. (2007). The practice of feminist oral history and focus group interviews. In S. Hesse-Biber & P. Leavy (Eds.), *Feminist Research Practice* (pp. 83–110). London: Sage. http://dx.doi.org/10.4135/9781412984270.n6

Lees, S. (1986). *Losing Out: Sexuality and Adolescent Girls.* London: Hutchinson.

Leira, A., & Saraceno, C. (2008). Childhood: Changing contexts. In A. Leira & C. Saraceno (Eds.), *Childhood: Changing Contexts* (pp. 1–26). Bingley: Emerald Group Publishing. http://dx.doi.org/10.1016/S0195-6310(07)00016-6

Lenz-Rashid, S. (2006). Employment experiences of homeless young adults: Are they different for youth with a history of foster care? *Children and Youth Services Review, 28*(3), 235–59. http://dx.doi.org/10.1016/j.childyouth.2005.03.006

Leslie, B., & Hare, F. (2000). Improving the outcomes for youth in transition from care. *Ontario Association of Children's Aid Societies Journal, 44*(3), 19–25.

Levenkron, S. (1998). *Cutting: Understanding and Overcoming Self-Mutilation.* New York: W. W. Norton and Company.

Lifson, A.R., & Halcón, L.L. (2001, Dec). Substance abuse and high-risk needle-related behaviors among homeless youth in Minneapolis: Implications for prevention. *Journal of Urban Health-Bulletin of the New York Academy of Medicine, 78*(4), 690–8. http://dx.doi.org/10.1093/jurban/78.4.690 Medline:11796815

Lindsey, E.W., Kurtz, D., Jarvis, S., Williams, N.R., & Nackerud, L. (2000). How runaways and homeless youth navigate troubled waters: Personal strengths and resources. *Child & Adolescent Social Work Journal, 17*(2), 115–40. http://dx.doi.org/10.1023/A:1007558323191

Link, B.G., & Phelan, J.C. (2001). Conceptualizing stigma. *Annual Review of Sociology, 27*(1), 363–85. http://dx.doi.org/10.1146/annurev.soc.27.1.363

Lister, R. (2008). Investing in children and childhood: A new welfare policy paradigm and its implications. In A. Leira & C. Saraceno (Eds.), *Childhood: Changing Contexts* (pp. 383–405). Bingley: Emerald Group Publishing. http://dx.doi.org/10.1016/S0195-6310(07)00013-0

Lorde, A. (1984). *Sister Outsider.* Berkeley: Crossing Press.

MacDonnell, S. (2007). *Losing Ground: The Persistent Growth of Family Poverty in Canada's Largest City.* Toronto: United Way of Greater Toronto.

Maher, L., Dunlap, E., Johnson, B., & Hamid, A. (1996). Gender, power and alternative living arrangements in the inner city crack culture. *Journal of Research in Crime and Delinquency, 33*(2), 181–2. http://dx.doi.org/10.1177/0022427896033002002

Mahoney, J. (2010, August 19). Rob Ford and a decade of controversy. *The Globe and Mail.* Retrieved from http://www.theglobeandmail.com/news/

national/toronto/rob-ford-and-a-decade-of-controversy/article1678543/
page2/

Mallett, S. (2004). Understanding home: A critical review of
the literature. *Sociological Review, 52*(1), 62–89. http://dx.doi.
org/10.1111/j.1467-954X.2004.00442.x

Mama, A. (1995). *Beyond the Masks: Race, Gender and Subjectivity*. London:
Routledge. http://dx.doi.org/10.4324/9780203405499

Mann, R.M., Senn, C.Y., Girard, A., & Ackbar, S. (2007). Community-based
interventions for at-risk youth in Ontario under Canada's Youth Criminal Justice Act: A case study of a "runaway" girl. *Canadian Journal of
Criminology and Criminal Justice, 49*(1), 37–74. http://dx.doi.org/10.3138/
K622-844X-3411-42H1

Mann-Feder, V., & White, T. (1999). Investing in termination: Intervening with
youth in the transition to independent living. *Journal of Child and Youth Care,
13*(1), 87–93.

Maracle, L. (1996). *I am Woman: A Native Perspective on Sociology and Feminism*.
Vancouver: Raincoast.

Martin, D. (2002). Demonizing youth, marketing fear: The new politics of
crime. In J. Hermer & J. Mosher (Ed.), *Disorderly People: Law and the Politics
of Exclusion in Ontario* (pp. 91–104). Halifax: Fernwood.

Martin, D.C. (1995). The choices of identity. *Social Identities, 1*(1), 5–20. http://
dx.doi.org/10.1080/13504630.1995.9959423

Martin, E. (1987). *The Woman in the Body*. Boston: Beacon Press.

Martin, J., & Pearson, M. (2005). Time to change: Toward an active social policy agenda. *OECD Observer, 248*.

Martineau, S. (1999). *Rewriting Resilience: A Critical Discourse Analysis of Childhood Resilience and the Politics of Teaching Resilience to "Kids at Risk."* PhD dissertation, University of British Columbia, Vancouver, BC.

May, J., Cloke, P., & Johnsen, S. (2007). Alternative cartographies of homelessness: Rendering visible British women's experiences of 'visible'
homelessness. *Gender, Place and Culture, 14*(2), 121–40. http://dx.doi.
org/10.1080/09663690701213677

Mayall, B. (1996). *Children, Health and Social Order*. Buckingham: Open University Press.

Maynard, M., & Purvis, J. (1994). *Researching Women's Lives from a Feminist Perspective*. London: Taylor and Francis.

McAdams, D.P., Josselson, R., & Lieblich, A. (Eds). (2006). *Identity and Story:
Creating Self in Narrative*. New York: American Psychological Association.
http://dx.doi.org/10.1037/11414-000

McCarthy, B., & Hagan, J. (1992). Surviving on the street: The experiences of homeless youth. *Journal of Adolescent Research, 7*(4), 412–30. http://dx.doi.org/10.1177/074355489274002

McClintock, A. (1995). *Imperial Leather: Race, Gender and Sexuality in the Colonial Context.* New York: Routledge.

McLane, J. (1996). The voice on the skin: Self-mutilation and Merleau-Ponty's theory of language. *Hypatia, 11*(4), 107–18. http://dx.doi.org/10.1111/j.1527-2001.1996.tb01038.x

McMurrich, W.B. (2008). *The School Law of Ontario.* Charleston: BiblioBazaar.

McNaughton, C. (2006). Agency, structure and biography: Charting transitions through homelessness in late modernity. *Auto/Biography, 14*(2), 134–52. http://dx.doi.org/10.1191/0967550706ab043oa

McRobbie, A. (2004). Post-feminism and popular culture. *Feminist Media Studies, 4*(3), 255–64. http://dx.doi.org/10.1080/1468077042000309937

Mehra, B., Merkel, C., & Bishop-Peterson, A. (2004). The internet for empowerment of minority and marginalized users. *New Media & Society, 6*(6), 781–802. http://dx.doi.org/10.1177/146144804047513

Mendelsohn, M. (2002). *Canadians' Thoughts on Their Health Care System: Preserving the Canadian Model through Innovation.* Saskatoon: Commission on the Future of Health Care in Canada.

Mental Health Commission of Canada. (2009). At Home/Chez Soi Research Demonstration Project in Toronto. Ottawa: Mental Health Commission of Canada.

Mental Health Commission of Canada. (2012). At Home/Chez Soi Early Findings Report. Ottawa: Mental Health Commission of Canada.

Miller, P., Donahue, P., Este, D., & Hofer, M. (2004, Winter). Experiences of being homeless or at risk of being homeless among Canadian youths. *Adolescence, 39*(156), 735–55. Medline:15727411

Mitchell, D. (2003). *The Right to the City: Social Justice and the Fight for Public Space.* New York: Guilford Press.

Modleski, T. (1991). *Feminism Without Women: Culture and Criticism in a "Postfeminist" Age.* New York: Routledge.

Mohanty, C. (2003). *Feminism Without Borders: Decolonizing Theory, Practicing Solidarity.* Durham: Duke UP.

Mohanty, C., Russo, A., & Torres, L. (Eds.). (1991). *Third World Women and the Politics of Feminism.* Bloomington: Indiana University Press.

Morrow, M., Hankivsky, O., & Varcoe, C. (2004). Women and violence: The effects of dismantling the welfare state. *Critical Social Policy, 24*(3), 358–84. http://dx.doi.org/10.1177/0261018304044364

Neal, R. (2004). *Voices: Women, Poverty and Homelessness in Canada*. Ottawa: National Anti-Poverty Organization.

Nehls, N. (2000, Jun). Recovering: A process of empowerment. *ANS. Advances in Nursing Science*, 22(4), 62–70. Medline:10852669

Nichols, N.E. (2008). Gimme shelter! Investigating the social service interface from the standpoint of youth. *Journal of Youth Studies*, 11(6), 685–99. http://dx.doi.org/10.1080/13676260802392957

Novac, S. (2006). *Family Violence and Homelessness: A Review of the Literature*. Ottawa: Public Health Agency of Canada.

Novac, S., Brown, J., & Bourbonnais, C. (1996). *No Room of Her Own: A Literature Review on Women and Homelessness*. Ottawa: CMHC.

Novac, S., Serge, L., Eberle, M., & Brown, J. (2002). *On Her Own: Young Women and Homelessness in Canada*. Ottawa: Status of Women Canada.

O'Connell, J.J. (2004, Apr 13). Dying in the shadows: The challenge of providing health care for homeless people. *Canadian Medical Association Journal*, 170(8), 1251–2. http://dx.doi.org/10.1503/cmaj.1040008 Medline:15078847

Office of Research Ethics, York University. (2010). Guidelines for Conducting Research with People who are Homeless. Toronto: York University.

O'Grady, B., & Gaetz, S. (2004). Homelessness, gender and subsistence: The case of Toronto street youth. *Journal of Youth Studies*, 7(4), 397–416. http://dx.doi.org/10.1080/1367626042000315194

Ontario Legislative Assembly. (1999). *Official Report of Debates (Hansard), 13 (2 November, 1999) at 32 (Hon. Jim Flaherty)*. Toronto: Government of Ontario.

Ontario Ministry of Community and Social Services. (2011). *Ontario Works Policy Directives*. Toronto: Government of Ontario.

Ontario Ministry of Health and Long-Term Care. (2008). *Results-Based Plan Briefing Book 2008–2009*. Toronto: Government of Ontario.

Ontario Ministry of Labour. (2010). *Your Guide to the Employment Standards Act, 2000*. Toronto: Government of Ontario.

Ostlin, P., George, A., & Sen, G. (2001). Gender, health and equity: The intersections. In T. Evans, M. Whitehead, F. Diderichsen, A. Bhuiya and M. Wirth (Eds.), *Challenging Inequities in Health: From Ethics to Action* (pp. 174–89). New York: Oxford University Press. http://dx.doi.org/10.1093/acprof:oso/9780195137408.003.0013

Pacom, D. (2001). Beyond positivism: A theoretical evaluation of the sociology of youth. In M. Gauthier & D. Pacom (Eds.), *Spotlight on Canadian Youth Research*. Quebec: University of Laval Press.

Pao, P.N. (1969, Aug). The syndrome of delicate self-cutting. *British Journal of Medical Psychology*, 42(3), 195–206. http://dx.doi.org/10.1111/j.2044-8341.1969.tb02071.x Medline:5808710

Passaro, J. (1996). *The Unequal Homeless: Men on the Streets, Women in Their Place*. New York: Routledge.

Patton, M.Q. (2002). *Qualitative Research and Evaluation Methods*. Thousand Oaks: Sage.

Peck, J. (2001). Neoliberalizing states: Thin policies/hard outcomes. *Progress in Human Geography, 25*(3), 445–55. http://dx.doi.org/10.1191/030913201680191772

Peressini, T. (2004). Canada's homeless: Patterns and policies. In J. Curtis, E. Grabb, & N. Guppy (Eds.), *Social Inequality in Canada: Patterns, Problems* (pp. 367–78). Toronto: PrenticeHall.

Personal Narratives Group. (1989). *Interpreting Women's Lives*. Bloomington: Indiana University Press.

Petchesky, R., & Judd, K. (1998). *Negotiating Reproductive Rights: Perspectives Across Countries and Cultures*. London: Zed.

Petchesky-Pollack, R. (2003). *Global Prescriptions: Gendering Health and Human Rights*. New York: Zed.

Phoenix, A. (2008). Analyzing narrative contexts. In M. Andrews, C. Squire, & M. Tamboukou (Eds.), *Doing Narrative Research* (pp. 64–77). London: Sage.

Pipher, M. (1994). *Reviving Ophelia: Saving the Selves of Adolescent Girls*. New York: Ballantine.

Plummer, K. (1995). *Telling Sexual Stories*. London: Routledge. http://dx.doi.org/10.4324/9780203425268

Poirier, M., Lussier, V., Letendre, R., Michaud, P., Morval, M., Gilbert, S. & Pelletier, A. (1999). *Relations et représentations interpersonnel es de jeunes adultes itinérants. Au-delà de la contrainte de la rupture, la contrainte des liens*. Montreal: Groupe de recherché sur l'itinérance des jeunes adultes.

Poland, B., Boutilier, M., Tobin, S., & Badgley, R. (2000). The policy context for community development practice in public health: a Canadian case study. *Journal of Public Health Policy, 21*(1), 5–19. http://dx.doi.org/10.2307/3343471 Medline:10754795

Porter, B. (2001). *ReWriting the Charter at 20 or Reading it Right: The Challenge of Poverty and Homelessness in Canada*. Plenary Presentation on the Canadian Charter of Rights and Freedoms. Canadian Bar Association.

Public Health Agency of Canada. (2006). *Street youth in Canada: Findings from the enhanced surveillance of Canadian street youth, 1999–2003*. Ottawa: Government of Canada.

Putnam, R. (1995). Bowling alone: America's declining social capital. *Journal of Democracy, 6*(1), 65–78. http://dx.doi.org/10.1353/jod.1995.0002

Qvortup, J. (Ed.). (2005). *Studies in Modern Childhood*. Basingstoke: Palgrave. http://dx.doi.org/10.1057/9780230504929

Raising the Roof. (2009). *Youth Homelessness in Canada: The Road to Solutions.* Toronto: Raising the Roof.

Ramazanoğlu, C., & Holland, J. (2002). *Feminist Methodology: Challenges and Choices.* London: Sage.

Raphael, D. (2004a). Introduction to the social determinants of health. In D. Raphael (Ed.), *Social Determinants of Health: Canadian Perspectives* (pp. 1–18). Toronto: Canadian Scholars' Press.

Raphael, D. (2004b). *Social Determinants of Health: Canadian Perspectives.* Toronto: Canadian Scholars' Press.

Raphael, D., & Curry Stevens, A. (2004). Addressing and surmounting the political and social barriers to health. In D. Raphael, (Ed.), *Social Determinants of Health: Canadian Perspectives* (pp. 345–60). Toronto: Canadian Scholars' Press.

Rapport, N. & Dawson, A. (Eds.). (1998). *Migrants of Identity: Perceptions of Home in a World of Movement.* Oxford: Berg Publishers.

Reid, S., Berman, H., & Forchuk, C. (2005, Oct-Dec). Living on the streets in Canada: A feminist narrative study of girls and young women. *Issues in Comprehensive Pediatric Nursing, 28*(4), 237–56. http://dx.doi.org/10.1080/01460860500396906 Medline:16356896

Reutter, L.I., Veenstra, G., Stewart, M.J., Raphael, D., Love, R., Makwarimba, E., & McMurray, S. (2005, Nov). Lay understandings of the effects of poverty: A Canadian perspective. *Health & Social Care in the Community, 13*(6), 514–30. http://dx.doi.org/10.1111/j.1365-2524.2005.00584.x Medline:16218981

Rew, L., Chambers, K.B., & Kulkarni, S. (2002a, May-Jun). Planning a sexual health promotion intervention with homeless adolescents. *Nursing Research, 51*(3), 168–74. http://dx.doi.org/10.1097/00006199-200205000-00005 Medline:12063415

Rew, L., Fouladi, R.T., & Yockey, R.D. (2002b). Sexual health practices of homeless youth. *Journal of Nursing Scholarship, 34*(2), 139–45. http://dx.doi.org/10.1111/j.1547-5069.2002.00139.x Medline:12078538

Rew, L., & Horner, S.D. (2003, Apr-Jun). Personal strengths of homeless adolescents living in a high-risk environment. *ANS. Advances in Nursing Science, 26*(2), 90–101. Medline:12795538

Rew, L., Taylor-Seehafer, M., Thomas, N.Y., & Yockey, R.D. (2001). Correlates of resilience in homeless adolescents. *Journal of Nursing Scholarship, 33*(1), 33–40. http://dx.doi.org/10.1111/j.1547-5069.2001.00033.x Medline:11253578

Rice, C. (2003). Becoming Women: Body Image, Identity and Difference in the Passage to Womanhood (Doctoral dissertation, York University, Toronto, 2003). AAT NQ99227.

Ritholtz, B. (2009). *Bailout Nation: How Greed and Easy Money Corrupted Wall Street and Shook the World Economy*. New York: John Wiley & Sons.

Robinson, C. (2002). "I think home is more than a building": Young home(less) people on the cusp of home, self and something. *Urban Policy and Research*, 20(1), 27–38. http://dx.doi.org/10.1080/08111140220131582

Robinson, C. (2003). Understanding Iterative Homelessness: The Case of People with Mental Disorders. Australian Housing and Urban Research Institute (AHURI) Final Report.

Robinson, C. (2005). Grieving home. *Social & Cultural Geography*, 6(1), 47–60. http://dx.doi.org/10.1080/14649360500200335964

Roe, E. (1994). *Narrative Policy Analysis: Theory and Practice*. Durham: Duke University Press.

Roschelle, A.R., & Kaufman, P. (2004). Fitting in and fighting back: Stigma management strategies among homeless kids. *Symbolic Interaction*, 27(1), 23–46. http://dx.doi.org/10.1525/si.2004.27.1.23

Roy, E., Haley, N., Leclerc, P., Sochanski, B., Boudreau, J.F., & Boivin, J.F. (2004, Aug 4). Mortality in a cohort of street youth in Montreal. *Journal of the American Medical Association*, 292(5), 569–74. http://dx.doi.org/10.1001/jama.292.5.569 Medline:15292082

Ruddick, S.M. (2002). Metamorphosis revisited: Restricting discourses of citizenship. In J. Hermer & J. Mosher (Eds.), *Disorderly People: Law and the Politics of Exclusion in Ontario*. Halifax: Fernwood.

Ruxton, S. (2005). *What About Us? Children's Rights in the European Union*. Brussels: European Children's Network.

Ryan, L., Leavey, G., Golden, A., Blizard, R., & King, M. (2006, Jun). Depression in Irish migrants living in London: Case-control study. *British Journal of Psychiatry*, 188(6), 560–6. http://dx.doi.org/10.1192/bjp.188.6.560 Medline:16738347

Saewyc, E., Bingham, B., Brunanski, D., Smith, A., Hunt, S., Northcott, M., & the McCreary Centre Society. (2008). *Moving Upstream: Aboriginal Marginalized and Street-Involved Youth in B.C.* Vancouver: McCreary Centre Society.

Safe Streets Act, S.O., 1999, c.8.

Saleebey, D. (Ed.). (1997). *The Strengths Perspective in Social work practice* (2nd ed.). London: Longman.

Salmon, P. (2008). Looking back on narrative research: An exchange. In M. Andrews, C. Squire, & M. Tamboukou (Eds.), *Doing Narrative Research* (pp. 79–85). London: Sage. http://dx.doi.org/10.4135/9780857024992.d6

Schafer, L.H. (2002). True survivors: East African refugee women. *Africa Today*, 49(2), 29–48. http://dx.doi.org/10.1353/at.2003.0015

Scheman, N. (1997). Queering the centre and centering the queer: Reflections on transsexuals and secular Jews. In D. Meyers (Ed.), *Feminists Rethink the Self* (pp. 123–62). Toronto: HarperCollins.

Schoppmann, S., Schröck, R., Schnepp, W., & Büscher, A. (2007, Sep). 'Then I just showed her my arms . . .' Bodily sensations in moments of alienation related to self-injurious behaviour. A hermeneutic phenomenological study. *Journal of Psychiatric and Mental Health Nursing, 14*(6), 587–97. http://dx.doi. org/10.1111/j.1365-2850.2007.01150.x Medline:17718732

Scott, S., Jackson, S., & Backett-Milburn, K. (1998). Swings and round-abouts: Risk anxiety and the everyday worlds of children. *Sociology, 32*(4), 689–91. http://dx.doi.org/10.1177/0038038598032004004

Sealy, P., & Whitehead, P.C. (2006). The impact of deinstitutionalizing psychiatric services on the accessing of mental health services by people with higher levels of psychological distress. *Canadian Journal of Community Mental Health, 25*(1), 1–15.

Serge, L., Eberle, M., Goldberg, M., Sullivan, S., & Dudding, P. (2002). *Pilot Study: The Child Welfare System and Homelessness among Canadian Youth.* Ottawa: National Secretariat on Homelessness.

Service Canada (2009a, 02 April). *The Extended Duration of Employment Insurance (EI) Regular Benefits.* Retrieved December 28, 2009, from http://www. servicecanada.gc.ca/eng/ei/information/extended_duration.shtml

Service Canada (2009b, 21 December). *Employment Insurance (EI) and Regular Benefits.* Retrieved December 28, 2009, from http://web.viu.ca/library/researchskills/citesources.htm#Govt%20Publ.

Sevenhuijsen, S. (1998). *Citizenship and the Ethics of Care: Feminist Considerations on Justice, Morality and Politics.* London: Routledge.

Shanahan, M. (2000). Pathways to adulthood in changing societies: Variability and mechanisms in life course perspective. *Annual Review of Sociology, 26*(1), 667–92. http://dx.doi.org/10.1146/annurev.soc.26.1.667

Shapcott, M. (2008). *Housing, Homelessness, Health, and the 2008 Federal Election.* Toronto: Wellesley Institute.

Shaw, M., & Dorling, D. (1998, Aug 29). Mortality among street youth in the UK. *Lancet, 352*(9129), 743. http://dx.doi.org/10.1016/S0140-6736(05)60868-9 Medline:9729028

Shaw, S.N. (2002). Shifting conversations on girls' and women's self injury: An analysis of the clinical literature in historical context. *Feminism & Psychology, 12*(2), 191–219. http://dx.doi.org/10.1177/0959353502012002010

Sherwin, S. (Ed.). (1998). *The Politics of Women's Health: Exploring Agency and Autonomy.* Philadelphia: Temple University Press.

Singer, J.A. (2004). Narrative identity and meaning making across the adult lifespan: An introduction. *Journal of Personality, 72*(3), 543–72. http://dx.doi.org/10.1111/j.0022-3506.2004.00268.x Medline:15102038

Sistering Toronto. (2002). *Common Occurrence: The Impact of Homelessness on Women's Health.*

Smith, C.A., Smith, C.J., Kearns, R.A., & Abbott, M.W. (1993, Sep). Housing stressors, social support and psychological distress. *Social Science & Medicine, 37*(5), 603–12. http://dx.doi.org/10.1016/0277-9536(93)90099-P Medline:8211274

Smith, D.E. (1999). *Writing the Social.* Toronto: University of Toronto Press.

Smith, J., & Gilford, S. (1998). Not only street sleepers are homeless: Issues of gender and ethnicity in researching youth homelessness. *Youth & Policy, 59,* 70–85.

Smith, N. (1993a). Homeless/global: Scaling places. In J. Bird (Ed.), *Mapping the Futures* (pp. 87–119). London: Routledge.

Smith, S. (1993b). *Subjectivity, Identity and the Body: Women's Autobiographical Practices in the 20th Century.* Bloomington: Indiana University Press.

Smith, S.J. (1990). Health status and the housing system. *Social Science & Medicine, 31*(7), 753–62. http://dx.doi.org/10.1016/0277-9536(90)90170-W Medline:2244217

Somerville, P. (1992). Homelessness and the meaning of home: rooflessness or rootlessness? *International Journal of Urban and Regional Research, 16*(4), 529-39.

Sproles, K.Z. (2006). *Desiring Women: The Partnership of Virginia Woolf and Vita Sackville-West.* Toronto: University of Toronto Press.

Stanley, L. (1992). *The Auto/Biographical I: Theory and Practice of Feminist Auto/Biography.* Manchester: Manchester University Press.

Steedman, C. (1995). *Strange Dislocations: Childhood and the Idea of Human Interiority.* London: Virago.

Steele, J., & Brown, J. (1995). Adolescent room culture: Studying media in the context of everyday life. *Journal of Youth and Adolescence, 24*(5), 551–76. http://dx.doi.org/10.1007/BF01537056

Stephen, D.E. (2000). Young women construct themselves: Social identity, self-concept and psychosocial well-being in homeless facilities. *Journal of Youth Studies, 3*(4), 445–60. http://dx.doi.org/10.1080/713684384

Stivers, C. (1993). Reflections on the role of personal narratives in social science. *Signs, 18,* 408–25. http://dx.doi.org/10.1086/494800

Street Health. (2005). *Research Bulletin: Majority of Homeless People Have Serious Health Conditions and Face Major Barriers to Health Care.* Toronto: Street Health.

Subrahmanyam, K., & Lin, G. (2007, Winter). Adolescents on the net: Internet use and well-being. *Adolescence, 42*(168), 659–77. Medline:18229503

Suyemoto, K.L. (1998, Aug). The functions of self-mutilation. *Clinical Psychology Review, 18*(5), 531–54. http://dx.doi.org/10.1016/S0272-7358(97)00105-0 Medline:9740977

Tamboukou, M. (2008). A Foucauldian approach to narratives. In M. Andrews, C. Squire, & M. Tamboukou (Eds.), *Doing Narrative Research* (pp. 102–20). London: Sage.

Tolman, D.L., Hirschman, C., & Impett, E.A. (2005). There's more to the story: The place of qualitative research on female adolescent sexuality in policymaking. *Sexuality Research & Social Policy, 2*(4), 4–17. http://dx.doi.org/10.1525/srsp.2005.2.4.4

Toronto Community Foundation. (2009). Independent Living Accounts: Leaving homelessness in the past. Toronto: SEDI.

Trinh, M.T. (1989). *Woman Native Other*. Bloomington: Indiana University Press.

Tudor Hart, J. (1971, Feb 27). The inverse care law. *Lancet, 297*(7696), 405–12. http://dx.doi.org/10.1016/S0140-6736(71)92410-X Medline:4100731

Tyler, K.A., Cauce, A.M., & Whitbeck, L. (2004, Mar). Family risk factors and prevalence of dissociative symptoms among homeless and runaway youth. *Child Abuse & Neglect, 28*(3), 355–66. http://dx.doi.org/10.1016/j.chiabu.2003.11.019 Medline:15066351

Tyler, K.A., Whitbeck, L.B., Hoyt, D.R., & Johnson, K.D. (2003). Self-mutilation and homeless youth: The role of family abuse, street experiences, and mental disorders. *Journal of Research on Adolescence, 13*(4), 457–74. http://dx.doi.org/10.1046/j.1532-7795.2003.01304003.x

Tyyska, V. (2001). *Long and Winding Road: Adolescents and Youth in Canada Today*. Toronto: Canadian Scholars' Press.

United Nations General Assembly Convention on the Rights of the Child, 20 November 1989, *United Nations, Treaty Series*, 1577, p. 3.

Ungar, M. (2007). Grow 'em strong: Conceptual challenges in researching childhood resilience. In A. Best (Ed.), *Representing Youth: Methodological Issues in Critical Youth Studies* (pp. 84–109). New York: New York University Press.

UNICEF. (1997). *Youth Health for a Change: A UNICEF Notebook on Programming for Young People's Health and Development*. New York: UNICEF.

UNICEF. (1999). *The Progress of Nations 1998*. New York: UNICEF.

Ussher, J.M. (1992). *Women's Madness: Misogyny or Mental Illness?* Amherst: The University of Massachusetts Press.

Vandemark, L.M. (2007, Oct). Promoting the sense of self, place, and belonging in displaced persons: The example of homelessness. *Archives of Psychiatric Nursing, 21*(5), 241–48. http://dx.doi.org/10.1016/j.apnu.2007.06.003 Medline:17904481

Varney, D., & van Vliet, W. (2008). Homelessness, children, and youth: Research in the United States and Canada. *American Behavioral Scientist, 51*(6), 715–20. http://dx.doi.org/10.1177/0002764207311983

Veness, A.R. (1993). Neither homed nor homeless: Contested definitions and the personal worlds of the poor. *Political Geography, 12*(4), 319–40. http://dx.doi.org/10.1016/0962-6298(93)90044-8

Votta, E., & Manion, I. (2004, Mar). Suicide, high-risk behaviors, and coping style in homeless adolescent males' adjustment. *Journal of Adolescent Health, 34*(3), 237–43. Medline:14967348

Walby, S. (1990). *Theorizing Patriarchy*. Oxford: Blackwell.

Walker, A. & Walker, C. (Eds.). (1997). *Britain Divided: The Growth of Social Exclusion in the 1980s and 1990s*. London: Child Poverty Action Group.

Walker, R.C. (2006). Interweaving Aboriginal/indigenous rights with urban citizenship: A view from the Winnipeg low-cost housing sector, Canada. *Citizenship Studies, 10*(4), 391–411. http://dx.doi.org/10.1080/13621020600858096

Walls, N.E., Hancock, P., & Wisneski, H. (2007). Differentiating the social service needs of homeless sexual minority youths from those of non-homeless sexual minority youths. *Journal of Children & Poverty, 13*(2), 177–205. http://dx.doi.org/10.1080/10796120701520309

Walters, A.S. (1999, Sep). HIV prevention in street youth. *Journal of Adolescent Health, 25*(3), 187–98. http://dx.doi.org/10.1016/S1054-139X(98)00155-4 Medline:10475495

Wardhaugh, J. (1999). The unaccommodated woman: Home, homelessness and identity. *Sociological Review, 47*(1), 91–109. http://dx.doi.org/10.1111/1467-954X.00164

Wardhaugh, J. (2000). *Sub City: Young Homeless People, Homelessness and Crime*. Brookfield: Ashgate Publishing.

Weare, K. (2000). *Promoting Mental, Emotional and Social Health*. New York: Routledge.

Weedon, C. (1987). *Feminist Practice and Poststructuralist Theory*. Oxford: Blackwell.

Weedon, C. (1999). *Feminism, Theory and the Politics of Difference*. Oxford: Blackwell.

Wengraf, T. (2000). Uncovering the general from within the particular. In P. Chamberlayne, J. Bornat, & T. Wengraf (Eds.), *The Turn to Biographical Methods in Social Science* (pp. 140–64). New York: Routledge.

Wesley-Esquimaux, C.C. (2007). Inside looking out, outside looking in. *First Peoples Child & Family Review, 3*(4), 62–71.

West, A., O'Kane, C., & Hyder, T. (2008). Diverse childhoods: Implications for childcare, protection, participation and research practice. In A. Leira & C. Saraceno (Eds.), *Childhood: Changing Contexts.* Bingley: Emerald Group Publishing. http://dx.doi.org/10.1016/S0195-6310(07)00009-9

Whitbeck, L.B., Hoyt, D.R., Johnson, K.D., & Chen, X. (2007). Victimization and posttraumatic stress disorder among runaway and homeless adolescents. *Violence and Victims, 22*(6), 721–34. http://dx.doi.org/10.1891/088667007782793165 Medline:18225385

Whitzman, C. (2006). At the intersection of invisibilities: Canadian women, homelessness and health outside the 'big city.' *Gender, Place and Culture, 13*(4), 383–99. http://dx.doi.org/10.1080/09663690600808502

Wiener, A. (1997). Making sense of the new geography of citizenship: Fragmented citizenship in the European Union. *Theory and Society, 26*(4), 529–60. http://dx.doi.org/10.1023/A:1006809913519

Wilkinson, R.G. (1996). *Unhealthy Societies: The Afflictions of Inequality.* New York: Routledge. http://dx.doi.org/10.4324/9780203421680

Williams, A. (2002, Jul). Changing geographies of care: Employing the concept of therapeutic landscapes as a framework in examining home space. *Social Science & Medicine, 55*(1), 141–54. http://dx.doi.org/10.1016/S0277-9536(01)00209-X Medline:12137183

Williams, D. (2006). Why game studies now? Gamers don't bowl alone. *Games and Culture, 1*(1), 13–16. http://dx.doi.org/10.1177/1555412005281774

Williams, D., Ducheneaut, N., Xiong, L., Yuanyuan, Z., Yee, N., & Nickell, E. (2006). From tree house to barracks: The social life of guilds in World of Warcraft. *Games and Culture, 1*(4), 338–61. http://dx.doi.org/10.1177/1555412006292616

Williamson, D.L., & Fast, J.E. (1998, Mar-Apr). Poverty and medical treatment: When public policy compromises accessibility. *Canadian Journal of Public Health, 89*(2), 120–4. Medline:9583254

Wingert, S., Higgitt, N., & Ristock, J. (2005). Voices from the margins: Understanding street youth in Winnipeg. *Canadian Journal of Urban Research, 14*(1), 54–80.

Wolcott, H.F. (1995). *The Art of Fieldwork.* New York: AltaMira Press.

Wolf, N. (1991). *The Beauty Myth.* Toronto: Vintage.

Woolf, V. (1948). The leaning tower. In V. Woolf (Ed.), *The Moment and other essays*. San Diego: Harcourt Brace.

World Health Organization. (2007). *Mental Health: Strengthening Our Response*. Geneva: World Health Organization.

Wyness, M. (2006). *Childhood and Society: An Introduction to the Sociology of Childhood*. New York: Palgrave Macmillan.

Yalnizyan, A. (2007). *The Rich and the Rest of Us: The Changing Face of Canada's Growing Gap*. Ottawa: Canadian Centre for Policy Alternatives.

Yee, J. (Ed.). (2011). *Feminism for Real: Deconstructing the Academic Industrial Complex of Feminism*. Toronto: Canadian Centre for Policy Alternatives.

Yoder, K.A. (1999, Spring). Comparing suicide attempters, suicide ideators, and nonsuicidal homeless and runaway adolescents. *Suicide & Life-Threatening Behavior, 29*(1), 25–36. Medline:10322618

Young, I.M. (2002). Lived body vs. gender: Reflections on social structure and subjectivity. *Ratio, 15*(4), 410–28. http://dx.doi.org/10.1111/1467-9329.00200

Zerger, S., Strehlow, A.J., & Gundlapalli, A.V. (2008). Homeless young adults and behavioral health: An averview. *American Behavioral Scientist, 51*(6), 824–41. http://dx.doi.org/10.1177/0002764207311990

Index